Dr. Katz's Guide to
Prostate Health
From Conventional to Holistic Therapies

by Aaron E. Katz, M.D.,
Director of the Center for Holistic Urology,
Columbia University Medical Center

Freedom
Press

Book design by Bonnie Lambert
Cover design by Nita Ybarra
Medical Illustrations by Tina Pavlatos, Visual Anatomy Limited
Cover photo by David M. Russell

ISBN 1-893910-39-3

Printed in Canada

Published by Freedom Press
1801 Chart Trail
Topanga, CA 90290

Bulk Orders Available: (800) 959-9797

E-mail: info@freedompressonline.com

 THIS WORK IS DEDICATED to my patients, who have trusted me with their health care; to my colleagues at Columbia, who inspire me daily; and to my loving family, whose support and guidance I treasure.

Foreword

I SHARE MUCH WITH AARON KATZ. We both practice at Columbia University Medical Center. We're about the same age and both of us are insanely busy maintaining surgical practices and teaching medical students about traditional and cutting-edge surgical therapies. Both of us strive to keep up with and contribute to medicine's answers to the unique health challenges of modern civilized life. We both perform clinical research and write up our results for publication in medical journals.

Our work has to do with some of the body's most important plumbing: I operate on hearts, and he operates on prostate glands and other vital parts down below. And both of us have taken it upon ourselves to try to clear up some of the myths and misinformation that abounds in the public mind about ways to maintain optimal health of these and other organ systems—by writing rather large but hopefully unintimidating books.

My recent book with colleague Mike Roizen, M.D., *You: The Owner's Manual* (HarperCollins, 2005), was successful in part because we made health fun with "news you can use." I'll never give up cardiovascular surgery or clinical research in favor of book tours or pounding away at the keyboard, but in this age—when overwhelming amounts of "info-tisement" for trendy supplements and foods clog lines of access to reliable, research-based information on treatment and prevention of disease—doctors need to stay involved with educating the public about these issues. This belief also drove Dr. Katz to stay up late at nights creating his masterpiece.

It's especially exciting to know that these new generations of books are being read by people who might not otherwise get "turned on" to a healthful lifestyle. We are not just preaching to the converted—those health food store denizens who devour every news tidbit on the hottest, latest supplements or meditative types who serenely munch on bowls of cooked kale and seaweed while yogic breathing ever so deeply. Instead we are reaching people who might not otherwise feel motivated to take better care of themselves. Since roughly half of the bodies on the planet contain prostate glands, and since the likelihood of every one of them having at least one prostate or (related) bladder difficulty at some point in life (assuming they live long enough) approaches 100 percent, I anticipate that Dr. Katz's book will fulfill this mantra also.

Dr. Katz is a world-class urologist who also does focused research into chemoprevention—the use of targeted nutrients and herbs to slow the growth of or prevent the formation of those hellion cells we know as cancer. In a world where watchful waiting or invasive, impotence-inducing surgery might appear to be a man's only choices if he has BPH or prostate cancer, Dr. Katz offers proactive and effective natural alternatives that offer big benefits without liabilities (otherwise known as side effects).

A lot of docs and other experts who write about medicine tend to take an "either-or" approach, demonizing the alternative methods and embracing the mainstream or vice-versa. Dr. Katz embraces it all, as long as it *works*, instead of only extolling what fits into one category or the other. He doesn't have a vested interest in the outcome of the alternative medical research he's doing; he isn't a vitamin peddler or a drug or surgical technology company CEO, he just wants to know what the science says about what helps and what doesn't. Dr. Katz is one of a new generation of doctors that is seeking to move into a truly integrative and holistic kind of medicine—the medicine that could play a role in rescuing us from the downward spiral of the money-gobbling health care system we have in place today. Coupled with patients who are willing to go the extra mile to educate themselves about their bodies and the illnesses they have the misfortune of developing—*that's you, sir or madam*—this approach shines a halogen beam down the dark and serpentine tunnel of today's sick-care system: a system that waits until you're good and broken, then patches you up with expensive technologies and side-effect-prone drugs that you're often told you will require for the rest of your days on Earth.

Sure, Dr. Katz knows all about the most high-tech medical options and has used most of them himself, with his own hands. In this book, he has successfully explained these approaches—and how they can be integrated with alternative medical approaches for the best possible outcome for this small but potentially troublesome organ.

If most people are ignorant in general about the overall workings of their bodies—the big topic we tackled in our recent book—they tend to be even more so when they are faced with an illness and have to make choices about treatment. This book demystifies that process for men who are dealing with prostate disease, gently guiding readers through both mainstream and alternative approaches to benign prostatic hyper-plasia (BPH), prostatitis, and prostate cancer.

It's tough as hell to get a guy to read a health book, even when it's talking about a part of his anatomy on which his gen-der has exclusive rights—a part that is integral to his sexual life, even. As a gender, if you will forgive the generalization, men like to feel invincible. They don't like to feel sick. They'll go to outrageous lengths to reassure themselves and their loved ones that they're just fine, thanks: "Oh, that basketball-sized growth on my back? It's nothing. Can't even feel it, nope. It's just a little sexy, don't you think, honey? C'mere..."

I know that in many cases, the women are the ones who pick up the health books, read them, and dispense advice and natu-ral prescriptions to their ailing male partners, or their brothers, or their fathers. If you are such a woman, I applaud you. This is the book you want to take home if your loved one has any decisions to make about treatments for or prevention of prostate disease, or if he flatly refuses to have a prostate evalu-ation despite his having to rise eight times a night to stand over the toilet, cursing his nether regions for not behaving as they should.

It's a resource that can serve to educate both patient and physician, because a lot of the therapies discussed—both main-stream and alternative—are still so new that they haven't hit the majority of urological practices. This is a very, very good book, and a necessary one, written by a doctor who is at the pinnacle of his field. It should be on every man's bookshelf.

All the best to you and your prostate,
Mehmet Oz, M.D.

Acknowledgements

THE AUTHOR would like to gratefully acknowledge David Steinman, Jeanne Ringe, Melissa Lynn Block, Cassandra Glickman, and the rest of the team at Freedom Press for their editing and publishing expertise. I would also like to thank Paul Schulick and Tom Newmark for teaching me about botanical medicine, my legal experts Eric Brown and Herb Sydney, and collaborating companies New Chapter, Natural Source, Amino Up, and Quality of Life Labs. For their valuable insight and support, I thank my colleagues Carl Olsson, M.D., Mitchell Benson, M.D., Steve Kaplan, M.D., James McKiernan, M.D., Brian Stone, M.D., David Samadi, M.D., Kimberly Cooper, M.D., Ridwan Shabsigh, M.D., Harry Fisch, M.D., Mantu Gupta, M.D., Erik Goluboff, M.D., Michael Wechsler, M.D., Ben Jacobs, M.D., and Jaime Landman, M.D., as well as my nurse who has helped me so much, Monica Johnson. In addition, the nurses in Cystoscopy, Marie Fatal, Robert Desjardins, Joseph Gonzaga, Young Soon Lee, Karen Johnson, and Okja Huh, my longtime secretary,

Mooneshwarie (Mona) Hanoman, Katie Khal for her secretarial help, and Kristofer Prepelica for his data collection on the cryosurgery patients. Thanks to Stephen Strum, M.D., for his editorial review. Thanks to Laura Chiappetta for helping me establish the Holistic Center and members of the Holistic Urology Advisory Board, especially Michael and Joan Schneeweiss, Phil Clark, Arthur and Karen Cohen, Fred Iseman, Jean-Pierre and Rose Benoit, and Charles Royce, for establishing the Charles Royce Holistic Research Fellowship. A special thanks to Dr. Debra Bemis, Dr. Ralph Buttyan, and Jillian Capodice who have worked countless hours in the Molecular Urology lab at Columbia and are the backbone of the Holistic Center research. Finally I would especially like to thank Mehmet Oz, M.D., for his foreword to this book.

Table of Contents

Foreword by Mehmet Oz, M.D.   v

Acknowledgements   ix

Introduction—Speaking Man to Man   xiii

PART I

Chapter 1: The Center for
Holistic Urology's Prostate Primer   3

Chapter 2: Enlarged Prostate—
Diagnosis and Mainstream Therapies   11

Chapter 3: BPH—The Holistic Approach   39

Chapter 4: Prostatitis   55

PART II

Chapter 5: Prostate Cancer—
What It Is, Who's at Risk, How It's Treated   81

Chapter 6: Chemoprevention and
Holistic Treatments for Prostate Cancer   129

Chapter 7: Nutrition—
Diet, Whole Foods and Supplements   165

Chapter 8: Lifestyle, Stress and Prostate Health   199

Chapter 9: In Conclusion   221

Resources   225

References   231

Index   243

About the Author   249

Speaking Man to Man

YOU KNOW, MEN DON'T LIKE to talk about their health problems, especially those that afflict us...*down there*. I guess it's that macho exterior of ours—a hardened shell we develop to succeed in our professional lives where admitting weaknesses can be certain death; but, often, even in our personal lives, we really don't like admitting our vulnerabilities.

But it's about time that we started talking about one of the key health issues men face, especially as they reach middle age: prostate cancer. Add to this the other problems that affect the nether regions of hundreds of thousands of men each year: benign prostatic hypertrophy (BPH), also known as enlarged prostate; and prostatitis, an inflammation of the prostate gland.

Prostate cancer is second only to lung cancer as the leading killer of men. More than 220,000 men will be diagnosed with prostate cancer in the United States this year, and more than 31,000 will die of the disease.

DID YOU KNOW?

According to Us TOO, the international men's prostate cancer support group, prostate cancer is:

- The single most common form of solid tumor in humans.
- Newly diagnosed every 2.6 minutes.
- Present in more than 9 million men.
- Predicted to be diagnosed 220,000 times—that's just new cases—and the cause of 31,000 deaths this year.
- A killer of one man every 13 minutes.
- Responsible for approximately 13 percent of cancer deaths in men.
- The most common cancer that afflicts men, aside from skin cancer.
- Likely to afflict 1 in 6 men in their lifetime.
- Second only to lung cancer in annual cancer deaths of U.S. men.
- As much as 50 percent more likely to strike and to kill African American men in comparison with other racial or ethnic groups.
- Proven to strike as many men (and cause almost as many deaths annually) as breast cancer does in women, but lacking the national awareness and research funding breast cancer currently receives.
- Nearly 100 percent survivable if detected early.

Did you read the last bullet point? It's 100 percent survivable if detected early. So let's let down our macho shield and confront this problem. When the talk turns to prostate health and disease, there's a lot that we can do. Even if you are currently problem-free down there or in your twenties or thirties, if you take steps now to preserve your health, you will have less risk of troubling prostate problems later in life.

Men of any age can develop prostate cancer. Most often, it is found in men who have been alive for at least 50 years, and 8 of 10 men who are diagnosed are 65 or older. Huge advances in diagnostic techniques and testing have increased prostate cancer detection in the past 15 years. Treatments are better than they've ever been. Still, we have a lot of work to do to eradicate this disease, or to at least ensure that if it afflicts men, that they can be treated and go on to live long, healthy lives.

OTHER PROSTATE PROBLEMS: MORE COMMON THAN YOU MIGHT THINK

Enlarged prostate—also known as benign prostatic hypertrophy, or BPH—and prostatitis, a painful inflammation of this male gland, are also extremely prevalent. They aren't cancer, but just about every man who walks the Earth will suffer from one or the other, either chronically or periodically, after he turns 50. Any man who cares about his prostate should know about these issues, too—and what can be done about them.

Once men find themselves confronting prostate health challenges, they quickly learn how difficult it is to get good information. Most physicians who treat prostate disease use drugs, surgeries, and other mainstream, allopathic treatments exclusively. Any patient who starts to look at books, news publications, and the Internet to fully educate himself about options ends up barraged with information about supplements, herbs, and other more natural healing methods. It's difficult to sort the hype from the help. This is partly because the research that has been done on many of the herbal compounds has not been subjected to the scientific testing that doctors require before they are willing to use them to treat patients. There have been cases where this reticence has paid off: A few herbal compounds have been found to be unsafe, and would have put patients at increased risk of side effects if they had been widely used by physicians.

However, there is a large body of research that supports some natural remedies for BPH and prostatitis, and favors the role of nutrients and herbs as complementary or integrative additions to other prostate therapies. They need to be used appropriately, in concert with your medical care. I wrote this book to tell you about my experience with some of these integrative therapies. It is my hope that this book can help guide you in the safe and effective use of nutritional therapies for prostate disease.

KNOWING YOUR OPTIONS

During my residency, which I finished in 1992, the approach to treating lower urinary tract symptoms that indicated BPH (frequent urination, up at night, urgency, incomplete emptying, blood in the urine, burning, weak stream, dribbling during or after urination, complete urinary retention) was limited to putting in a catheter and counseling patients to have their prostate glands removed. Today, if you visit your doctor with these kinds of complaints, your medical options are vastly improved.

Most doctors don't routinely use herbs, diet and lifestyle changes, or supplements to heal prostate disease. It just hasn't hit their radar yet. If you use this book to become an expert on prostate disease and on the various treatment options, both allopathic (drugs, surgeries) and alternative (herbs, diet changes, lifestyle changes, supplements), you'll be able to understand and communicate about them with your medical team in an educated way.

If your doctors don't know yet about saw palmetto, or pygeum, or antioxidants, or natural anti-inflammatory therapy—all of which are covered in this book—you can help them see what we're finding in our research efforts at Columbia: These natural substances can help. In many men with early-stage prostate cancer, particularly those who are older, who have small volume cancers, or have been diagnosed with less aggressive cancer (Gleason score of 6 or less, PSA values under 10 ng/ml), one of the options is to "watch and wait."

A Brief Glossary of Medical Schools of Thought

Holistic medicine: The word "holistic" is defined as follows in *Webster's New World Dictionary*: "of or dealing with wholes or integrated systems rather than with their parts." Holistic medicine regards the patient not as a collection of symptoms, but as a well-rounded and complex organism, comprised of many interdependent physiological systems that cannot be treated one at a time. The holistic approach sees how body, mind, spirit, and environment coalesce in ways that promote disease, and works with all of these systems in each individual patient to move the body back towards health. Holistic medicine prefers to use natural substances (*nutra*ceutical rather than *pharma*ceutical), such as nutrients, and encourages lifestyle changes. Although synthetic drugs tend to rein in symptoms quickly, there may be a price of promoting imbalances that can give rise to side effects or illness later on. Holistic medicine may also be referred to as "naturopathic," "natural," or "integrative" medicine (see below for more on the integrative approach).

Allopathic (mainstream) medicine: This is the most prevalent school of medical thought in Western nations. Allopathic medicine is heavy on the use of pharmaceuticals and high-tech testing, diagnostic, and surgical techniques.

Integrative medicine: This kind of medicine is destined to create the gold standard sometime in the future. It employs aggressive allopathic therapies, but conservatively, only when absolutely necessary. It takes the best scientific and technological information and incorporates it with ages-old traditional healing practices and remedies and modern research into nutritional supplements and herbal remedies. Integrative medicine gives the physician that much more to choose from when he or she is trying to discover the best possible way to help his or her patient heal. Some refer to this kind of medicine as "complementary," as in a complementary joining of allopathic and holistic medicine. To make matters more confusing, integrative medicine can also be called holistic. Although I run the Center for *Holistic* Urology, we do embrace an integrative approach—the best of allopathy and the best of naturopathy.

I don't use watchful waiting in my practice. I take a more active role with my patients. The role of holistic therapies in this disease is rapidly expanding, and I firmly believe that there is lots to gain. Why not watch, wait, and intelligently use targeted nutrition and herbal medicines at the same time?

I have experienced the great benefits firsthand at the Center for Holistic Urology. My patients who use both holistic and allopathic treatments enjoy excellent quality of life. Many have been taken off hormonal therapies, maintained low PSA values, and have a renewed sense of hope—a new lease on life.

Doctors and health professionals alike often lack a balanced view of nutrition, herbal medicine, acupuncture, and mind-body therapies. Since formal training in the application of complementary therapies is extremely hard to find, physicians are left to their own devices to seek out the science and the practical knowledge that will help them to better help their patients. My purpose in writing this book is to increase awareness in this area.

Attitudes towards natural medicine are polarized in America. To many, leaves, roots, and berries hold no appeal compared to high-tech pharmaceutical and surgical science. Those who scoff at herbal and nutritional medicine usually hold an image of it as unscientific, something that comes from little thatched huts in the wilderness, inert or possibly harmful concoctions created by the greedy or the uneducated. Others stand firmly in the opposite corner, demonizing mainstream medicine as slash-and-burn, accusing the medical profession of hurting more than it helps.

Neither of these perspectives are accurate, as is the case with just about every extreme perspective since the dawn of history. The answers don't come exclusively from one healing perspective or the other, but from a melding of the two.

Herbal and nutritional medicine has become highly scientific and rigorous over the past few years. There are medical schools in the United States that are now offering elective courses to students in integrative medicine. (Columbia University is one of them!) Every day new and exciting research is being performed by scientists at leading institutions around the United States and the world. Some of this work is being published in the most prestigious allopathic medical journals, increasing the credibility of these therapies. In 1998, Congress established national funding for CAM therapies, and established the National Center for Complementary and Alternative Medicine (NCCAM). NCCAM is one of the 27 institutes and centers that make up the National Institutes of Health (NIH).

NCCAM is dedicated to exploring complementary and alternative healing practices in the context of rigorous science, training complementary and alternative medicine (CAM) researchers, and disseminating authoritative information to the public and professionals. In 1999, Congress appropriated 50 million dollars for NCCAM. This year, in 2005, the funding has expanded: 123 million dollars! In just a few years, the funding has more than doubled complementary research. In time, with more research and efforts in this area, I believe that some of the these holistic therapies will be considered by allopathic physicians and become incorporated into "mainstream" medicine. This is the dawn of a new era in medicine and research—a time when the two worlds seem to be converging.

There is definitely a place for standard allopathic medicine and surgery in the treatment of prostate problems. I am trained in the use of these practices. I teach them to medical students at Columbia University. Anyone who has been in the trenches, dealing with prostate disease, recognizes that allopathic medicine can be the smartest course of action. Having studied complementary medicine and the inclusion of scientifically validated methods from natural health, however, I am convinced that it is in our patients' best interests if we follow a balanced approach that utilizes what is proven in both allopathy and naturopathy.

Here, at the Center for Holistic Urology at Columbia University Medical Center, we are probably now the world's leaders in accumulating information on complementary forms of medicine, and on how they can be integrated with the mainstream. You'll see in this book that this research evidence is just too compelling to be overlooked.

If we don't help patients take advantage of what natural remedies can offer when integrated with allopathic treatments—if we compel men to believe that surgery, medication, radiation or doing nothing are their only choices—we are not doing all we can for our patients.

Dr. Katz's Guide to
Prostate Health

PART I

Chapter 1

The Center for Holistic Urology's Prostate Primer

THE BIGGEST ASSET to empowered patient decision-making is information. Men newly diagnosed with prostate cancer may spend precious days, weeks or months searching for definitive and reliable information upon which to make a treatment-option decision, trying to piece together information from several (possibly conflicting) sources.

You hold in your hands the first truly comprehensive guide to help you navigate this complex decision-making process. In addition, this "resource kit" will also help anyone looking to learn more about prostate cancer and available treatment options, as well as other medical and emotional aspects of the disease, which affect every man diagnosed with prostate cancer, his spouse or partner, and the rest of his family.

I know how your doctor feels when he shakes his head at patients who ask questions about the use of herbs and nutrients. At one time, I felt the same way. Just like them, I went through pre-med in college, then to medical school, then into a urology residency where I did two years of general surgery and four years of urological surgery. Like some of those who chose this specialty, I went on to a fellowship in oncology after finishing my residency. No one said a word about using herbs or diet to treat urological conditions.

My training embraced a very conservative, traditional allopathic approach, but I was given a golden opportunity when I started my academic practice at Columbia University: I worked with Dr. Robert Atkins at his famous Atkins Center in Manhattan. There, they were educating patients about low-carbohydrate diets and alternative medicine. Once a week, between 1993 and 1997, I went there to consult with patients who had prostate and urological problems.

With my conservative training, I looked at what the Atkins physicians were advising patients to use—herbs and nutrients, mostly—and at first thought to myself: "This is a bunch of (mild expletive)! It's not going to work. Why are these people wasting their money on this stuff?"

But I was careful to do something my professors had told me I must do to be a good doctor: I listened to my patients, even though I was skeptical. And my patients were telling me, "I was on this medication, my doctor wanted me to have my prostate out, and instead I was taking this herb or that herb, and I'm doing fine." And it wasn't just one patient, it was a lot of patients. When I turned to the medical literature, I was surprised to find that although some science was there to support these patients' claims, the majority of these herbals were not studied in true clinical trials, the gold standard for allopathic medicine.

In 1998, having convinced myself that integrative, natural therapies could hold an important place in urology, I opened the Center for Holistic Urology at Columbia University Medical Center. I was unsure of myself, because I had a feeling that my colleagues would receive it with great suspicion. I didn't particularly want my colleagues to think I was doing something crazy. But I did have the support of my chairman, Dr. Carl Olsson, who is a world-renowned urologic surgeon and a world leader in urology. As it turned out, the other urologists in my department were glad to have somewhere to send patients who wanted to try holistic therapies.

Today, I am one of the few urologists involved in clinical and laboratory studies of natural formulas. From the dual perspective of a holistic physician and mainstream, allopathic physician, I am in a unique position to help you make a thoroughly informed decision on how best to support the health of your prostate. At the Center for Holistic Urology, we have found that natural healing is often strikingly effective for many men's health conditions, both malignant and non-malignant, especially those for which allopathy offers little help. We base this conclusion on clinical and scientific backing from our Center and from published research studies.

The science of herbal and nutritional medicine is advancing rapidly. I have found that allopathic doctors can do best for patients when both allopathy and natural health measures are combined—especially when it comes to urology and men's health.

Think of our Center—and, by association, this book—as this balanced place: a home, if you will, for men seeking help and advice about a critical area of their lives, central to their manhood. There's no denying that this is a sensitive topic for most men, and they deserve to be told, based on in-depth research, what really works. We tell our patients about all of their treatment options, both allopathic and naturopathic, and we're honest about the risks and benefits of each option.

UROLOGY 101

Before we focus on the prostate, let's look at the branch of medicine that deals with the diagnosis and treatment of diseases of the prostate: urology.

Urologists:

• diagnose and treat diseases of the kidney, bladder, and urethra (internal urinary organs), and of the penis, testicles and scrotum (external urinary organs);

• deal with disease processes that are relatively benign, such as prostate enlargement, prostatitis (infection or inflammation of the prostate), kidney and bladder stones, and urinary tract and bladder infections;

• deal with cancers of these organs, particularly of the prostate, bladder, testicle, and kidney;

• treat pediatric urological problems, usually due to congenital physical deformities;

• treat problems that affect women's urological health; and

• treat erectile dysfunction and male infertility.

In this book, we will focus largely on diseases and conditions of the prostate. Along with heart disease, these are among the leading health challenges men face today. If men can maintain or regain their prostate health, very often we find that the other conditions men face—including erectile dysfunction, a major quality-of-life issue for many men—can also be improved.

AND NOW, PRESENTING...YOUR PROSTATE

It's amazing how many men really aren't sure what this vital gland actually is and what it does. (Some even think it's called the "prostrate.")

The prostate is:

• a gland that wraps around the upper part of the urethra, a tube that carries urine from the bladder out through the tip of the penis;

- the source of a thick fluid that both transports and nourishes sperm on its journey towards attempted procreation;
- about the size of a walnut;
- located below the bladder and in front of the rectum.

The prostate needs male hormones to function. The main male hormone is testosterone, which is made mainly by the testicles. Some male hormones are produced in small amounts by the adrenal glands.

A combination of connective tissue, gland, and muscle, the prostate provides the power that propels semen through the urethra and out the penis. Within the stroma lie smooth muscle cells that allow the gland to contract during ejaculation. The prostate plays a key role in men's sexuality, providing more than 90 percent of his ejaculate, including semen, the enzyme-filled fluid required for fertilization of the ovum.

There are three ways in which the prostate gland can become diseased: 1) benign enlargement; 2) infection/chronic inflammation; and 3) cancer.

Benign prostatic hyperplasia (BPH) is the abnormal, non-cancerous growth of prostate cells. In BPH, the prostate grows larger and pushes against the urethra and bladder, blocking the normal flow of urine. More than half of the men in the United States between the ages of 60 and 70, and as many as 90 percent between the ages of 70 and 90, have symptoms of BPH. Although this condition is seldom a threat to life, it may require treatment to relieve symptoms. BPH can be a source of much suffering and embarrassment, and it's the most common disorder of the prostate.

For some men, there may be only a minor discomfort and the symptoms can be stoically shrugged off—"just part of getting older." Men with more severe symptoms will probably require medical help.

Prostatitis is inflammation of the prostate gland characterized by pain in the perineal area (between the testicles and the anus), irregular urination, and (in more severe cases) chills and fever. It usually affects men who are younger than 45. Both bacterial and nonbacterial forms of the disease exist.

Some men are chronically afflicted with prostatitis. Considering the advances urology has made in the treatment of other prostate disorders, the science and treatment of chronic prostatitis is far from where it should be. Most physicians with patients who turn out to have chronic prostatitis have trouble diagnosing and treating this condition. Even when the problem is correctly diagnosed, many patients get no improvement despite repeated courses of antibiotics and anti-inflammatories. The research on how to treat chronic prostatitis doesn't give physicians much guidance. Only a handful of small studies have been done, and most of those are for documented bacterial prostatitis, a form of the disease that comprises less than 10 percent of the patients seen by urologists. At this writing, complementary medicine is an important part of treatment for many men with chronic prostatitis that doesn't respond to mainstream therapies.

Prostate cancer is the most common type of cancer (excluding skin cancer) among American men. According to the American Cancer Society, men aged 50 and older, and those over the age of 45 who are in high-risk groups, such as African American men and men with a documented family history of prostate cancer, should have a prostate-specific antigen (PSA) blood test and digital rectal exam (DRE) once every year.

All of these conditions can affect men's overall health and well-being. It isn't any fun to stand at the toilet, unable to urinate. Really, it's downright uncomfortable. Prostatitis can go for years without being detected or effectively treated. Prostate cancer is so common, it must (or should) be on every man's mind. Taking care of your prostate can extend your longevity. It can enhance your potency and virility.

Each of these conditions is best dealt with by drawing from the best of all facets of medicine. Often, we find herbal medicines can do wonderful things for patients with any of these conditions. They offer efficacy without risk, or with very little risk. That's what's so exciting to both practitioners and patients who stay informed about the latest breakthroughs in holistic urology.

The best treatments from natural health heal more than the prostate issue that led you to use them; they heal and support other body systems, too. Certain herbs used for prostate health reduce overall inflammation or inhibit prostate cancer. Some herbs that are good for the prostate are also great for the heart. Some even affect the same toxic enzyme that leads to male pattern baldness (although, to be honest, I have not seen any patients grow back their hair).

This book will also educate you about surgery, medication and radiation, and other allopathic treatments (for example, a new method where diseased tissue is frozen, called cryosurgical ablation). You will learn when these therapies are appropriate and when they might not be. I'll also cover the latest breakthroughs in nutritional, hormonal, and "mind-body" treatments.

Chapter 2

Enlarged Prostate— Diagnosis and Mainstream Therapies

JOE GETS UP fix or six times, at all hours of the night, waking his wife up in the process. He stumbles to the toilet, and then...nothing. No stream. When finally there's a dribble, Joe has difficulty stopping and start- ing it; there's a throbbing sensation, and he feels like he hasn't finished what he felt he needed to do.

In the morning, Joe's back is aching. His sexual drive isn't what it used to be, and he's exhausted from waking up so often during the night, as is his wife, who can't get any sleep either.

Who wants to be going to the bathroom fix or six times a night and repeating this scenario? Not Joe, and not the millions of older men across America who are doing exactly this.

Joe, like any other man suffering these symptoms, needs help. He definitely should not take the "macho" route, keeping his symptoms to himself, hoping they will resolve on their own. That could be the quickest, most certain way of doing himself serious harm.

If you are reading this book, you are probably less than trusting of the more conventional allopathic medical approach taken by most urologists. Even if you want a more holistic approach, and your doctor chooses not to take one, take care to listen seriously to the diagnosis, advice and prescriptive help given to you by your medical team. They know what they are doing. Once you have consulted with other qualified health experts and done all your research, you may decide to reject or accept any or all of the prescriptions made by your doctor(s).

However, I can't stress enough how important it is to work with your urologist, particularly in reaching an accurate diagnosis that will ensure the condition is an enlarged prostate, and not prostate cancer or another disease. Hear your urologist out, and don't argue with him if he chooses not to employ holistic methods.

If your urinary condition is serious, such as urinary retention, holistic therapies are not going to give you the help you need at that time. You may need to be catheterized, and started on medicine right away to restore your bladder function. Use the advice of a well-respected urologist in your community. God has given you one bladder, and if it gets damaged and is no longer able to function, you could be on a catheter for life. I have seen this firsthand in a few patients who did not take the advice of their doctors.

Consider the bladder a muscle, like the heart. If a patient develops heart failure, they could get a heart transplant. There is no such thing as a bladder transplant (although there are some bladder substitutions, which require major surgery). If you develop bladder failure, you will require a catheter for life, affecting the quality of your life significantly. However, if your condition is mild, and you are not in a serious situation, and desire another opinion regarding your care, go elsewhere to receive advice from other qualified experts. You can always add this information to your decision-making process.

WHAT IS ENLARGED PROSTATE?

As a man matures, the prostate goes through two main periods of growth. The first occurs early in puberty, when the prostate doubles in size. During his mid-twenties, this gland begins to grow again. This second growth phase often results, years later, in BPH. In fact, the prostate continues to grow during most of a man's life, but this gradual enlargement doesn't usually cause problems before age 40.

As the prostate enlarges, the layer of tissue surrounding it stops it from expanding. The gland begins to press inward against the urethra like a clamp on a garden hose. The bladder wall thickens and becomes irritable, so that it begins to contract even when the bladder contains small amounts of urine. At first, frequent urination is the main symptom, but eventually, the bladder weakens and loses the ability to empty itself. Urine remains in the bladder after urination.

Prostate enlargement is almost as common a part of aging as gray hair. As life expectancy rises, so does the occurrence of BPH. In the United States in 2000, there were 4.5 million physician visits due to BPH.

WHY BPH OCCURS

The cause of BPH is not well understood. We don't know much about risk factors for the disease. For centuries, it has been known that BPH occurs mainly in older men and that it doesn't develop in men whose testicles were removed before puberty (and I'd hazard a guess that these men had other issues to worry about). An as-yet-incompletely understood interplay between hormonal factors and aging is the most likely culprit.

Throughout their lives, men produce both testosterone, an important male hormone, and small amounts of estrogen, a female hormone. As men age, the amount of active testosterone in the blood decreases, leaving a higher proportion of estrogen.

Studies done with animals have suggested that BPH may occur because the higher amount of estrogen within the gland increases the activity of substances that promote cell growth. For this reason, there is some speculation that specific foods, such as crucifers—broccoli, cauliflower, cabbage, brussels sprouts—and phytonutrients they contain, particularly indoles, might help to prevent the accumulation of estrogen. Supplements containing absorbable forms of cruciferous indoles might be helpful. (See also Chapter 7.)

Another theory focuses on dihydrotestosterone (DHT), a substance derived from testosterone in the prostate, which may help control its growth. Most animals lose their ability to produce DHT as they age. However, some research has indicated that even with a drop in the blood's testosterone level, older men continue to produce and accumulate high levels of DHT in the prostate. This accumulation of DHT may encourage the growth of cells. Scientists have also noted that men who do not produce DHT do not develop BPH.

Some researchers suggest that BPH may develop as a result of "instructions" given to cells early in life. According to this theory, BPH occurs because cells in one section of the gland follow these instructions and "reawaken" later in life. These "reawakened" cells then deliver signals to other cells in the gland, instructing them to grow or making them more sensitive to hormones that influence growth.

BPH SYMPTOMS

Many symptoms of BPH stem from obstruction of the urethra and gradual loss of bladder function, which results in incomplete emptying of the bladder. The symptoms of BPH vary, but the most common ones involve changes or problems with urination, such as:

• hesitant, interrupted, weak stream;

- urgency and leaking or dribbling; and
- more frequent urination, especially at night.

The size of the prostate does not always determine how severe the obstruction or the symptoms will be. Some men with greatly enlarged glands have little obstruction and few symptoms. I once had a patient with a prostate that weighed in at an astonishing 180 grams (normal adult male prostatic weight: 20 to 35 grams) who had no symptoms of BPH whatsoever. Others, whose glands are far less enlarged, have more blockage and greater problems.

Sometimes a man may not know he has any obstruction until he suddenly finds himself unable to urinate at all. This condition, called acute urinary retention, may be triggered by taking over-the-counter cold or allergy medicines. Such medicines contain a decongestant drug known as a sympathomimetic. This type of drug can prevent the bladder opening from relaxing and allowing urine to empty. When partial obstruction is present, urinary retention also can be brought on by alcohol, cold temperatures, or a long period of immobility.

It is important to tell your doctor about urinary problems like those described above. In 8 out of 10 cases, these symptoms suggest BPH, but they also can signal other, more serious conditions that require prompt treatment. These conditions, including prostate cancer, can be ruled out only by a doctor's exam. Then again, you may have a simple urinary tract infection, which can easily be detected by a urine culture.

Severe BPH can cause serious problems over time. Urine retention and strain on the bladder can lead to urinary tract infections, bladder or kidney damage, bladder stones, and incontinence. If the bladder is permanently damaged, treatment for BPH may be ineffective. It's essential to get treatment for BPH in its earlier stages to avoid these kinds of complications. On the other hand, you and your doctor may decide together that your condition is mild and doesn't yet need aggressive treatment. This "watchful waiting" approach may be fine, as long as you remember that the key word is watchful. If symptoms begin to worsen, it's time to get back to thinking about treatment.

While you watchfully wait, be sure to try the herbal and other natural remedies I will tell you about throughout this book. They may prevent your ever having to have surgery or take drugs to treat your BPH.

DIAGNOSIS

You may first notice symptoms of BPH yourself, or your primary care doctor may find that your prostate is enlarged during a routine checkup. Once you've been referred to a urologist, you'll receive several tests that will help the doctor identify the problem and decide whether any treatment or further evaluation is needed. He will take a detailed medical history focusing on the urinary tract, previous surgical procedures, and other general health issues, such as current use of prescription or over-the-counter medications (some drugs can impair urination). Expect a digital rectal exam (DRE) and urinalysis to help rule out the possibility of prostate infection and bladder or prostate cancer. Your doctor should be especially careful to rule out prostatitis, which often masquerades as BPH.

Digital Rectal Exam (DRE)

This exam, a favorite of men everywhere, is usually the first test done. The doctor inserts a gloved finger into the rectum and feels the part of the prostate next to the rectum. This exam gives the doctor a general idea of the size and condition of the gland. If he finds any irregular or abnormally firm areas, he will do further testing to figure out whether cancer is the cause. This exam can also determine if there is any tenderness or fullness of the prostate, indicating an inflammation in the gland (prostatitis).

Prostate Specific Antigen (PSA) Blood Test

The PSA measures blood levels of a protein made in the cells of the prostate. A normal result will fall below 4 ng/ml (nanograms per milliliter). In the past, this value of 4 ng/ml was considered to be the standard cut-off value. However, with more testing and studies, we've found that this cut-off point may be too high, as many patients have been found to have cancer with lower PSA values. This is especially important for younger patients (below 50 years) and African American men, whose PSA values may be different than Caucasians. However, most urologists agree that results between 4 and 10 are considered borderline high, and anything above 10 is a strong indication that cancer is present. The American Cancer Society recommends that all men aged 50 and up have yearly PSA tests performed. African American men may be advised to be tested starting at 40 or 45.

The higher the PSA, the more likely that you're dealing with prostate cancer—but this test alone does not give all the information needed to make a prostate cancer diagnosis. Even if the PSA comes back low, this doesn't rule out cancer of the prostate. Your urologist will need to account for your age (there are age-specific PSA ranges), and additional blood tests can be performed to help clarify what you're dealing with: the percent-free PSA test, PSA velocity, and the PSA density (PSAD). In the end, if cancer is suspected, the only way to definitively confirm the diagnosis is to perform a biopsy of the suspicious tissue. (See Chapter 5 for more information on the PSA and prostate cancer.)

Urine Flow Study

Sometimes a doctor will ask a patient to urinate into a special device that measures how quickly the urine is flowing. A reduced flow may help with a BPH diagnosis, although it doesn't give us enough information to make a conclusive diagnosis. Reduced flow can suggest a BPH problem, but it may have other causes—urethral stricture, for example, or perhaps an impaired bladder. Understand that the uroflow is just a screening test that allows doctors to check whether the bladder is contracting and the sphincter is relaxing—both hallmarks of normal urination, known jointly as the *micturition reflex*. An abnormal uroflow indicates a voiding dysfunction and should be followed up with further testing.

Show up for your uroflow test with a full bladder. A small amount of urine voided will make the test inaccurate and the urologist will not be able to interpret the results properly.

The results of your uroflow will come back in terms of:
• Maximum Flow Rate
• Volume Voided
• Voiding Time (always)
• Flow Time (if intermittent)
• Average Flow Rate (cc/sec)

Cystoscopy

In this exam, the doctor inserts a small fiber optic tube through the opening of the urethra in the penis. (If the very thought of this causes you to wince and cross your legs, don't worry—the inside lining of the penis, called the urethra, is numbed first with a topical anesthetic solution.) The tube, called a cystoscope, contains a lens and a light system, which help the doctor see the inside of the urethra, prostate and bladder. This test allows the doctor to determine the size of the gland and to see exactly where and how severe the obstruction is. This is done routinely for patients that have a history of blood in the urine, as the cystoscopy remains the gold standard for detecting bladder cancer. This test should not take more than 5 to 10 minutes to perform, and is done in the doctor's office.

In addition to bladder cancer, which may also show urinary symptoms, cystoscopy helps us to detect bladder stones and other lesions in the bladder. If there is a narrowing in the urethra, known as a stricture, this can also be detected by the cystoscope, and if the stricture is small, it can be dilated or stretched at that time.

Ultimately, your best diagnosis will come from the use of at least two of these tests, and possibly more. Once a diagnosis of BPH is confirmed, it's time to decide what treatment, if any, is necessary.

Urodynamic Testing

If, after the tests already mentioned, the cause of urinary symptoms is unknown or unclear to the urologist, a test to examine the functioning of the bladder may be ordered. Earlier, I mentioned that the bladder is a muscle, just like the heart. Think of bladder function in two ways: It stores urine and empties urine. The muscle to the bladder works because it is controlled by a series of nerves, which are connected to your brain and spinal cord. If a patient has an underlying neurological problem, such as diabetes, Parkinson's disease, stroke, transient ischemic attack (TIA, a form of stroke), or spinal cord injury, these could all affect the functioning of the bladder.

Urodynamic testing is comprised of a series of individual tests:

1. A cystometrogram (CMG), where a very small catheter is inserted into the bladder to measure pressure during various stages of urination. CMG tests how well the bladder muscle stretches during filling, how well it stores fluid, and how well you empty your bladder. During the test, a small tube is placed in your rectum so that we can isolate the pressure of the bladder muscle itself. Although this doesn't sound all that pleasant, the test is over in about 20 to 30 minutes, and most patients

find it only slightly bothersome. I think the worst part of the exam is having to urinate in front of the professional staff that is doing the testing. That's not always so easy.

There are times when we need to perform video urodynamics. This uses a contrast dye to fill your bladder and an x-ray procedure known as fluoroscopy. During video urodynamics, you will be able to see your bladder on a TV-like screen during each stage of the procedure. The size of the bladder can be determined, and we can determine whether there are any abnormalities to the structure of the bladder. If there has been long-standing high pressure in the bladder, the wall of the bladder can become weakened, and pouches (diverticula) may form. Bladder diverticula may trap urine and debris, possibly leading to infections, bladder stones, or cancers.

2. Electromyograph (EMG) involves the placement of skin patches on either side of the rectum to test the muscle activity of the external sphincter muscle. The EMG is done at the same time as the CMG. During urination, the bladder should contract and the sphincter muscle should relax. This coordinated activity between the sphincter and the bladder muscle requires proper neurological functioning. Some conditions can affect the sphincter muscle, including certain medications, neurological conditions and previous surgery on the lower urinary tract. The EMG can help the physician determine if the urination problem is related to the sphincter, and can aid in treatments like pelvic exercises and biofeedback.

TREATMENT FOR BPH

Men who have BPH with symptoms usually need some kind of treatment at some time, but several recent studies have questioned the need for early treatment, especially when the gland is just mildly enlarged and the symptoms are mild. We're finding that the symptoms of BPH can clear up without treatment in as many as one-third of all mild cases. If you have a mild case, your urologist may recommend regular checkups: the "watchful waiting" approach. If the condition becomes a more serious inconvenience or poses a danger to your health, treatment usually is recommended at that point. At the Center for Holistic Urology, we have found that these milder cases lend themselves particularly well to the use of herbs, nutrients, and other aspects of integrative medicine.

Since BPH may cause urinary tract infections, a doctor will usually clear up any infection with antibiotics before treating the BPH itself. Although the need for treatment is not usually urgent, doctors generally advise going ahead with treatment once the problems become bothersome or present a health risk.

Here's a listing of the types of allopathic treatments most commonly used for BPH:

Drug Treatment

Over the years, researchers have tried to find a way to shrink the prostate, or at least stop its growth, without using surgery. The FDA has approved four drugs to relieve common symptoms associated with an enlarged prostate.

Among the most widely prescribed drugs today for the treatment of BPH are 5 alpha-reductase inhibitors, such as finasteride and dutasteride (Proscar and Avodart), and the alpha-blockers, also known as smooth-muscle relaxants.

Drugs to Shrink Your Prostate. Finasteride (Proscar), FDA-approved in 1992, and dutasteride (Avodart), FDA-approved in 2001, inhibit production of the hormone DHT, the form of testosterone that increases with age and that has growth-promoting effects on the prostate. They do so by inhibiting the enzyme, 5 alpha-reductase, that converts testosterone into DHT; as a class, the drugs are called 5 alpha-reductase inhibitors.

The use of either of these drugs can prevent progression of prostate growth; in some men, these drugs actually shrink the gland. By 1994, finasteride was being used by some half-million men in 25 countries.

Unfortunately, these drugs haven't earned rave reviews. Some doctors say that they're a bust. In a 1994 report in the *New England Journal of Medicine*, researchers note that improvement in symptoms of men suffering BPH—including urinary flow— was "not impressive." Although rapid regression of the enlarged prostate occurs in most men, fewer than 50 percent show improvement in the realm of increased urinary flow and improvement of BPH with 12 months of finasteride treatment. Men with mild symptoms appear to have the slimmest chance of benefiting from these drugs. Medical experts now say that finasteride might help only, at best, a "small number of men." And, to add insult to injury, no published study has addressed the question of whether finasteride prevents long-term progression of the disease.

When I was training, if a patient showed up with a large prostate, we took it out. Now, we only remove a prostate gland when it is causing symptoms. If the patient has only obstructive symptoms (problems with emptying the bladder) and the gland is enlarged, we have a good chance of reducing symptoms with drugs. Sometimes we get decent results with a combination of a 5 alpha-reductase inhibitor like Proscar and an alpha-blocker like Flomax. But not all prostate drugs have the same results on each patient. We can't rely on them to fix this growing problem.

Another nail in finasteride's coffin: Another report, this one in 1996 from the *New England Journal of Medicine*, confirmed finasteride's lack of efficacy. In fact, drugs like terazosin (Hytrin), not originally developed for prostate but rather for blood pressure problems, worked better than finasteride, even though Hytrin and its ilk present a witches' brew of complications men also need to know about (more on this below).

Some 10 percent of men who use finasteride experience short-term side effects like decreased sex drive and impotence. And, an important precaution for men who are still interested in having children: Finasteride tablets should not be handled by pregnant women or those who may become pregnant. Men who want to try to conceive should stop taking the drug several weeks before doing so, and they should take care that no woman who could become pregnant handles the tablets. The drug can be absorbed through the woman's skin. If a pregnant woman has contact with this drug, the result may be major malformations of the fetus's sexual organs. Finally, anyone considering the use of a 5 alpha-reductase inhibitor should know that the drug will reduce PSA even if prostate cancer is present; in other words, finasteride may "mask" the presence of prostate cancer.

Recently, the results of the Prostate Cancer Prevention Trial (PCPT) were published in the *New England Journal of Medicine*. The purpose of the trial was to find out whether finasteride could prevent prostate cancer. In order to answer this question, nearly 18,000 men were enrolled in a national clinical trial in the United States. Men were randomized to take either finasteride or placebo for seven years. The trial was terminated early because of the significant findings: Men taking the finasteride had a 25 percent reduction in the incidence of prostate cancer. This was a very positive finding in the trial.

Unfortunately, in the men that did develop prostate cancer and were taking finasteride, the cancers were more aggressive than the cancers that developed in the men taking the placebo. Initially positive results have now been revealed to merit a great deal of caution. Urologists are still debating the role of finasteride at conferences and in medical literature, and the verdict is still unclear. Should we place men—especially those who are at higher risk for developing prostate cancer—on Proscar?

At this point in time, taking into account all of the data, I would personally not take the medication to prevent prostate cancer. It is possible that Proscar may be killing off the low-grade cancers, and leaving the more aggressive ones to live. But, as you may suspect, the low-grade, non-aggressive cancers are rarely a concern for most patients, and I would be concerned about developing an aggressive form of the cancer with this medication.

Smooth Muscle Relaxants: The Alpha-Blockers. The FDA has also approved four alpha-blocker drugs for the treatment of BPH: terazosin (Hytrin) in 1993, doxazosin (Cardura) in 1995, tamsulosin (Flomax) in 1997, and alfuzosin (Uroxatral) in 2003. All four drugs, which are part of a class known as alpha-blockers, relax the smooth muscle of the prostate and bladder neck, improving urine flow and reducing bladder outlet obstruction. Hytrin and Cardura were first developed to treat high blood pressure; Flomax and Uroxatral were developed specifically to treat BPH.

According to the results of the National Institute of Diabetes & Digestive & Kidney Diseases (NIDDK) Medical Therapy of Prostatic Symptoms (MTOPS) Trial, using Proscar and Cardura (doxazosin) together is more effective than either drug alone for the relief of symptoms and prevention of BPH progression. The two-drug regimen reduced the risk of BPH progression by 67 percent, compared to 39 percent for Cardura alone and 34 percent for Proscar alone.

The FDA has noted that urinary flow rate and symptom relief were improved more rapidly in Hytrin patients than in those using finasteride. Similar drugs, such as prazosin (Minipress), have also been shown to improve BPH symptoms in the short term. The real question, however, is their long-term effectiveness. Nobody knows whether they stop the progression of the disease.

The FDA approved Uroxatral (alfuzosin) in 2003 for the treatment of BPH, based on three 12-week studies involving 1,608 subjects, 473 of whom received 10 mg of Uroxatral daily. All of the subjects filled out the International Prostate Symptom Score (IPSS, or AUA Symptom Score) survey, consisting of seven questions that assess the severity of both irritative (frequency, urgency, nocturia) and obstructive (incomplete emptying, stopping and starting, weak stream, and pushing or straining) symptoms, with possible scores ranging from 0 to 35.

All three studies showed significant reduction in symptoms between the study's outset and the last assessment in subjects using Uroxatral. Improvement in urinary flow rates was also found in two of the three studies. These are promising results.

The FDA has warned that you should not take Uroxatral if you:

- have liver problems;
- are taking antifungal drugs like ketoconazole or HIV drugs called protease inhibitors;
- are already taking an alpha-blocker for either high blood pressure or prostate problems;
- are a woman;
- are a child under the age of 18;
- are allergic to Uroxatral's active ingredient, alfuzosin hydrochloride.

Some special warnings should be heeded with regard to this medication. Uroxatral can cause a sudden drop in blood pressure, possibly leading to fainting, dizziness, or lightheadedness, especially at the beginning of treatment. This is a possibility with all drugs in the alpha-blocker class.

Do not drive, operate machinery, or do any dangerous activities until you know how the medicine affects you. If you already have a problem with low blood pressure or take medicines to treat high blood pressure, this side effect is more likely to be a problem for you. If you begin to feel dizzy or light-headed, lie down with your legs and feet up, and if your symptoms do not improve, call your doctor. Other common side effects with Uroxatral are headache and tiredness.

One potential advantage of Uroxatral over the other alpha-blocker medications is relatively normal ejaculation. Other alpha-blockers are often associated with retrograde ejaculation, which means that no semen is propelled from the urethra during climax. This may be uncomfortable for some men, and may deter them from using the medication.

With any alpha-blocker, patients should avoid driving or hazardous tasks for 12 hours after the first dose, after a dosage increase, and when treatment is stopped and started again. Other adverse reactions to alpha-blockers may include weakness, headache, nasal congestion, heart palpitations (flutters), rapid pulse, nausea, swelling of the ankles, abnormal neurological sensations, sleepiness, shortness of breath, and blurred vision.

Alpha-blockers, such as Flomax or Uroxatral, may be required to quickly clear a blockage of the urethra in cases of acute urinary retention. As soon as it is practical, however, men should work with their doctor to reduce their dosage and replace its use with our recommended safer alternatives for long-term care.

Minimally Invasive Therapy

Swollen prostate tissues can be removed by one of two routes: through the urethra (transurethrally) or through an incision in the abdomen (open prostatectomy).

You can think of the prostate as an orange; the peel is the capsule, and the inner part is the adenoma. For enlargement, we only need to open the peel and remove some or all of the fruit. If we need only to remove some of the fruit, we can do it transurethrally, but if we need to remove all of it, we will do an open simple prostatectomy. With these procedures, the capsule still produces the fluids that go into the ejaculate, and regrowth can occur. In the case of cancer, it may be necessary to remove the entire gland, peel and all, in a process called radical prostatectomy.

When we are dealing with BPH, the choice of surgery depends upon the size of the gland. If it weighs less than 60 grams, and medical therapy (5 alpha-reductase inhibitors and smooth-muscle relaxants) has failed and the patient still has significant urinary tract complaints, the gold standard is transurethral resection of the prostate (TURP). This procedure gives the best results.

Other transurethral therapies can work well on smaller glands, including microwave, transurethral needle ablation (TUNA), or laser (all of which are discussed in greater detail below). These therapies can be done in an office setting without general anesthesia or a hospital stay. While they are probably not as good at fixing BPH as TURP, they may be the best option for men with mild symptoms.

Here are the procedures that have been developed to relieve BPH symptoms without open prostatectomy:

Transurethral Microwave Procedures. In May 1996, the FDA approved the Prostatron, a device that uses microwaves to heat and destroy excess prostate tissue. In transurethral microwave thermotherapy (TUMT), the Prostatron sends computer-regulated microwaves through a catheter to heat selected portions of the prostate to at least 111 degrees Fahrenheit. A cooling system protects the urinary tract during the procedure.

A similar microwave device, the Targis System, received FDA approval in September 1997. Like the Prostatron, the Targis System delivers microwaves to destroy selected portions of the prostate and uses a cooling system to protect the urethra. A heat-sensing device inserted in the rectum helps monitor the therapy.

Both procedures take about one hour and can be performed on an outpatient basis with local anesthesia. Neither procedure has been reported to lead to impotence or incontinence.

Although microwave therapy does not cure BPH, it reduces urinary frequency, urgency, straining, and intermittent flow. It does not correct the problem of incomplete emptying of the bladder. Ongoing research will determine any long-term effects of microwave therapy and who might benefit most from this therapy.

Transurethral Needle Ablation (TUNA). In October 1996, the FDA approved VidaMed's minimally invasive transurethral needle ablation (TUNA) system for the treatment of BPH. The TUNA system delivers low-level radio frequency energy through twin needles to burn away a well-defined region of the enlarged prostate. The thermal ablative therapy can reach temperatures as high as 110 degrees Celsius. Shields protect the urethra from heat damage. In the TUNA procedure, obstructive prostate tissue is destroyed (ablated) using radio frequency (RF) energy. Only the obstructive tissue is destroyed. The urethra and the rest of the prostate remain intact. The procedure can be performed without general or spinal anesthesia, and is considered an outpatient procedure.

The TUNA system improves urine flow and relieves symptoms with fewer side effects when compared with transurethral resection of the prostate (TURP). No incontinence or impotence have been observed. About 40 percent of the patients need to be catheterized for three days on average. About 60 percent of patients do not require catheterization. TUNA therapy is covered by Medicare in all 50 states and Puerto Rico.

Surgery

Most doctors recommend removal of the enlarged part of the prostate as the best long-term solution for patients with BPH.

With surgery for BPH, only the enlarged tissue that is pressing against the urethra is removed; the rest of the inside tissue and the outside capsule are left intact. Surgery usually relieves the obstruction and incomplete emptying caused by BPH.

Some 25 to 30 percent of men with BPH ultimately require surgery. Compared with other treatments, surgery often offers the most promise for relief of BPH symptoms and, ultimately, the lowest cost. Men should recognize, however, that some surgical procedures offer only temporary benefits, and that complications can lead to incontinence and impotency.

There are a few surgical options to choose from:

Transurethral Resection of the Prostate (TURP). This is the gold standard urological procedure for men who need to have obstructing prostate tissue removed. There has been a significant evolution in the way that the TURP is performed over the past 40 years, owing mostly to improved instrumentation and light sources. Currently, the procedure is usually performed with the aid of a video camera, and the magnification from the lens allows the urologist perfect vision. As a resident, I stayed up all night with many patients who were bleeding after a TURP. Today, bleeding after this procedure is extremely rare, and the transfusion rate is nearly zero percent. Today the TURP is used for 90 percent of all BPH surgeries.

Patients that choose a TURP come to the hospital on the day of the procedure. After the patient receives anesthesia, the surgeon inserts a resectoscope into the urethra through the penis. The resectoscope, which is about 12 inches long and a half an inch in diameter, contains a light, valves for controlling irrigating fluid, and an electrical loop that cuts tissue and seals blood vessels. During the 30- to 60-minute operation, the surgeon uses the resectoscope's wire loop to remove the obstructing tissue one piece at a time. The pieces of tissue are carried by the fluid into the bladder and then flushed out at the end of the operation.

The benefit here is that no incision through the skin is necessary. The patient will stay in the hospital usually overnight with a catheter to wash and clear the bladder of any clots and debris, and then will be sent home the next morning. Most patients are sent home without needing a catheter.

TURP has long-term benefits for most patients. In the past, the TURP was associated with incontinence and impotency in nearly 20 percent of patients. This is rare these days. The most common side effect with the TURP today remains retrograde ejaculation, which is harmless (if a bit uncomfortable). However, the studies do reveal that up to 15 percent of men who undergo this procedure require repeat surgery within eight years.

Transurethral Incision of the Prostate (TUIP). Another surgical procedure is called transurethral incision of the prostate (TUIP). It is used when the prostate is only mildly enlarged. Instead of removing tissue, this procedure widens the urethra by making a few small cuts in the bladder neck, where the urethra joins the bladder, and in the prostate gland itself. These cuts reduce the prostate's pressure on the urethra, making it easier to urinate. Although TUIP is often slightly less effective than TURP, most patients will show symptom improvement. There is minimal chance of becoming impotent after surgery. About 1 in 10 men may require retreatment within the first five years following this procedure. Still, its advantages and long-term side effects have not been clearly established, although there is a clear reduction in the risk of retrograde ejaculation. I believe that this form of treatment should be used in the younger patient with a smaller prostate, who is concerned about maintaining normal ejaculation.

Open Simple Prostatectomy. Open prostatectomy is the surgical procedure of choice when the prostate gland is very enlarged, or if the bladder has been damaged and needs surgical repair. An incision is made in the lower abdomen to remove part of the inside of the prostate. Most patients show improvement with this surgery, but there can be a cost: Depending on the specific type of procedure used, the risk of impotency following surgery can be as high as about one in three, and there may be a period of time when the patient experiences mild urinary leakage. The surgery is also the most traumatic of the available treatments, requiring a longer hospital stay and more extended recuperation once home. There may also be bleeding during the surgery, and the transfusion rate can be as high as 20 to 30 percent. This surgery was very common when I was training, especially since we did not have drug treatments to shrink the gland as we do today. Currently, at our hospital, this surgery is rarely performed.

Before submitting to this open prostate surgery, men should get a second opinion, and should seriously consider other options. Many urologists are now performing the TURP procedure instead of open prostatectomy. In addition, the new vaporization and green-light procedures are being performed on very large prostates, which may make this surgery even more obsolete.

Laser Surgery. In March 1996, the FDA approved a surgical procedure that employs side-firing laser fibers and Nd:YAG lasers to vaporize obstructing prostate tissue. The doctor passes the laser fiber through the urethra into the prostate using a cystoscope and delivers several bursts of energy lasting 30 to 60 seconds. The laser energy destroys prostate tissue and causes shrinkage. Like TURP, laser surgery requires anesthesia and a hospital stay. One advantage of laser surgery over TURP is that laser surgery causes little blood loss. Laser surgery also allows for a quicker recovery time. But laser surgery may not be effective on larger prostates.

In a multicenter randomized trial at six U.S. hospitals, 72 men with bladder outflow obstruction due to benign prostatic hyperplasia were treated with either TURP or laser. Of the 35 men who had TURP, 6 required retreatment within the first year, and after two years, the TURP patients had slightly better median peak flow rates than the men who had laser treatment. Symptom indexes and quality-of-life measures were similarly improved in both groups. Of 37 laser patients, 6 (16 percent) were retreated with TURP in the first year. Sexual function declined in the TURP group but remained stable in the laser group. Adverse event rates were similar, although the events were more serious in the TURP group.

Overall, given the advantages of an outpatient procedure, similar results in symptom reduction and quality-of-life measures, and less severe adverse effects, laser treatment for patients with relatively small prostates can be an acceptable alternative to TURP.

The latest laser to hit the wire for the treatment of an enlarged prostate is the GreenLight PVP (photoselective vaporization of the prostate) Laser, which received FDA clearance in May 2001. The new GreenLight PVP system uses a special, patented green-light laser, which appears to have a more effective wavelength than other lasers when it comes to removing excess prostate tissue. The procedure is minimally invasive: A laser fiber is threaded into the urethra to deliver the green-light energy through a cystoscope, then removed. GreenLight treatment appears to have the same success rate as standard TURP in alleviating symptoms, with less bleeding and a shorter hospital stay.

This is clearly an advance in technology for urologists, and can be performed even on very large prostates. Many patients do not require a catheter after PVP, and those who do typically are catheterized for less than 24 hours. Patients are advised to avoid strenuous exercise for two weeks following the procedure and can usually resume regular activities the next day. PVP provides immediate and long-lasting results comparable with other minimally invasive procedures, and may become the leader in this area of surgery over the next few years.

An additional benefit of laser surgery: Patients who are taking blood thinners, such as aspirin and coumadin, can stay on these medications and have the procedure performed.

WHAT YOU CAN EXPECT POST-SURGERY

If you have surgery, you'll probably need to stay in the hospital. The length of your stay depends on the type of surgery you had and how quickly you recover.

At the end of surgery, a catheter tube is inserted through the opening of the penis to drain urine from the bladder into a collection bag. This device, called a Foley catheter, is kept in place by a small, water-filled balloon on the end of the tube that is inserted into the bladder. This catheter is usually left in place for several days. Sometimes, the catheter causes painful bladder spasms the day after surgery. Urine may leak around the catheter, and there may be pain with bowel movements. If you ask for medication for catheter-related discomfort, you'll probably receive bladder antispasmodics like Detrol LA or Ditropan. Spasms will eventually disappear on their own.

You may also be given antibiotics while you are in the hospital. Many doctors start giving this medicine before or soon after surgery to prevent infection. However, some recent studies suggest that antibiotics may not be needed in every case, and your doctor may prefer not to prescribe these medications unless an infection develops.

After surgery, you will probably notice some blood or clots in your urine as the wound starts to heal. If your bladder is being irrigated (flushed with water), you may notice that your urine becomes red once the irrigation is stopped. Some bleeding is normal, and it should clear up by the time you leave the hospital. During your recovery, it is important to drink a lot of water (up to eight cups a day) to help flush out the bladder and speed healing.

AFTER LEAVING THE HOSPITAL

Take it easy the first few weeks after you get home. You may not have any pain, but you still have an incision that is healing—even with transurethral surgery, where the incision can't be seen. Since many people try to do too much at the beginning and then have a setback, it is a good idea to talk to your doctor before resuming your normal routine. During this initial period of recovery at home, avoid any straining or sudden movements that could tear the incision. Here are some guidelines:

- Continue drinking a lot of water to flush the bladder. Avoid aspirin or vitamin E; they may promote bleeding.
- Don't do any heavy lifting.
- Don't drive or operate machinery.
- Avoid straining when moving your bowels. Eat a balanced diet to prevent constipation. If constipation occurs, ask your doctor if you can take a laxative.

GETTING BACK TO NORMAL

Even though you should feel much better by the time you leave the hospital, it will probably take a couple of months for you to heal completely. During the recovery period, you might experience some of these common problems:

Problems urinating. You may notice that your urinary stream is stronger right after surgery, but it may take a while before you can urinate completely normally again. After the catheter is removed, urine will pass over the surgical wound on the prostate, and you may initially have some discomfort or feel a sense of urgency when you urinate. This problem will gradually lessen, though, and after a couple of months you should be able to urinate less frequently and more easily.

Inability to control urination (incontinence). As the bladder returns to normal, you may have some temporary problems controlling urination, but long-term incontinence rarely occurs. Doctors find that the longer problems existed before surgery, the longer it will take for the bladder to regain its full function after the operation.

Bleeding. In the first few weeks after transurethral surgery, the scab inside the bladder may loosen, and blood may suddenly appear in the urine. Although this can be alarming, the bleeding usually stops with a short period of bed rest and drinking fluids. However, if your urine is so red that it is difficult to see through, if it contains clots, or if you feel any discomfort, be sure to contact your doctor.

SEXUAL FUNCTION AFTER SURGERY

Many men worry about whether surgery for BPH will affect their ability to enjoy sex. Some sources state that sexual function is rarely affected, while others claim that it can cause problems in up to 30 percent of all men who undergo surgery. However, most doctors say that even though it takes awhile for sexual function to return fully, most men are able to enjoy sex again, with time.

Complete recovery of sexual function may take up to a year, lagging behind a person's general recovery. The exact length of time depends on how long symptoms were present before surgery was performed, and on the type of surgery that was performed. Surgery for BPH may affect:

Erections. Most doctors agree that if you were able to maintain an erection shortly before surgery, you will probably be able to have an erection afterward. Surgery rarely causes a loss of erectile function, but surgery cannot usually restore function that was lost before the operation.

Ejaculation. Although most men are able to continue having erections after surgery, any surgery on the prostate—both minimally invasive therapies and prostatectomy—is likely to cause retrograde ejaculation or "dry climax." (With radical prostatectomy for cancer, where the entire gland and the seminal vesicles are removed, no semen is produced at all.) During sexual activity, sperm from the testes enters the urethra near the opening of the bladder. Normally, a muscle blocks off the entrance to the bladder, and the semen is expelled through the penis. The coring action of prostate surgery cuts this muscle as it widens the neck of the bladder. Following surgery, semen takes the path of least resistance and enters the wider opening to the bladder rather than being expelled through the penis. Later, it is harmlessly flushed out with urine.

In some cases, this condition can be treated with a drug called pseudoephedrine, found in many cold medicines, or another drug called imipramine. These drugs improve muscle tone at the bladder neck and prevent semen from entering the bladder.

Men who wish to conceive despite retrograde ejaculation can urinate into a sterile container after ejaculating, and sperm can be collected, alkalinized, and used for *in vitro* fertilization.

Orgasm. Most men find little or no difference in the sensation of sexual climax before and after surgery. Although it may take some time to get used to retrograde ejaculation, you should eventually find sex as pleasurable after surgery as before.

Many men find that concerns about sexual function can interfere with sex as much as the operation itself. Understanding the surgical procedure and talking over any worries with the doctor before surgery often help men regain sexual function sooner afterwards. Many men also find it helpful to talk to a counselor during the adjustment period after surgery. I often prescribe some of the oral agents like Viagra (100 mg, not more than three times per week) or Levitra for patients during this time to help them regain confidence and erectile function during sex.

IS FURTHER TREATMENT NEEDED?

In the years after your surgery, it is important to continue having a rectal exam once a year and to have any symptoms checked by your doctor.

Since surgery for BPH leaves behind a good part of the gland, it is still possible for prostate problems, including BPH, to develop again. Surgery usually offers relief from BPH for at least 15 years. Only 10 percent of the men who have surgery for BPH eventually need a second operation to treat further enlargement. Usually these are men who had their first surgery at an early age.

It is possible that scar tissue from BPH surgery will require treatment in the year after surgery. In rare cases, the opening of the bladder becomes scarred and shrinks, causing obstruction. This problem may require a surgical procedure similar to transurethral incision (TUIP). More often, scar tissue forms in the urethra and causes narrowing. This problem can usually be solved during an office visit, where the doctor stretches or dilates the urethra.

PROSTATIC STENTS

A stent is a small device that, when inserted through the urethra, expands like a spring to open up a narrowed area. The FDA approved the UroLume endoprosthesis in 1996 to relieve urinary obstruction in men and improve their ability to urinate. The device is approved for use in men for whom other standard surgical procedures to correct urinary obstruction have failed.

BPH AND PROSTATE CANCER:
NO APPARENT RELATION

Although some of the signs of BPH and prostate cancer are the same, having BPH does not seem to increase the chances of getting prostate cancer. A man who has BPH may have undetected prostate cancer at the same time, or may develop prostate cancer in the future, but no causal relationship between the two has been found. For this reason, the National Cancer Institute and the American Cancer Society recommend that all men over 50 have a rectal exam once a year to screen for prostate cancer.

Tissue removed during BPH surgery is routinely checked for hidden cancer cells. In about 1 out of 10 cases, some cancer tissue is found, but often it is limited to a few cells of a nonaggressive type of cancer, and no treatment is needed.

SMART CONSUMERS GET A SECOND OPINION ON DOCTORS' TREATMENTS

Before committing to your doctor's recommendation—unless, of course, you are in a life-threatening situation—take a step back and examine your options. The options are so extensive that it is important for you to know about both the benefits and risks associated with conventional treatments, so that you can make an informed medical choice.

If symptoms are only mild, "watchful waiting" may be appropriate. Simply doing nothing may be too passive, however; you will likely want to do something to improve your chances of avoiding medications and surgery. Here is where I believe that you should consider some natural formulas that, in my opinion and that of a growing number of U.S. medical experts, are showing some benefit for patients with mild forms of BPH. I want to review with you now the alternative approaches to BPH.

Chapter 3

BPH—
The Holistic Approach

THE HOLISTIC APPROACH to prostate health attempts to correct underlying conditions through many different modalities. It involves diet, nutritional habits, natural medicines, lifestyle, stress levels, exercise, and personal hygiene. Men in other parts of the world, particularly Europe, commonly use natural medicines and successfully avoid prostate surgery and drugs. Even mainstream urologists are starting to hear about these therapies, because the science is sophisticated and the results are impressive.

Why haven't you heard more about these therapies, then? Because these natural medicines, which cannot be patented, simply aren't profitable enough to the large drug companies. Since drug companies can't make big profits on natural substances, they don't put the money into the research or the advertising necessary to put a natural medicine on the map.

Doctors who want to know more about natural medicines have to do their own homework—not an easy task when added to the huge amount of allopathic research in which they are expected to stay current, not to mention learning how to do new procedures or finding out about new drugs. The allopathic community is only just beginning to embrace alternative medicine (herbs, nutrients) rather than expeditiously shunning any colleague who dares suggest that roots and leaves might be medicine every bit as good as chemical pharmaceuticals.

In many instances, doctors first learn of alternative therapies through their patients—just as I did back at the Atkins Center. Help your doctor help you by staying abreast of the latest research into alternative therapies for your condition, and letting him or her know what you would like to try and what seems to work well for you. Or, hand your doctor a copy of this book.

I also believe that it is important to inform your physician of the alternative therapies that you are taking, just as you would for pharmaceuticals. The reason for this is that some of these may interfere with medications that you are taking. In addition, if you are planning to have a surgical procedure, it may be necessary to stop taking certain vitamins and herbs as they may cause more bleeding. Vitamin E, for example, should definitely be stopped, for at least a week before the procedure.

THE SAFE AND NATURAL
PATHWAY TO PROSTATE HEALTH

In recent years, mainstream medicine has rediscovered the wisdom of ancient healers, proving that the efficacy and safety of many traditional, natural remedies can easily stand up to the rigors of controlled trials. Plant medicines, long used by native healers to treat genitourinary problems, are being discovered by modern science.

You can put these botanical medicines from nature's pharmacy to work for you. Recent evidence of their power to maintain prostate health has been demonstrated in clinical trials, and has demonstrated activity similar to the 5 alpha-reductase inhibitors or alpha-blockers. Generally, men show improvement, although it may take weeks to months for supplements to "kick in" and yield benefits. I have yet to see a man experience unpleasant side effects from the herbs discussed below.

HERBAL REMEDIES
Saw Palmetto Berry Extract

One important healing herb that should be in a natural men's support formula is *Serenoa serrulata sabal*: the saw palmetto berry. Saw palmetto is a dwarf palm that grows to be 6 to 10 feet tall, and can be found in sandy, wind-swept coastal areas of the southeastern United States, especially Florida, Louisiana, Georgia, and South Carolina.

Native Americans have long used saw palmetto as an invigorating tonic for the entire genitourinary system. In 1892, an article by A. L. Marcy appeared in the *American Journal of Urology*. The author noted that 9 of 10 men eventually will suffer an enlarged prostate, and that saw palmetto had been proven especially effective in treating this problem.

In my own urological practice, I prefer to start patients with minimal lower urinary tract symptoms with saw palmetto. For example: If the patient is just starting to notice that his stream has diminished, or perhaps he is getting up one to two times per night, he would be an ideal patient to start with herbals rather than medications. In cases where the symptoms worsen, and the patient is experiencing more discomfort, I add medicines like Proscar and an alpha-blocker (Flomax or Uroxatral). In rare cases where these combinations do not help, or there is bleeding from the prostate, I recommend surgery—minimally invasive, if possible.

Medicinally, the most important part of the plant is its wrinkled, oval-shaped, red-brown berries. This powerful plant's effectiveness in the treatment of BPH has been extensively studied by the modern European medical community, with favorable results. Use of this plant extract has been shown to be effective in terms of improving urinary flow rate and decreasing residual urine volume. Moreover, *Serenoa serrulata* is effective over extended periods of time.

Saw palmetto works in a manner similar to that of finasteride, inhibiting the enzyme responsible for the formation of DHT and preventing uptake of DHT by prostatic tissue. As for side effects, there are none, and no known cases of drug interactions.

The authors of a report in the Italian medical journal *Terapia Medica* note, "In view of the almost complete absence of side effects, the lack of [negative] changes produced in terms of sexual activity, and the clear improvement in [symptoms], we believe *Serenoa* [*serrulata*] to be a useful drug, and one which in particular should be adopted in the early phases of [enlarged prostate]."

Buyer Beware

Keep in mind as you read on that a lot of companies are trying to make a quick dollar on this hugely popular herbal healer, but only a few are paying attention to producing a quality product that really works.

The amount generally recommended corresponds to the degree of standardization of the extract. In fact, if you don't purchase a broad-spectrum extract that provides the fatty acid fraction required for clinical efficacy, you may not get the results you expect.

The major studies on saw palmetto were all conducted using a specific concentrated extract form of the plant's berries. The berries are a rich source of oils, powerful fatty acids that have shown a remarkable affinity for the male genitourinary tract and for inhibiting excesses of the testosterone by-product DHT.

Saw palmetto works by:

- helping to rebalance the body's hormones and the ratio of testosterone to DHT;
- reducing the body's concentration of DHT;
- interfering with DHT's binding to prostate tissue;
- inhibiting alpha receptors, a mechanism similar to that of the alpha-blocker drugs currently prescribed, without the side effects caused by those medications.

As a result, the patient's prostate may shrink back to a presumably more youthful state, reducing blockage of the urethra and eliminating symptoms of enlarged prostate without surgery or medical drugs.

Saw palmetto is an herbal remedy that holds great promise for men. Currently, the NIH is about to initiate a large clinical trial in the United States to determine the efficacy and safety of this compound alone, and in combination with another herb, *Pygeum africanum*. The results of this study may not be available for several years. If you hear about this study in your community, I would urge you to participate if you meet the entry criteria.

A Note on Clinical Trials

Doctors rely on large, multicenter trials to prove that a medication or an herbal compound is safe and effective. This is the manner by which medications achieve FDA approval. For herbs, which do not require FDA approval, these standards do not have to be met. Herbal compounds can just appear on the shelf in the health food store. However, the only way that physicians in the United States will believe that herbs work will be from the results of large clinical trials. From my own experience, and reviewing the literature, I believe that the results will show that in the patient with mild symptoms, saw palmetto is safe, effective, and likely to be as good as the medications out on the market.

I've seen saw palmetto work again and again. Within two months, about 70 percent of my patients respond favorably. This natural healer has saved many of my patients from having to use prescription medicine or undergo surgery. Standardized saw palmetto has no known drug interactions; this has been demonstrated in a large number of well-conducted studies. I can say with complete assurance that saw palmetto is totally safe.

Pygeum africanum

In the 1990s, the natural medicine *Pygeum africanum* arrived in the U.S. It has long been a popular natural remedy for prostate enlargement in France, and it is well validated by current science. At the Center for Holistic Urology, men who have been doing their own research into natural remedies often ask whether they should use saw palmetto berry extract, *Pygeum africanum*, or both.

Pygeum africanum is derived from the bark of an African evergreen tree, growing to a height of more than 100 feet. This species of tree is found on the high-elevation plateaus of southern Africa, the island of Madagascar, and in Central Africa, particularly in Cameroon and Kenya. Scientific evidence from European studies shows that *Pygeum africanum* consistently and reliably reduces symptoms of BPH.

Other evidence suggests that pygeum inhibits prostate cell proliferation that is at the root of both BPH and prostate cancer. The positive effects of pygeum have been found to last for at least one month after stopping its use.

Medical studies indicate that pygeum may improve fertility in cases in which diminished prostatic secretion plays a significant role. Specifically, when men with diminished prostatic secretion use pygeum regularly, the volume of seminal fluid in their ejaculate increases. So do proteins in the semen that help nourish sperm.

A 1991 double-blind study conducted by Italian investigators indicates that men with either BPH or prostatitis who use pygeum may enjoy better, stronger erections. Pygeum also appears to enhance and renew sexual vigor by acting as a tonic, improving the underlying health of the genitourinary system.

Pygeum appears to work by:

- inhibiting formation of hormones known as prostaglandins that are responsible for painful inflammation of the prostate;
- acting as a diuretic to relieve bladder pressure;
- and (possibly) by inhibiting absorption and metabolism of prostatic cholesterol, which some researchers suggest is part of the BPH pathology.

Pygeum has become one of the urologist's drugs of choice in France and other European nations. No interactions of pygeum with any drug have been reported. As researchers noted in a 1990 report, "Use of the extract of *Pygeum africanum* seems justified especially due to its extremely favorable benefit-risk ratio as part of drug therapy."

Pygeum for Bladder Dysfunction

Often accompanying BPH, bladder dysfunction is a major— but often overlooked—affliction associated with male aging. As men age, they often suffer severe, irreversible alterations in bladder function, including partial or complete obstruction. Researchers have identified major cellular changes in the bladder that result from such obstruction. These include progressive free radical-related damage to the nerves and cellular mitochondria (energy factories) of the bladder.

A recent experimental study from Albany College of Pharmacy, New York, shows that pretreatment with pygeum significantly reduced the severity of metabolic dysfunction associated with partial outlet obstruction. Hopefully, more research

will be done to demonstrate the utility of pygeum in the prevention of bladder dysfunction in aging men.

To Replace Saw Palmetto with Pygeum?

The question many men will have is whether to replace saw
palmetto extracts with pygeum as part of their daily prostate
health regimen. These two herbs have slightly different modes
of action, according to recent studies from research centers,
such as the Department of Urology, University of Essen,
Germany. Saw palmetto blocks the enzyme responsible for con-
verting free testosterone to the toxic dihydrotestosterone
(DHT) molecule. Pygeum works by enhancing prostatic secretions, acting as a diuretic, and decreasing inflammation. Nettle,
another prostate-health herb that I'll discuss in the next section, has anti-inflammatory effects. Your wisest course of
action might be to combine these herbs and cycle them, or take
them together.

One study by Swiss researchers examined the interactive
effects of pygeum and nettle root (see below) on the action of
two enzymes involved in production of dihydrotestosterone
and estrogen. (Increased ratio of estrogen to testosterone in elderly men has been linked with BPH.) In the lab, they found
that both plant extracts effectively inhibited DHT and aromatase, the enzyme that transforms testosterone into estrogen.
A combination of both extracts was significantly more effective
than either extract alone at blocking the activity of aromatase.

MORE GREAT NATURAL MEDICINES FOR BPH

Here are some other compounds you can look for in your herbal
remedy. They all have varying degrees of scientific support, but
all are backed by considerable traditional and anecdotal evidence.

Nettle root. The use of stinging nettle (*Urtica dioica*) has its
origins in Indian medical history, where it was used to relieve

the stinging, prickling sensations of prostate infection and enlargement. Some unpublished data indicate it could work by inhibiting 5 alpha-reductase, or by inhibiting the aromatase enzymes that convert testosterone to estrogen in the male body. Nettle root appears to work synergistically with *Pygeum africanum*.

Flower Pollen. Cernilton® is a flower pollen extract manufactured by Swedish company AB Cernelle. This natural medicine is made from cernitin, a mix of rye pollen from several different plants grown in the southern part of the country. It has a relaxant effect on the smooth muscle that surrounds the urethra, and has been reported to slow the growth of prostate cells. Cernilton was introduced to the European market over 30 years ago and continues to be used as a first-line defense for patients with prostatitis.

In 1990, British physicians tested Cernilton's effectiveness in treating BPH-related impaired urine flow. Sixty patients were involved in the study, half receiving Cernilton and the other half placebo. After six months, 69 percent of the patients reported improvement in symptoms. Researchers also found a decrease in residual urine and prostate diameter.

In another study, 79 patients with BPH were treated with 126 mg of Cernilton three times a day for more than 12 weeks. Their symptoms included urinary flow obstruction, increased prostatic volume, and residual urine. Scientists reported that the extract produced a statistically significant improvement of 69 percent of the symptoms compared with an improvement of 30 percent with placebo. A decrease in residual urine volume and in prostate volume was observed.

Finally, in a Japanese study published in 1990, 192 patients were treated with Cernilton. After four weeks, moderate or great improvement was seen. Patients improved in terms of residual urinary volume, average urine flow rate, maximum flow rate, and prostate weight.

Cernilton is available at health food stores and natural product supermarkets throughout the country. There are no reports of toxicity tied to this product. However, some users may experience mild to moderate heartburn and nausea.

Beta-sitosterol. This compound is found in many of the plant foods we eat, including rice, soy, corn, wheat, and peanuts. It appears to help relieve symptoms in men with BPH. (It is also being studied as a natural remedy for high cholesterol, and as an aid to recovery from intense exercise.) One study found that when 200 men with BPH were given 20 mg of beta-sitosterol three times daily for six months, urinary flow and other symptoms improved significantly. The placebo group in this study demonstrated no improvement. In another double-blind study, 130 mg per day of beta-sitosterol yielded similarly encouraging results.

Vitamin B_6. The intake of this B vitamin is commonly low; it is scarce in modern processed-food diets. Its scarcity poses a risk to the prostate because it—along with zinc, discussed below—is needed to create and maintain hormone balance and to make testosterone. More specifically, vitamin B_6 is needed to produce a substance called picolinic acid, which in turn is needed for the utilization and absorption of zinc, and to convert zinc into forms that the body needs. Both zinc and vitamin B_6 work together to rebalance the body's hormones and build testosterone.

Zinc. The secretions of the prostate gland contain an abundance of this mineral, which strongly suggests that zinc plays a role in prostate function. Zinc supplements have been found to help shrink the prostate and to relieve symptoms of BPH. The usual recommendation is 30 to 50 mg daily of zinc. In a study presented at a meeting of the American Medical Association, 19 men with BPH took 150 mg of zinc per day for two months, then lowered their dosages to 50 to 100 mg per day; 74 percent of the men in this preliminary study experienced shrinkage of the prostate.

The research evidence that zinc alone is effective is not all that strong, and taking too much zinc can cause copper deficiency. Ensure that you are getting 2 to 3 mg of copper each day through a multivitamin and mineral supplement.

Amino acids. A combination of three amino acids (glycine, alanine, and glutamic acid) has been found to improve BPH symptoms. Men with BPH were given a total of approximately 760 mg of these amino acids three times daily for two weeks, after which their dosages were ramped down to 380 mg three times a day, with the therapy lasting three months total. Half of the subjects reported that they had less urinary urgency and frequency, and/or that they had less trouble starting the flow of urine. Only 15 percent of the placebo subjects reported improvements.

Why would amino acids help? No one knows for certain, but they appear to shrink swelling of prostatic tissue.

Pumpkin seeds. The seeds of pumpkins and other winter squash, all members of the genus *curcubita*, were used by Native American Indians to heal prostate problems. In Europe today, pumpkin seeds are a widely used therapy for urinary symptoms of BPH and to calm overactive bladder. They are nutrient-dense, containing protein, B vitamins, fiber, iron, manganese, copper, calcium, and magnesium. Interestingly, pumpkin seeds are also an effective natural remedy for intestinal parasites. They contain a unique amino acid called *curcurbitin*, which has been found to paralyze intestinal parasites so that they can be expelled by the body.

In countries where pumpkin seeds are eaten often, there is a lower incidence of prostate problems. It's believed that these seeds contain fatty acids that block the action of DHT on the prostate. You can eat pumpkin seeds raw, or toast them in the oven; or if pumpkin seeds aren't on your short list of favorite foods, you can take a supplement that contains concentrated pumpkin seed oil.

Essential fatty acids (EFAs). The importance of adequate essential fatty acid nutrition is becoming evident in a great many so-called "diseases of aging." Modern diets are very low in EFAs, or contain unbalanced amounts of these fats. The EFAs are transformed into hormone-like biochemicals in the body, and these biochemicals have enormous impact on inflammation, blood clotting, and a host of other processes that can dictate whether we're chronically sick or chronically well. We'll talk in much greater detail about inflammation and prostate health later in this book. For now, suffice it to say that proper fatty acid nutrition can help to reduce the size of the prostate by reducing inflammation.

Not much research has been published on the effects of EFA supplements on BPH. We do know that proper EFA balance promotes better heart and joint health; it may help to prevent allergies, autoimmune disease, and even some cancers. More research is needed, but in the meantime, getting more of the omega-3 fatty acids—those found abundantly in flaxseeds and fish—is helpful in so many ways that it won't hurt to add them to your prostate health regimen. Most experts recommend a tablespoon of flaxseed oil per day, or two to four tablespoons per day of ground flaxseeds. Ground flaxseeds have the added bonus of being high in beneficial fiber.

Fish oil is an excellent source of EFAs; choose oils from deep-water fish, such as salmon, sardines, or anchovies, and aim for a dosage of about 600 to 1,000 mg of omega-3 fats per day. If you do add extra EFAs to your diet, also add a vitamin E supplement (200 IU daily).

Exercise. A higher level of physical activity appears protective against BPH. A study published in the *Archives of Internal Medicine* found that men who did more physical activity had decreased likelihood of BPH symptoms, diagnosis, and surgery. Men who walked for two to three hours per week lowered their risk of BPH by 25 percent compared to men who did not exercise.

WHEN TO USE ADDITIONAL HERBS & NUTRIENTS:
Our Best Advice from the Center for Holistic Urology

There is no question that remedies like saw palmetto and pygeum have a place for men with BPH. Many men can gain big benefits from herbal remedies. However, each person is different, and different herbs and nutrients bring with them specific qualities that may help an individual. Give these formulas a few months and keep track of your urinary symptoms. If your frequency has diminished, your urine stream grown stronger, and congestion declined, then the product may be all that your system requires.

Start with saw palmetto berry. If additional help is required, use nettle, pygeum and pumpkin to augment your saw palmetto supplement. Take three to four capsules daily to achieve the therapeutically proven dosage for pygeum (which is 100 mg daily).

If you feel that your symptoms are about the same or only showing slight improvement, then you should next combine ingredients in various formulas. For example, another formula that many of my patients like combines nettle with pygeum and pumpkin. This formula from Enzymatic Therapy is great! It may produce results when other formulas do not.

New Chapter makes a product called Prostate 5LX®, which contains several herbs that support prostate health: a supercritical extract of solvent-free saw palmetto, green tea, nettles (*Urtica dioica*), ginger, rosemary, and selenium. Green tea, ginger, and rosemary all have natural antioxidant and anti-inflammatory effects; not only do they directly inhibit prostate enlargement, but they also downregulate specific inflammatory pathways that are being increasingly implicated in the development of prostate cancer. You will learn a great deal about these pathways—which are referred to as COX and LO—in the chapter on prostate cancer and prostatic intraepithelial neoplasia (PIN).

In Chapter 7, I will tell you more about how to use diet and specific kinds of supplemental nutrients to protect your prostate against BPH, prostatitis, PIN, and prostate cancer.

Here's a chart to help you compare and evaluate the nutrients I've recommended for BPH.

HERB/ NUTRIENT	DOSAGE	SIDE EFFECTS/ DRUG INTERACTIONS
Saw palmetto	160 mg twice a day	rarely, mild gastrointestinal upset or abdominal pain; dizziness and headache have been reported rarely; and in rare cases there may be decreased libido or male breast enlargement (the latter goes away when the supplement is stopped)
Pygeum	50 mg twice daily or 100 mg once daily	possible gastrointestinal discomfort
Nettle root	300 to 600 mg extract twice a day; especially good combined with pygeum	mild gastrointestinal upset, diarrhea; take with food to prevent this; rash if the extract is applied topically—which you should never do
Cernilton	126 mg three times a day	possible gastrointestinal discomfort

HERB/ NUTRIENT	DOSAGE	SIDE EFFECTS/ DRUG INTERACTIONS
Beta-sitosterol	20 mg three times a day	rarely, mild gastrointestinal upset
Vitamin D$_6$	50 mg daily	none reported
Zinc	30 to 60 mg daily (make sure you also get 2 to 3 mg copper)	immune system suppression with long-term doses over 100 mg
Amino acids: glycine, alanine, glutamic acid	380 to 760 mg three times a day	not advisable in men with kidney disease; otherwise, no adverse effects reported
Pumpkin seed oil	160 mg three times per day, with meals	none reported
Essential fatty acids	Choose a supplement that gives you 150 mg per day of the omega-3 fatty acids EPA, DHA, and/or ALA; fish oil should come from Arctic fish (salmon, sardines); any EFA supplement should also contain an herbal or antioxidant vitamin preservative (e.g., vitamin E, rosemary)	fish oils may have a fishy repeat if taken without food; consult your doctor if you are on any kind of blood-thinning drug, including aspirin

Chapter 4

Prostatitis

PROSTATITIS, OR INFLAMMATION of the prostate, is said to account for up to 25 percent of all office visits related to genital and urinary complaints in young and middle-aged men. The prostate receives a plentiful blood supply, and periodically becomes congested—two of the characteristics of organs that are vulnerable to infections, both acute and chronic.

About 30 percent of men between the ages of 25 and 40 years who have prostate complaints have true prostatitis. Another 30 percent have genitoanal syndromes—chronic discomfort that is difficult to diagnose and treat, such as chronic pelvic pain syndrome. The other 40 percent turn out to have other prostatic conditions. Because of the similarity of symptoms, it is difficult even for experts to differentiate the various clinical syndromes.

Prostatitis is classified as either *acute* or *chronic*. In addition to the usual symptoms, acute prostatitis usually involves fever and chills. We use painkillers and antibiotics to treat acute prostatitis. It is important to bring the inflammation under control quickly to prevent the development of abscesses. Acute prostatitis may evolve into a chronic form, even if it is quickly treated. Chronic prostatitis comes on more gradually and does not cause fever.

TYPICAL PROSTATITIS SYMPTOMS

- Pain in the penis and/or testicles
- Pain above the pubic bone
- Pain in the lower back, down the leg, or in the perineum or groin, during or following ejaculation
- Pain while sitting
- General pelvic discomfort
- Frequent/urgent urination; feeling of incomplete voiding
- Sensation like you're sitting on a golf ball, or like you have a golf ball in your rectum that won't come out

THE FOUR FORMS OF PROSTATITIS

The two subtypes of prostatitis are further divided into four specific disorders:

Acute bacterial prostatitis is the least common of the four types but also the easiest to diagnose and treat effectively. Symptoms include lower back and genital pain, fever, chills, body aches, frequent (and often burning or painful) urination, and urinary urgency (often at night). The diagnosis is confirmed by the detection of white blood cells and bacteria in the urine. It is usually treated with an antibiotic.

Chronic bacterial prostatitis, also uncommon, is actually acute prostatitis that affects a defective area of the prostate. This defect has a vulnerability to bacterial attack. To treat it effectively, we must first identify and remove the defect, and then we try to clear up residual infection with antibiotics. (Antibiotics often do not cure this condition, however.)

Chronic prostatitis/chronic pelvic pain syndrome is the most common but least understood form of prostatitis. It may also be called *prostatodynia*. Men of all ages can develop it. The symptoms come and go without apparent cause. This syndrome can be inflammatory, meaning that urine, semen, and other prostatic fluids do not contain evidence of an infectious organism, but they do contain signs that the body is producing infection-fighting cells in the prostate and/or bladder. The non-inflammatory form is even more mysterious, because there are symptoms, but no evidence of inflammation or infection.

Because there are no bacteria involved in this form of prostatitis, antibiotics will not help. There is no one solution that works in every case. You will need to work with your urologist to settle on the best possible treatment. Holistic therapies may include dietary changes and warm baths. Alpha-blocker medications like Hytrin and Flomax may be used to relax the smooth muscle tissue in the prostate.

Asymptomatic inflammatory prostatitis is usually discovered when a man is undergoing an infertility evaluation or prostate cancer testing. He has had no pain or other discomfort, but tests reveal that his semen contains immune cells that fight infection.

CAUSES OF PROSTATITIS

There is controversy even between the most highly regarded experts when it comes to the causes of prostatitis. In the end, it looks as though any one patient can fall prey to the disease for one or more of several reasons. We may be dealing with several diseases, all of which present with identical or similar symptom profiles.

Bacterial infection. If you have had acute prostatitis with a fever, and you had tests that demonstrated the presence of bacteria in the prostate, and it went away when you took antibiotics, you likely have had bacterial prostatitis. This would place you in the 5 to 10 percent of prostatitis patients who have had prostatitis of certifiably bacterial origin.

Heated debate rages in urological circles about the importance of bacteria in the big picture of prostatitis. It isn't as straightforward as taking a semen or urine sample and checking for bacteria; tests don't always find bacteria even when they are there. Many urologists simply try a trial of a broad-spectrum antibiotic and see whether it eliminates the patient's symptoms, without first testing to see whether bacteria are present.

Sometimes physicians assume that bacteria are not the cause when antibiotics don't solve the problem. This is not a safe assumption, due to increasing numbers of antibiotic-resistant bacteria that can survive even the most powerful onslaught of antimicrobial artillery. Besides, there is no hard and fast way to prove that bacteria, even when present, are the cause of a man's prostatitis symptoms. Nonbacterial prostatitis can evolve from the bacterial variety, and some even suggest (based on anecdotal evidence) that multiple courses of antibiotics lead to imbalances that *cause* prostatitis.

It is known that *E. coli*, klebsiella, and *Proteus mirabilis* are common bacteria found in cases of bacterial prostatitis. In hospitals, catheters can infect men's prostates with staphylococci and gram-negative pathogens, such as pseudomonas. There is debate over whether some cases of prostatitis previously thought to be nonbacterial could involve chlamydia or other bacteria, although most researchers do not feel that chlamydia plays a major role in this disease.

Should you submit yourself to extensive tests to try to determine whether your prostatitis is caused by bacteria? There is no harm in doing so, but there is no evidence that treatment based upon the results of bacterial cultures yields a better response rate than so-called *empiric* treatment. In other words, if your doctor just treats you with antibiotics without doing the tests first, your end results will probably be the same. If antibiotics don't work, we just move on to the next thing. Curtis Nickel, M.D., professor of urology and director of the Prostatitis Clinical Research Centre at Queen's University in Kingston, Ontario, has said that "...we are questioning now whether the standard evaluation—very uncomfortable and expensive and cumbersome—of looking at prostate-specific specimens after prostate massage is really indicated in clinical practice."

Still, based on what we know at this writing, your doctor should do the following tests for bacterial infection:

• Urethral swab
• Voided urine
• Expressed prostatic secretions or post-prostate massage urine ("VB3")

I like to do a culture of the semen, as well, particularly in men who have post-ejaculatory pain and/or changes in the appearance of semen. This test may determine the type of bacteria present. This may be especially helpful in men that have been previously treated with multiple antibiotics in the past and remain symptomatic.

Zinc has been studied for the treatment of chronic bacterial prostatitis. In one recent Chinese study, researchers used biological organic zinc in one group of 39 patients with this disease, along with antibiotic therapy. The other group, 22 in number, got only antibiotics. Compared with the group that did not use zinc, the zinc group showed significantly more symptom improvement.

Out-of-whack immune response. Prostatitis may, in some cases, be caused by autoimmunity, a misguided attack by your own immune system against your urinary tract. The result is inflammation that is not caused by bacteria or injury.

Some patients with nonbacterial prostatitis also complain of joint pain, rashes, and inflammatory bowel disease that tend to flare at the same time as their prostatitis. This suggests an autoimmune component to the disorder, but this nugget of evidence is undermined by the fact that few of these patients get better when given steroid drugs.

According to Cleveland Clinic, Florida, urologist Daniel Shoskes, M.D., "…it is unlikely that 'true' nonbacterial chronic prostatitis represents a classical autoimmune disease…it more likely represents a disorder of regulation of the inflammatory response." In other words, the immune system goes after a true

Why Would Your Immune System Turn on You?

Autoimmune diseases are poorly understood. Mainstream treatment options are limited to steroids and nonsteroidal anti-inflammatory drugs (such as naproxen, indomethacin, and ibuprofen). In more severe cases, physicians turn to powerful drugs with a high incidence of adverse effects, including immunity-suppressing drugs also used in transplant patients to prevent their bodies from rejecting new organs, and drugs used for cancer chemotherapy (e.g., methotrexate). Many people with autoimmune disorders, including rheumatoid arthritis, asthma, lupus, allergies, and Graves' disease (a thyroid disorder), find that changes in diet and lifestyle and nutritional supplements help them halt or reverse the course of their disease.

Theories abound as to what causes autoimmune disease, and many of them are backed by solid science. Some of the evidence indicates that bacterial *antigens*—parts of the bacteria that are recognized by the immune system, helping target them for destruction—can, in susceptible people, stimulate the immune system to also attack antigens that are made by healthy cells. Other evidence suggests that an overly active immune system can cause inflammation in the prostate (or elsewhere) by stimulating *mast cells*, which make the inflammatory biochemical histamine.

enemy in the prostate, but doesn't stop once all of those bacteria have been eradicated, and inflammation (and accompanying pain and other symptoms) lingers.

"A headache in the pelvis." Researchers at Stanford have just released a book by this name. The book outlines their proposal that in many cases, chronic nonbacterial prostatitis is a result of tension in the pelvic muscles. According to this theory, this muscular tension eventually causes the urinary tract to become irritable. When nerves involving urination, ejaculation, and defecation are impinged upon by tensed pelvic muscles, prostatitis symptoms result.

Some of the recent work that has been done at my institution seems to link this form of prostatitis to pelvic floor spasms. My colleague, Dr. Steven Kaplan, is a well-known urologist in the field of BPH, prostatitis, and bladder testing. He routinely recommends that men with this form of prostate congestion undergo the urodynamics testing described on pages 19-20. Dr. Kaplan has found that an overwhelming number of men with prostatitis between the ages of 20 and 40 have a tightening in the pelvic floor muscles, not a problem in the prostate itself. Relaxation techniques and biofeedback may be very helpful for men who have this kind of prostatitis.

This theory makes sense intuitively. Chronically tensed jaw muscles lead to TMJ pain and inflammation; chronically tensed upper back, facial, or neck muscles can lead to headaches. And it may well be that men with chronic prostatitis end up with an escalating cycle of tension and pain that brings muscle tension into the mix, even if it was not a causative factor in the first place.

According to clinical psychologist David Wise, Ph.D., a visiting scholar at Stanford, prostatitis "usually tends to occur in men who hold their tension and aggression inside. They squeeze themselves rather than lashing out at others. Often they have work in which they sit for long periods of time and the only way they have found to express their frustration is to tense their pelvic muscles. This tension has become a habit with them. Often they do not know they tense themselves in the pelvic floor."

Dr. Wise is quoted further at www.prostatitis.org: "We have identified a group of chronic pelvic pain syndromes that are caused by the overuse of the human instinct to protect the genitals, rectum and contents of the pelvis from injury or pain by contracting the pelvic muscles. This tendency becomes exaggerated in predisposed individuals and over time results in pelvic pain and dysfunction. The state of chronic constriction creates pain-referring trigger points, reduced blood flow, and an inhospitable environment for the nerves, blood vessels and structures throughout the pelvic basin. This results in a cycle of pain, anxiety and tension which has been previously unrecognized and untreated."

If your chronic prostatitis is the result of pelvic floor tension, drugs and surgeries won't help. Dr. Wise mentions several patients at Stanford who had their prostates removed or who have taken huge doses of antibiotics over extended periods in desperate attempts to be rid of their symptoms. Still, their symptoms persisted.

A pilot study at Stanford showed that men with abacterial prostatitis or prostatodynia often have "trigger points," muscle fiber that is extremely painful when pressed. These trigger points actually refer pain to the pelvic floor, and by pressing them, investigators were able to reproduce the men's typical pain sensations that they attribute to prostatitis. A technique called *myofascial release* or *soft tissue mobilization* can be used to release these trigger points. It involves pushing against the trigger points to stretch the contracted tissue. As you might imagine, this is a painful process, but one that can reduce symptoms after a few sessions. Once treatment ends, it's the patient's responsibility to learn relaxation techniques that will allow the pelvic floor to remain relaxed.

Unfortunately, insurance companies haven't been convinced that myofascial release is a valid therapy for abacterial prostatitis. It most likely will not be covered by your insurance company, so if you choose to go this route, be prepared to pay out-of-pocket.

Acupuncture is a natural direction for treatment of chronic abacterial prostatitis, also known as chronic pelvic pain syndrome (CPPS). Dr. Nickel, quoted earlier, says that "[p]atients have neuropathic pain which is reflected in voiding and sexual disturbances and musculoskeletal pain. And that's why instead of using prostate-centric treatment, we should probably be using something a little more broad, such as acupuncture."

Dr. Nickel sent 12 of his most difficult patients—men who had not found relief with antibiotics, alpha-blockers, anti-inflammatories, or herbal therapy—to acupuncturist and urologist Richard Chen, M.D. The men received acupuncture treatment, including electroacupuncture (where a mild current is sent through the needles), twice weekly for six weeks. Of the 12 patients, 11 had greater than 50 percent improvement in symptoms based on the National Institutes of Health chronic prostatitis symptom index. And of those 11, 10 men had at least a 75 percent improvement in subjective symptoms with the acupuncture treatment. Even better: Following treatment, their improvements were maintained for 24 to 52 weeks of follow-up.

At the Center for Holistic Urology, we have started a clinical trial using acupuncture on patients with chronic prostatitis. This trial has been approved by the Institutional Review Board at Columbia University. Although the trial has just begun, I am impressed with the early results. Our patients are treated once a week for 10 weeks, and fill out questionnaires before and after treatment. This is another example of how treatments used in the alternative medicine world can play a role in allopathic medical centers.

Uric acid. Uric acid is a natural by-product of the breakdown of body cells that have served their purpose. It is also created when we digest and assimilate protein-rich foods. Normally, the kidneys filter out any excess and send it to the bladder to be excreted in the urine. In some people, this process doesn't happen as smoothly as it should, and uric acid levels rise too high. (This may be due to genetics, or to the use of diuretics or certain anticancer drugs.) Stones (calculi) may form in the urinary tract, or the person may develop gout, a type of arthritis caused by the accumulation of uric acid in the joints. Allopurinol is the drug of choice for the treatment of gout and chronic development of urinary tract stones. It inhibits an enzyme necessary for uric acid synthesis.

A small 1996 study published in the *Journal of Urology* found that the drug allopurinol at a dose of 300 or 600 mg per day for 240 days helped a significant proportion of men with abacterial prostatitis. In a previous study, this Swedish research team had found that urinary reflux (the backflow of urine into the prostatic ducts) is not uncommon in men with abacterial prostatitis. They hypothesized that the uric acid in this refluxed urine might be causing the men's prostatitis symptoms. Some weight has been lent to this hypothesis by the finding of uric acid by-products in expressed prostatic secretions. On message boards at the Prostatitis Foundation website, a few men have posted their success stories with allopurinol, saying that it's the only thing that has significantly reduced their symptoms. But we know little to nothing about how these people will do once the drug is withdrawn. So far it looks as though the drug's effects are only temporary—three months or so on average.

Why haven't you heard about allopurinol? Because, although the study from Sweden did show improvement, it was small.

On a scale of 1 to 12, the patients who improved only did so by a maximum of one-and-a-half points. When the results of one small study are this unremarkable, the research community tends not to get too excited, particularly when we're talking about the use of a drug that lost its patent protection a long time ago.

Any responsible physician will tell you that allopurinol is not a drug to be taken lightly. It can cause some serious side effects. The most common adverse effect of this drug is a skin rash. Such rashes can get pretty bad, so if one appears while you are on allopurinol, stop using the drug at once. Other possible side effects include fever, chills, arthralgia (pain in the bones and joints), jaundice, imbalances of red or white blood cells, diarrhea, nausea, and acute attacks of gout.

Prostatic stones. It is estimated that 75 percent of middle-aged men have calcified stones in their prostate glands. They are believed to form due to "backed-up" prostatic secretions that cannot get out of the gland due to structural changes caused by BPH. Stones may also form in the ejaculatory ducts. In some men, the stones cause no symptoms, but in others, chronic prostatitis can arise due to their presence. In other men, undrained infection from bouts of bacterial prostatitis can also serve as raw material for calculi. In my own personal experience, these stones have proven to be a cause of elevated PSA in a subset of men.

Prostatic stones may or may not create obstructions; they also may or may not provide fertile breeding grounds for bacteria. When infection is present, it may cause symptoms that don't seem to be due to any detectable bacteria; this may be because the infected part of the gland is sealed off by a stone or by scar tissue.

Lithotripsy—the process used to break up kidney stones— doesn't work with prostatic stones. In the kidney, stones are surrounded by fluid, and so the fragments can drain out easily. (If kidney stones are in areas that aren't well drained, they don't respond well to lithotripsy, either.) In the prostate, there is no fluid sitting there to help the fragments drain, and so they would probably just reform into stones.

Some physicians recommend aggressive prostatic massage to break up the stones. (This may be recommended for other types of prostatitis that involve inflammation or infection.) This can be quite painful during, but can provide some relief afterwards. Unfortunately, that relief tends to be temporary.

Urethral strictures. A percentage of the patients with chronic prostatitis have urethral strictures, areas of the urethra that are partially closed off by fibrotic tissue buildup. When there is a partial blockage of the urethra, voiding the bladder completely may be impossible, and bladder hypertrophy may end up further compromising the man's ability to empty his bladder. If the condition is not treated, prostatitis, urinary tract infections, and even kidney failure can result.

Initial diagnosis may be made because of a significant decrease in the power of the urine stream, or the first visit to the doctor may be due to prostatitis or other UTI symptoms. Measurements of urine flow rate are used to help diagnose stricture, and x-ray and cystoscopy are used to locate the stricture along the urethra. These tests help to rule out cancer and prostatic obstruction as causes of the diminution in urine flow.

Strictures are usually caused by infection or trauma. Patients in whom these are found and repaired may find themselves cured, but some stricture-repair surgeries don't cure them. Unfortunately, there's no way to predict who will or won't be helped by urethral stricture repair. Treatment of severe stricture may involve dilation, where filiforms or narrow rods are threaded through the urethra to expand the opening gradually. (Yes, this smarts a bit, and can also cause bleeding.) We start with a very narrow dilating instrument and as the urethra stretches, we place wider ones in their place. Unfortunately, once the rods are removed, the stricture can return.

The gold standard treatment (it has a 70 to 80 percent success rate, and can be performed a second time if necessary) is the urethrotomy, where an endoscope with a tiny, sharp knife on its end is used to cut out fibrotic tissue inside the urethra. If urethrotomy fails, surgery can be performed to remove the urethral segment with the stricture and sew together the two loose ends; or, if a urethral segment longer than two centimeters is involved, a skin graft (usually from the penis) is used to perform patch graft urethroplasty. The surgeon cuts the urethra lengthwise in the fibrotic area and uses the graft to create a wider tube. Even with these extreme measures, additional surgeries may eventually be necessary.

Cancer. Sometimes, but not often, chronic prostatitis can be due to rare types of cancer or undetected cancer. Be prepared for your urologist to do tests to rule out cancer, including PSAs and biopsies, if your prostatitis proves to be intractable.

BPH. In some men, changes in the prostate over time can lead to prostatitis due to the retention of prostatic fluid, which can then become calcified and form stones or serve as a breeding ground for infection.

Food allergies, yeast infections. In some alternative health circles, food allergies and/or overgrowth of yeasts have been blamed for chronic nonbacterial prostatitis. While there is little concrete, peer-reviewed scientific evidence to support these theories, it may help your prostate health (and your overall health) to eliminate allergenic foods from your diet and to support the growth of "friendly" probiotic bacteria that are the natural enemy of yeasts in your body. You will find out how to do this in Chapter 7.

"YOU'LL JUST HAVE TO
LEARN TO LIVE WITH IT"

If you've been in and out of doctor's offices many times in search of answers about theories I've just finished explaining, you may even have been told by one or more well-meaning (but stumped) physicians that "you'll just have to learn to live with it."

The sad truth about many cases of prostatitis is that we can't figure out what causes it. And even if we could, this might not lead us to a cure.

Men whose prostatitis is caused by bacteria can at least hang their hopes on antibiotic therapy. While some doctors don't test carefully enough for the presence of bacteria, even those who do are not always able to cure the patient by obliterating the bacteria. Symptoms can persist even after several courses of antibiotics. In cases where prostatitis is believed to be based in a disordered immune system, there is no clear agreement on how to deal with the problem, either.

Patients with chronic prostatitis often end up trying a slew of different drugs, including pain medications (aspirin, ibuprofen, naproxen, acetaminophen) and stool softeners (to ease the discomfort of straining to pass stool when the whole pelvis hurts). Bacterial prostatitis patients may have to undergo multiple courses of fluoroquinolone antibiotics, such as Cipro (ciprofloxacin)—not a good idea because of the risk of breeding resistant bacteria and because antibiotics kill off "friendly" bacteria in the GI tract, where they are needed.

Symptom control is more easily attainable than a cure in many cases. Relaxation techniques and muscle-strengthening techniques can help relieve pain by relaxing or repairing problems in the muscles that comprise the pelvic floor. But, again, there is no standard of care that is going to help every patient get back to normal.

When a man ejaculates, his genitourinary tract is bathed in a substance called *prostatic antibacterial factor*. It does a good job of killing off pathogens. In a study of men with prostatitis who abstained from sex, a prescription of twice daily masturbation for six months provided moderate to complete relief for 78 percent of the 18 subjects. If this sounds like a prescription you can live with, go for it...you certainly don't have anything to lose!

Bottom line: Men who struggle with chronic prostatitis must take their health into their own hands. They end up having to become the world's leading experts on their disease, with their doctors running a close second. They find out which questions to ask and what tests they should be given.

And, for many, their most effective answers come from their research into alternative methods of dealing with prostatitis.

AND YET ANOTHER THEORY: ATTACK OF THE BIOFILMS!

Let's journey back in time to 1684. Anton van Leeuwenhoek, a dry-goods merchant who would leave his mark on history as inventor of the microscope, is viewing a miniscule world no one has ever seen before. With his eyes alone, the man is dissecting everything—including the hidden biological world adhering to his own teeth—what he calls "animalcules," a sort of film adhering to the enamel.

Appalled at his own dirty dental health, he grabs a nearby bottle of vinegar and engages in a thorough cleaning of the teeth, and then does another scraping. The vinegar has killed only the outer film. In the incrustation, a well-colonized tenacious layer of "animalcules" remains.

How is this relevant to the man with prostatitis? It turns out that what Leeuwenhoek was viewing was what scientists now call biofilms—entire bacterial communities that can take up residence almost anywhere—in machinery, plumbing, ships' hulls, catheters and stents used for medical procedures and in the human body...and—you guessed it—in the prostate and urinary tract.

Scientists believe that biofilms are the cause of many chronic infectious disease states—including chronic ear and urinary-tract infections (UTIs) as well as gum disease. In fact, biofilms may be involved in as many as 65 percent of all human bacterial infections, according to the Centers for Disease Control and Prevention in Atlanta.

In its early stage of development, a biofilm is actually just a group of disparate, unorganized cells on the surface. As their population grows, the cells prove to have an almost insidious survival instinct. The groups send out signals and begin to reorganize into colonies shaped like pillars, minarets and other structures, forming a veritable city of scum. Banded together, their resistance to antibiotics and antimicrobials becomes greatly magnified—perhaps as much as 1,000 times greater, scientists estimate. They even alter proteins in their cell walls to evade antibiotics that would have targeted those particular proteins. Furthermore, the slime that they secrete acts much like a coat of armor, lending them even greater protection.

FOILING THE BIOFILM
WITH NATURAL MEDICINE

Modern science is working hard to find ways to counter biofilm. One thought is to disrupt the communications of the biofilm colonies, thus interfering with genetic alterations that stimulate release of protective slime and changes in protein structure.

Other researchers have discovered a plant that grows in saltwater, *Delisea pulchra*, that resists biofilm formation. Its protective chemical is a furanone. Scientists have since created more than 60 different types of furanones, all of which inhibit biofilm formation.

Several natural medicines may be more effective than antibiotics and antimicrobials against formation of biofilm by preventing adherence of initial cells to bodily tissues. Using these natural medicines may benefit your prostate health, but it is also likely to protect against gingivitis and other types of chronic infection. These include isoquinoline alkaloids from goldenseal, barberry and Oregon grape; and cranberry.

The most widely studied of the isoquinoline alkaloids is berberine. Although berberine is known to have a very pro-nounced antibiotic effect, its ability to vanquish strains of bacteria may be more related to inhibition of the adhesion of pathogens to host tissues. For example, berberine causes certain bacteria, such as streptococci, to lose their lipoteichoic acid, the major chemical that enables the bacterium to attach to the body's tissues and, even more important to fighting biofilm, dissolves the chemicals already connecting bacteria to tissues. This may be why these herbs, rich in berberine, are ideal for treating so many common infectious states, including strep infections in the throat.

Cranberry's chemicals also inhibit the initial adherence of bacterial plaque. For example, in the case of gum disease, den-tal plaque depends initially on bacterial adhesion. However, cranberry's active constituents were able to reverse the coag-gregation of 49 (58 percent) of 84 coaggregating bacterial pairs tested in a recent experimental study.

Sometime in the not-too-distant future, modern medicine may be able to vanquish biofilm. But for now, if your doctor prescribes antibiotics or if you are simply dealing with chronic infections, try using cranberry or berberine formulas, either alone or with antibiotics, to prevent further bacterial adhesion and to help dissolve some of the already existing adhesions. Or, use barberry bark root, Oregon grape root or goldenseal root, separately or in combination. Take one or two capsules three times daily either alone or with antibiotics.

ALTERNATIVE MEDICINE RECOMMENDATIONS FOR PROSTATITIS

Here are some of the natural remedies that have worked for men with refractory or chronic prostatitis. First, I'll tell you about lifestyle changes and natural therapies that can ease symptoms or even set the disease's course in reverse. Then, I'll give you some advice on using herbal and nutritional medicine to support and heal your prostate.

Lifestyle Changes and Natural Therapies

Stay hydrated. Often, men with urinary symptoms try to get relief by drinking less water. But keeping your system flushed with plenty of pure water sets the foundation for better prostate health. Try natural, herbal diuretics, such as couch grass, pipsissewa, and watermelon seed. (I'll discuss these and other herbs for prostatitis in more detail below.)

Eat lightly. Your prostate health will improve when you shift to a diet comprised mostly of whole grains, steamed vegetables, fresh fruit, and herbal tea.

Take a daily complement of vitamins and minerals. Be sure to include antioxidants like vitamin E, vitamin C, and beta-carotene. Lycopene, quercetin, and other carotenoid and bioflavonoid nutrients have powerful antioxidant action. Selenium and zinc are also important for improving prostate health.

Try hydrotherapy. Water therapy can improve blood flow through the prostate and perineum, which may in turn open up a clamped-down urinary tract. Sit in a tub or sitz bath containing water that is as hot as you can tolerate. Stay there for 15 to 30 minutes. (If you have acute prostatitis or other infection, don't do a hot soak; it can aggravate the inflammation.) For more aggressive treatment, try alternating hot and cold soaks; do the cold soaks for a fourth of the time you do the hot soaks. Try to do them two to three times daily. Or, you can follow this same regimen by applying hot and cold packs to the perineum (between the testicles and the anus).

Take steps to reduce stress. Learn how to manage stress and find some form of exercise that you enjoy.

More Herbal and Nutritional Medicine for Prostatitis

Since aging men have suffered from prostate troubles for millennia, medicine has had plenty of time to figure out which plants are helpful and how to use them. I use mainly saw palmetto and pygeum in the treatment of prostate disorders, but a long herbal tradition—and, increasingly, modern scientific methods—is illustrating the potential value of other medicinal plants for the treatment of prostatitis and other prostate disorders. Many of these herbs are available in the form of nutritional supplements; some formulations contain several of them. If you'd rather use them in more traditional ways (as teas, tinctures, infusions, decoctions, dried herbs, or suppositories), consult with an herbalist, Traditional Chinese Medicine (TCM) physician, or naturopathic doctor (ND).

None of the herbs below has been tested in a true "clinical trial." I am passing on to you mostly anecdotal information, and although I have provided references, the studies are of short-term duration, and not placebo-controlled—in other words, they have not been measured by the gold standard of medical research. Having said that, I believe that most of these are relatively safe; whether they can be relied upon to improve your symptoms is unknown. The website www.prostatitis.org, a resource I strongly recommend to prostatitis patients, provided me with a good deal of the information on the herbs below.

Buchu. The leaves of this African plant help relieve painful muscle spasms. Buchu also has analgesic and antimicrobial effects.

Chamomile. This mild sedative herb is sold as a tea in most supermarkets. It has been said to have relaxant effects on spasms and cramps, particularly in the genitourinary system. Chamomile also has antiseptic and anti-inflammatory properties.

Chinese goldthread. This herb contains anti-inflammatory and antibiotic properties and is effective for infections, fevers, abscesses, hemorrhage, nervousness, anxiety, and insomnia.

Comfrey. Long used as a topical remedy to speed healing of cuts and scrapes, comfrey contains a phytochemical called allantoin that reduces inflammation and promotes the growth of new cells. It has been found to cause rare blood vessel disorders if taken internally in high doses for long periods, but these problems have never been reported in people using the herb as directed.

Couch grass. This plant has a long tradition of use by herbalists for the treatment of prostate enlargement and infection. It is a diuretic, and has antimicrobial properties.

Cramp bark. As the name suggests, this herb is well suited for the treatment of painful pelvic floor and prostate muscle spasms. It also has sedative effects. Herbalists recommend using it in conjunction with chamomile and dong quai (which is discussed below) for best results.

Cranberry. Phytochemicals found in cranberry juice have been found to help prevent the binding of bacteria to the bladder wall. It can prevent the spread of a bladder infection into the prostate, or vice versa. It also has a deodorizing effect on urine, which might be helpful if you are dealing with incontinence. If you prefer juice, choose one that contains no refined sugar (it can be mixed with other juices); or you can take pills or chewable tablets with concentrated doses of these cranberry phytochemicals.

Dong quai. Useful to men with prostatitis because of its antispasmodic and diuretic properties. It can raise blood sugar, however, so don't use it if you are diabetic.

Echinacea. This herb is a research-tested natural antibiotic and immune stimulant. It is toxic to both bacteria and viruses. For chronic infectious prostatitis, add this when you first feel the symptoms coming on. Take it every hour or two, as a tincture or dried root in a capsule, until symptoms resolve.

Garlic. Whether you adore the smell of garlic or would rather avoid it, your prostate (and the rest of you) will thank you for including it in your diet. Garlic has stimulant, antispasmodic, and antimicrobial effects. It also has been found to help prevent heart disease and may even support the body's defenses against cancer.

Goldenseal. This herb's astringent, antiseptic qualities combine well with saw palmetto and echinacea. Avoid using it for prolonged periods at high doses; it can raise blood pressure and kill off the "good" intestinal bacteria that aid digestion. Those with heart disease, hypertension, glaucoma, diabetes, or history of stroke should avoid goldenseal.

Juniper. Herbal lore says that using this herb gives urine the fragrance of violets—a benefit for men who have problems with urinary incontinence. It's also used in herbal medicine to treat genitourinary infections, and for its diuretic properties. If you have a kidney infection or other kidney disease, don't use it.

Pipsissewa. This tongue-twisting plant is mostly known in herbalism as a treatment specifically for chronic prostatitis and other disorders of the genitourinary system.

Queen of the meadow. Another diuretic herb that is said to be especially good for genitourinary problems.

Saw palmetto. This herb has been found to help men with prostatitis improve urine flow, relieve pain, and aid in eradicating infection. Herbalists sometimes suggest combining saw palmetto, echinacea, and buchu.

Scullcap. Men with chronic pelvic pain can, understandably, end up becoming tense and irritable, and this becomes part of a vicious, escalating cycle of pain and tension. Baikal scullcap is an herbal sedative and antispasmodic that can help to break this cycle.

Siberian ginseng. Although not a true ginseng, Siberian ginseng, also known as eleuthero, has similar effects on the body. It is an overall tonic that supports and balances immune function and helps to regulate blood pressure. It is also considered to lend support to optimal reproductive and prostate health. Some people use eleuthero on a regular basis, to counteract the effects of stress, boost energy, and improve resistance against disease.

Valerian. This is another sedative herb that helps relieve cramping and pain. Especially good for helping you relax and sleep at day's end.

Acupuncture and TCM for Prostatitis

As with other prostate problems—perhaps, more so than any other of the common disorders of the genitourinary tract—acupuncture and Traditional Chinese Medicine (TCM) may be useful adjunctive treatments for chronic prostatitis. Jillian Capodice and I are conducting acupuncture research at the Center, and one of our current studies aims to assess whether acupuncture can be effective for chronic prostatitis. Having seen patients get better with acupuncture therapy, we've concluded it should definitely be researched further.

As I mentioned earlier in the chapter, a current challenge concerning treatment for chronic prostatitis is in the fact that there are many symptoms present besides prostate pain alone. And since acupuncture is a "holistic therapy" that treats the whole person—not just discrete symptoms—it makes sense that it could be a viable treatment option for this complex syndrome.

For example, according to TCM, prostate dysfunction is generally related to a deficiency or blockage of *qi* (also spelled *chi*), the vital energy of every living organism and the source of all movement and change in the universe. When qi becomes static or deficient in the body, it may result in an enlargement or dysfunction of the prostate. According to TCM, some of the symptoms that may be exhibited when qi is lacking or stagnant mirror the symptoms of chronic prostatitis: generalized pain; pain during or after intercourse; or perineal, penile, pelvic, lower back, and anal pain. Additional, related symptoms might include excessive day- or nighttime sweating, fatigue, stress, depression, premature ejaculation, no sensation with ejaculation, erectile dysfunction, loss of appetite, feeling of incomplete voiding, painful urination, weak stream, and getting up often at night to urinate.

If this sounds complex or confusing to you, don't worry. In TCM, diagnosis is an extremely complex process—in ways that differ from the complexities of more technologically based allopathic diagnosis. Hearing a TCM practitioner discuss your condition may end up being more confusing than clarifying if you don't know the terminology or the theoretical basis of this ancient science. The *treatment* of prostatitis with acupuncture is somewhat easier to understand: The practitioner uses extremely fine needles to puncture specific points related to the blockage or deficiency of qi. This, in turn, may help decrease some of the symptoms related to chronic prostatitis. To the average Westerner, this might sound far-fetched, but so far our research and clinical experience suggests that this therapy can do a lot of good in patients with prostatitis. We hope to learn more about its effectiveness in our studies.

CYSTITIS AND LOWER
URINARY TRACT INFECTIONS (UTIs)

When complete draining of the bladder is obstructed because of BPH or prostatitis, the risk of urinary tract infection (UTI) rises dramatically. Even in the general population, despite ever-improving antibiotic therapy, 10 percent of the population is affected by infections of the urinary tract. These infections often afflict the bladder as well. When the bladder lining becomes inflamed or infected, the diagnosis is acute primary or secondary cystitis. UTI is a blanket term for all infections of the urinary tract, including *cystitis* and *pyelonephritis* (infection of the kidneys) and *urethritis* (infection of the urethra).

Symptoms to look for:

Urethritis: Burning during urination; rarely there may be blood in the urine.

Cystitis: Frequent urge to pass urine, with only small amounts passed each time; pain and/or burning or stinging with urination; sometimes, blood in the urine or foul-smelling urine, or fever and chills with lower abdominal discomfort.

Kidney infection: pain in the loins, high fever.

When the urinary tract becomes infected, the usual suspects—bacterial pathogens that can crop up nearly anywhere in the body—are often to blame: *E. coli*, enterococci, proteus bacteria and *Staphylococcus aureus*. One or more may be present at the site of infection. When cystitis occurs, it can spread throughout the system, so it's important to get good treatment quickly. A course of antibiotics usually takes care of the problem in the short term. Unfortunately, cystitis and UTIs tend to become chronic, and end up involving the deeper layers of the bladder wall.

Cernilton for Prostatitis and UTI

The flower pollen extract Cernilton has been studied as a remedy for chronic prostatitis. In a Chinese study, researchers analyzed prostatic fluids in men with chronic prostatitis before and after therapy with Cernilton. Before, their prostatic fluids had elevated measurements of leukocyte activity (immune cells) and elevated measures of free radical formation (oxidative stress). The fluids were also lower in zinc and the antioxidant substance superoxide dismutase (SOD). Therapy with Cernilton turned most of these variables around, reducing leukocytes and oxidative markers, elevating zinc levels, and (in men who were also infertile) improving sperm motility and viability and enhancing SOD levels.

In a German study, researchers evaluated six months of therapy with Cernilton on men with chronic prostatitis or prostatodynia (prostate pain). Of 72 men with uncomplicated prostatitis, 56 (78 percent) had a favorable response, and 26 (36 percent) were cured of symptoms and signs. Thirty (42 percent) demonstrated improved urine flow rate and decreased immune and inflammatory signs in their ejaculate. (Note, however, that of 18 additional subjects who had complications, such as urethral stricture, prostatic calculi, and bladder neck sclerosis, only one responded to Cernilton therapy.)

Yet another research team did a small study on Cernilton therapy of prostatitis, involving 15 men. Thirteen had lasting, complete relief or marked improvement. The researchers attribute these effects to the extract's anti-inflammatory or antiandrogenic properties. More rigorous research is needed to ascertain the mechanism of flower pollen therapy for prostatitis.

PART II

Chapter 5

Prostate Cancer—
What It Is, Who's at Risk,
How It's Treated

IF THE PREVIOUS CHAPTERS didn't already give you the impression that you have a walnut-sized ticking time bomb wrapped around your urethra, keep reading. There's more to be concerned about with this particular gland: prostate cancer.

Men in the United States are more likely to get prostate cancer than lung cancer. Nearly 31,000 men die each year of prostate cancer in the U.S.

If you are of African American descent, you have an especially high risk of developing prostate cancer, and it can be more aggressive. If you are still a young man, you have less to worry about than if you are elderly: The median age at which the prostate cancer diagnosis is made is 72. However, due to widespread PSA screening, we are seeing younger men diagnosed these past few years. I have treated men in their early 40s with early-stage prostate cancer.

If you are Asian, and living in Japan, you can relax a little, because people of your racial descent have the lowest rate of prostate cancer diagnosis and mortality. But if you are Asian and living in the U.S., keep in mind that Japanese in Hawaii have prostate cancer rates that fall between those of Japanese living in Japan and white Americans living in Hawaii. Race appears to influence prostate cancer risk, but when a person of a lower-risk race moves to a part of the world where risk is higher, their risk tends to rise, too. This suggests that environmental and dietary factors play an important role in the development and progression of prostate cancer.

Early detection and advanced treatment modalities have helped catch cancer earlier. The rate at which prostate cancer is diagnosed has risen 67 percent since the middle of the twentieth century. Unfortunately, mortality (the number of deaths) from prostate cancer has not declined much in recent years. Between the years of 1990 and 1998, in white men, deaths from prostate cancer fell only 2.8 percent per year (roughly 500 fewer deaths in 1998 than 1990). In black men during this time span, prostate cancer deaths fell only 1.5 percent per year, with less than 300 fewer prostate cancer deaths in 1998 than 1990.

According to the Centers for Disease Control and Prevention 2003 Fact Sheet on prostate cancer:

- Among all racial and ethnic groups, prostate cancer death rates were lower in 1999 than they were in 1990.
- Decreases in prostate cancer death rates during 1990 to 1999 were almost twice as great for whites and Asian/Pacific Islanders as they were for African Americans, American Indian/Alaska Natives, and Hispanics.

We are making headway, but we still have a lot of work to do on behalf of men who are at risk.

RISK FACTORS FOR PROSTATE CANCER

When you hear the term "risk factor," you can bet that you're going to hear information that is just specific enough to scare you, but not specific enough to give you any exact idea of how to protect yourself. And there are risk factors that are utterly out of your control, such as age, race, and family history.

Keep in mind that risk factors are identified by looking at large populations of people and determining the incidence of the disease in question. Then, the researchers go backwards to see whether any dietary habits, environmental influences, or lifestyle patterns can be associated with the incidence of that disease. When we can find a trend among populations, and we find similar association in two or more different populations, we are fairly sure we've got another risk factor on our hands.

Having one or more of the following risk factors isn't a certain death sentence, and neither is the absence of these risk factors a promise of protection. When we identify risk factors, what we are really doing is trying to identify groups of people who would be best served by increased vigilance. In the case of prostate cancer, for example, men who are in higher-risk groups might have PSA tests more often, and a high measurement of PSA might be more aggressively followed up.

The identification of risk factors is also important for research purposes. Once we have an idea of what puts certain groups of people at increased risk of certain diseases, that helps us know how we might treat or prevent those diseases through dietary changes or medical means.

So...with all of that in mind, here are the risk factors for prostate cancer:

Family history. If you have a relative who has had the disease, be sure you are evaluated regularly to detect it early in yourself, should it arise. Having a first-degree male relative (a father or brother) with the disease doubles the risk of developing prostate cancer. Your risk is greater if several of your relatives have been diagnosed, especially if they were diagnosed while young (under 50). Men diagnosed with prostate cancer at a young age are likely to have a more aggressive form of the disease.

Age. Over 80 percent of prostate cancer patients are over 65, and risk spikes in men over 50.

Geography and race. Prostate cancer incidence is highest in North America and western Europe. Denmark has the highest rate in the world. Asians, native Africans, and Central and South Americans have lower risk, but their risk rises if they move to other parts of the world where risk is higher. African American men have the highest rate of prostate cancer in the world, and are more likely to develop more aggressive forms of the disease.

Animal fat. Countries with diets higher in animal fat tend to have higher rates of prostate cancer, and case-control studies show that men who have prostate cancer have eaten more animal fat-rich diets than their counterparts who are cancer-free. It is not currently known whether this relationship is due to the physiological effects of fat in the diet, or to fatty foods replacing vegetables and fruit. Contrary to evidence from studies of other cancers, no correlation has been drawn between vegetable fat consumption and prostate cancer. However, several recent studies have revealed that men that are heavier and have a higher body mass index are more likely to have a worse pathology report after surgery. In addition, these men are also more likely to have a PSA recurrence after surgery.

Low antioxidant intake. Studies show that a diet high in lycopenes (found in vegetables and fruit) and vitamin E and selenium (found in whole grains) is protective against prostate cancer.

Vasectomy. Some research suggests a link between vasectomy and prostate cancer—up to a 50 percent increase in risk. The jury is still out on this, however, and if there is a relationship, it doesn't appear to be a strong one.

Too much vitamin A—or not enough? Greater dietary intake of vitamin A (found primarily in flesh foods and supplements that contain retinol, unlike its precursor, the carotenes, which are found in vegetables and fruits and have been correlated with reduced risk) has also been associated with an excess risk for prostate cancer in some studies, although high blood levels of retinol appear related to a decreased risk for this disease.

Sexual activity, venereal disease. Studies have found that men with prostate cancer have histories of greater sexual activity and more bouts of venereal disease than men who don't have prostate cancer. This suggests a possible role for a sexually transmitted agent.

BPH and prostatitis. Some studies suggest that a history of some benign prostatic disease, including prostatitis and some types of hyperplasia, may increase prostate cancer risk. This may be due to problems with detection of cancerous growths in swollen or inflamed prostatic tissues.

Obesity. Obesity has been associated with many cancers, particularly those that are related to hormone levels. Extra body fat doesn't just sit there, taking up space; it's metabolically active and can alter hormone production and action. Men who carry around a lot of extra fat make extra estrogens, for example, and this hormone is linked with increased prostate cancer risk. One research group found a strong link between childhood obesity and adult risk of prostate cancer.

Physical inactivity. In a nationwide Swedish study, researchers investigated the effects of occupational physical activity on relative risk for prostate cancer. They used census data to divide roughly one-and-a-half-million men into three groups, each with different levels of physical activity on the job. (The researchers accounted for changes in physical activity levels over the ten years studied, as well.) They found that the relative risk for prostate cancer decreased with increasing levels of occupational physical activity. Men who were sedentary had about a 111 percent risk of ending up with prostate cancer in comparison to men who were active. Other studies have suggested the same, but more research is needed to elucidate the couch potato-prostate cancer connection.

Pesticide exposure. Farmers are consistently at elevated risk of developing cancer of the prostate. This could be due to the chemicals they come into contact with, or some other unidentified factor. In a National Cancer Institute study, Michael Alavanja and co-workers followed 55,332 Iowa and North Carolina farm or plant-nursery workers who had regular contact with pesticides while on the job. During the course of the study, which ran from 1993 to 1999, 566 new prostate cancers developed in this group of men, much more than the 495 men that would be expected to do so in these parts of the country. Men who applied pesticides (including methyl bromide, chlorpyrifos, coumaphos, fonofos, phorate, permethrin, and butylate) as part of their jobs were 14 percent more likely to get prostate cancer compared with the general population. Interestingly, only methyl bromide raised risk for all the men who used it; the others on the list only appeared to raise risk in men with a family history of the disease.

Cadmium exposure; rubber industry work. Men who work in iron or steel foundries, and rubber and other types of manufacturing plants have a slightly increased risk. Workers exposed to cadmium during welding, electroplating, or making batteries may have an increased risk of cancer of the prostate.

Agent Orange exposure. In a 1993 report entitled "Veterans and Agent Orange—Health Effects of Herbicides Used in Vietnam," the National Academy of Sciences concluded that men who were exposed to Agent Orange appear to have "some elevated risk" of developing prostate cancer. A follow-up report in 1996 found slightly stronger evidence in favor of a link. Men who were exposed to Agent Orange may want to be more vigilant with early detection measures.

THE ROLE OF TESTOSTERONE
AND OTHER HORMONES

Without testosterone, your prostate wouldn't develop or function normally, but some evidence suggests that this hormone isn't always on the side of good when it comes to prostate cancer. Lowering testosterone levels and manipulating its metabolism are important treatments for existing prostate cancer, and we can fairly reliably *cause* prostate cancer in experimental animals by altering hormone concentrations or metabolism.

Our diets and lifestyles can powerfully influence our hormone levels. Some men may have hormonal patterns that are by their nature higher-risk, and these patterns may be encoded in their DNA from the moment they are conceived.

Rather than a simple black-and-white relationship between one hormone and increased risk, the overall tone of the recent studies is that the interrelationships between hormones and prostate cancer are complex and still not well understood.

WHAT IS CANCER?

Cancer is much more than a single disease. It is actually a group of many different diseases, but all of them have a few important things in common. Finding cures for cancer is an excruciatingly tough task because of the ways in which different cancers form and progress. One drug won't work the way another drug might, and one drug might work initially for a patient and then stop working as the cancer morphs into a newer, more virulent form.

The best thing to do is prevent it (more on this later), and if we can't do that, we need to catch cancer as early as possible and (1) get rid of it with the most advanced methods in our possession, and then (2) do all we can through integrative medicine to try to prevent a recurrence.

In order to understand what cancer is, let's look at the life cycle of healthy, non-cancerous cells. Normal cells grow and divide, producing new, healthy cells as the body needs them. Old, "used-up" cells are destroyed and broken down to make way for the new. The balance between the formation of new cells and the elimination of old cells maintains the body in its healthy state.

Sometimes, cells keep dividing despite the fact that no more new cells are needed, and the excess cells end up forming a mass called a tumor. Some tumors are benign, which means they are not cancerous and will not spread.

Malignant tumors are those that do spread and are cancerous. The origin of the word *cancer* is credited to the Greek physician Hippocrates (460-370 BC), considered the "Father of Medicine." He named the disease *karkinos*, Greek for "crab," because he noticed that the blood vessels around a malignant tumor looked like the claws of a crab. Celsus (28 BC-50 AD), a Roman doctor, translated the Latin adaptation of the Greek word *carcinos* into the Latin word cancer.

What is the insult that sparks the formation of a malignancy? What causes that malignancy to grow and spread instead of being attacked and eliminated by the immune system, which has the equipment to do just this? These are enormous questions that, in the "War Against Cancer" that began while I was still in elementary school, we are still struggling to answer. In sections to come, I will tell you more about what is known about risk factors for prostate cancer, and about what you can do to better manage your risk. But first, let's finish our lesson on the basics of cancer.

When malignant tissue forms, the cells that comprise it divide in an out-of-control fashion, invading and destroying

When Death Is Good: Apoptosis

Most scientists, like most people, abhor the thought of death. Yet, sometime in the 1970s, researchers began pioneering the notion that a state of health in living organisms is actually a balance between life and death—cellular death, that is. Large numbers of our cells must die for us to go on living.

Cells are programmed to die after a period of time that is specified in their genetic material. Changes in that genetic material can render cells immortal, but there's a price to pay: It foreshadows death of the organism. The only immortal cell is a cancerous cell. We can take some cancerous cells from a tumor and put them in a petri dish, and as long as we maintain the right temperature and give them fuel, they will continue to thrive and multiply. We use cell cultures like these to do research. We have cancer cell lines sitting around in labs that were originally taken from people who have been dead for decades.

The immortal cell is the basis of the cancerous cell, and cells that die on schedule are part of the genetic programming that keeps us healthy. The process of genetically programmed cell death is called *apoptosis* (from the Greek *ApoPtosis*, for "falling off").

Until around 1991, there was little awareness or study of apoptosis. Only around 300 total papers on this topic could be found on medical databases. By early 1995, this had changed markedly, with the number of papers soaring to more than 3,000. Today, much of the research being done to find effective cancer treatments has to do with turning on the cellular machinery responsible for apoptosis.

Part of our knowledge of apoptosis stems from the work of H. Robert Horvitz of the Massachusetts Institute of Technology. Dr. Horvitz researched a tiny segmented worm, *C. elegans*, consisting of fewer than 1,000 cells. During his postdoctoral fellowship work in Britain, Dr. Horvitz was able to trace the appearance and fate of every one of these cells from fertilized egg to adult. Many more cells were produced than managed to survive. Later, Dr. Horvitz proved that this cell death was not random but geneti-

continued on next page

When Death Is Good: Apoptosis *continued*

cally programmed; that it was not an aberration, but was at the very heart of the worm's orderly development.

We all have these same basic genes that lead to programmed cell death. But what happens when our cells forget to die—when that genetic programming fails us? Many cancers today, we now believe, result because our cells have forgotten how to bow out gracefully, and have instead opted for immortality. That cellular immortality comes at the expense of the body of the person in which these immortal (cancerous) cells grow and divide.

Apoptosis and Chemotherapy

Cell death in general follows two distinct pathways: passive necrosis or active apoptosis. Either something kills the cells—bacteria, viruses, cancer, inflammation, chemotherapy drugs, or trauma—or the cells walk the plank, so to speak, for the good of the organism as a whole. We can use natural substances to induce apoptosis, or we can use toxic chemotherapeutic agents to kill off cells in a disorganized, chaotic manner. We may destroy some cancer cells, but with the drugs currently used, we always do a lot of damage to non-cancerous cells as well.

When caused by chemotherapy, passive necrosis—the alternative to apoptosis as a means of cell death—might be considered "random cell murder." Chemotherapy releases cytotoxic materials through sudden cell rupture, with randomly adverse effects on healthy cells. The resulting secondary inflammation of adjacent and distant cells is a major problem with such necrotic cell death, and is responsible for the side effects of chemotherapy.

In contrast, apoptosis is a highly organized biochemical process. Only those cells programmed to die (or to "commit suicide") will do so, without rupture or release of cytotoxic substances, leaving all neighboring cells intact. Treatment regimens specifically triggering the targeted apoptosis of cancer cells may represent a great advance over standard chemotherapeutic regimens in terms of reducing side effects.

healthy tissue all around itself. Cancer cells may also break off of the tumor and enter the circulatory system or the lymphatic system, both of which can transport malignancy to other parts of the body, where they form new tumors. Metastases, as these new tumors are called, can show up in the lymph nodes, bone, bladder, rectum, or other organs.

Even when a cancer has spread, it is named for the cell or organ in which it began its formation. If prostate cancer has spread to the bones, for example, we can still identify those cells as prostate cancer cells, and it is called metastatic prostate cancer.

SYMPTOMS OF PROSTATE CANCER

If you are diagnosed with prostate cancer, it may come as a complete surprise. Early prostate cancer causes no symptoms in most cases, and the first you may hear about the possibility is at a follow-up to your physical, where you are informed that your PSA came back high. Then, you're scheduled for tests and biopsies that make you wince when you think about them.

However, some men do experience symptoms. They resemble symptoms of BPH and/or prostatitis, and may include:

- A need to urinate frequently, especially at night;
- Difficulty starting urination or holding back urine;
- Inability to urinate;
- Weak or interrupted flow of urine;
- Painful or burning urination;
- Painful ejaculation;
- Blood in urine or semen; and/or
- Frequent pain or stiffness in the lower back, hips, or upper thighs.

I can't emphasize enough that men with these kinds of symptoms need to see a urologist right away to rule out prostate cancer. A lot of men try to shrug off or ignore symptoms, or they dig in their heels and refuse to see a doctor because they are, deep down, afraid of what they might be told. But generally, when it comes to prostate cancer, the earlier we detect it, the higher the likelihood of cancer cure. And if it turns out to be BPH or prostatitis that we are dealing with, we are better able than ever before to restore your urinary tract health with a combination of allopathic and holistic therapies.

PSA TESTING: SHOULD YOU OR SHOULDN'T YOU?

Much remains unknown about the interpretation of PSA levels. The test has limited ability to distinguish cancer from benign prostate conditions. According to a study by Stanford University researchers that was published in the *Journal of Urology*, the PSA exam causes many men who have slow-growing prostate cancers to have their prostates removed, even though they would most likely never have died from their cancer. (After all, according to statistics from the American Cancer Society, only 1 in 32 men who get prostate cancer ever dies from the disease.) These men have a chance of ending up impotent or incontinent as a direct result of their treatment, and they may not have truly needed the treatment in the first place. Treatments can be costly in dollars and cents, too. Some radical experts believe that the PSA is not a useful test, because it leads to too many men having unnecessary, invasive treatments, and as a screening test it has not proved its efficacy in decreasing death rates from prostate cancer.

How good is the PSA at detecting cancer? From what we know now, it detects about 70 percent of prostate cancers. One recent trial, which involved 18,000 subjects, looked at prostate cancer prevention using finasteride (Proscar). Overall, there was a 25 percent reduction in prostate cancer, but when the results were stratified by PSA and the investigators looked at the lower ranges, 15 to 18 percent of patients with "normal" PSAs (PSA less than 4.0 ng/ml) had prostate cancer.

There are also a lot of false positives when it comes to PSA. It can be elevated in men with large prostates but without cancer; if there are precancerous cells; or within 48 hours of ejaculation or prostate manipulation. In fact, if you have had a prostate biopsy, I would recommend that you wait at least 6 weeks before having another PSA as it may be falsely elevated during that time.

A urinary tract infection can markedly elevate PSA. I recently saw a patient who had a PSA of 35 ng/ml. I routinely perform urine cultures on these men, and in fact this patient had a severe urinary infection. After treating him with the appropriate antibiotics, his PSA came down to 3 ng/ml. Bottom line: A man with a high PSA doesn't always have cancer, and a man with a low PSA isn't always cancer-free.

The real question is: Why do we screen? The idea is that we can use a test to screen normal, healthy individuals, or individuals at high risk for a disease, and use that test to detect the disease early. Ideally, this will translate into improved mortality. Today, it's still questionable whether we are seeing a reduced mortality from prostate cancer screening. If there is any, it's around 6 or 8 percent, which may be significant and may translate into saving thousands of men from dying of this disease. By detecting patients earlier, we have seen much less lymph node involvement at the time of surgery. We have fewer patients presenting with bone metastases. With a cancer such as prostate, it may take a while to translate into reduced mortality.

I'm in favor of PSA screening, as long as we are conscientious about what we do once the results come back. It is particularly useful for men in high-risk groups, such as African Americans and men with a family history of the disease. The American

Urological Association and the American Cancer Society both recommend that men over 50 be offered screening each year. In addition, those men at increased risk (family history, African American) should be tested earlier, starting at the age of 40. On the other hand, the National Cancer Institute has made recommendations *against* routine PSA screening.

Those who are in favor of screening don't recommend mass testing of an uninformed male population. They recommend that patients be completely informed of the PSA's potential risks and benefits, and most do not support mass screening of all men over 50. A man who is not well-informed about how to interpret the results of his PSA test is not equipped to work with his doctor to make the best treatment decisions.

Men aged 50 to 65 benefit most from screening, and those over 70 to 75 the least. If we find prostate cancer in a man over 80, it is not likely to grow large enough to cause problems before something else causes his death. As I mentioned above, African American men or men whose immediate family members have had prostate cancer should talk with their doctors about starting screening earlier, at age 40.

There is considerable debate about the best course of action following a finding of elevated PSA. It is not always reliable when it comes to making a distinction between BPH and early prostate cancer.

One final point: If you do have an elevated PSA, and you are found to have a small cancer, your medical team may advise you to "watch and wait" to see whether the cancer grows or not. Urologists use your age, the Gleason score of the cancer, the amount of cancer present in the cores, the number of cores involved, the size of your prostate, any preexisting medical conditions, and the rate of change in your PSA over six months to evaluate how benign the cancer is to avoid unnecessary treatments. There is a small risk that the cancer will grow quickly and possibly move beyond the limits of the prostate during this time. Discuss this carefully with your medical team.

DIAGNOSIS

Prostate cancer diagnosis includes the digital rectal exam, blood tests, urine testing, and some other tests. What to expect:

Blood tests. First, drawn blood will be sent to a lab for measurement of prostate-specific antigen (PSA). Keep in mind that a high PSA can be due to BPH, prostatitis, ejaculation within the past 48 hours, urinary tract infection, trauma, bicycle riding...or prostate cancer.

Digital rectal exam. The doctor inserts a gloved, lubricated finger into the rectum and feels the prostate through the rectal wall. If he feels any hard or lumpy areas, he may suspect cancer or BPH. All prostate nodules should be biopsied, regardless of the PSA value. So, even if your PSA is normal, or below normal, if there is a nodule on exam, a biopsy should be performed.

Urinalysis. The lab will check a urine sample for blood or infection.

Transrectal ultrasonography. With this test, we insert a rectal probe and use ultrasound to create a sonogram picture of the prostate. The volume of the prostate can be determined. The ultrasound can guide us as to where to place the needles in the gland. Some have used a color doppler to locate cancer. This may be helpful in experienced hands, but for the most part the color doppler in urology practices has not gained large support in detecting cancers.

Intravenous pyelogram. A fancy name for x-rays of the urinary tract organs. It is rarely used today to detect or stage prostate cancer. This test can detect a small tumor in the kidney, or in the tube leading from the kidney to the bladder known as the ureter.

Cystoscopy. A thin tube with a light at its end is inserted into the penis to look into the urethra and bladder. This is rarely required today in the evaluation of a patient with prostate can-cer. Even in patients with prostate cancer, the gland itself may appear normal by cystoscopy. Rarely, prostate cancer can invade the bladder, pushing up against the ureters, preventing urine from passing freely into the bladder. Again, this is rare and was seen more commonly years ago before the PSA was avail-able. During those days, patients would present with back pain and kidney failure as the urine put pressure against the kidneys.

Probably the only reason to do cystoscopy to look for prostate cancer is in patients with severe urinary symptoms or blood in the urine. This visual inspection of the internal anatomy (urethra, prostate and bladder) is routinely used to detect and monitor bladder cancer patients. There are some cases where the cystoscopy can reveal large, bulky tumors that are invading the urethra or bladder.

Biopsy. If the results of the PSA and/or rectal exam are sus-picious for the presence of prostate cancer, we then schedule the patient for a biopsy. In the end, this is the only way to know for certain whether we are dealing with cancer. We perform this test by removing a small amount of tissue from the prostate with a needle. A pathologist then uses a microscope to look for cancer cells.

When you are told that you need a biopsy, ask your doctor about what to expect from the procedure: Will you be awake or asleep? Will it hurt? How soon will you have the results? And if cancer is found, what will be the next step, and who will talk to you about treatment options? The more information you have going in, the better.

BIOPSY: WHAT TO EXPECT

There have been some incredible improvements in prostate biopsy techniques over the past decade. When I was a resident, all patients scheduled for prostate biopsy were admitted to the hospital. The biopsy was performed somewhat blindly with a needle guide placed over the doctor's finger, directing the needle into the prostate gland. Today, the majority of the prostate biopsies are done in the physician's office in an outpatient setting. Patients are fully awake.

It is important that you inform your doctor if you are taking any blood thinners, or if you have a history of bleeding or easy bruising. You will be required to stop taking blood thinners (i.e., aspirin, coumadin, Plavix, vitamin E, even some blood-thinning herbs) for at least a week beforehand.

An enema is routinely given on the morning of the biopsy. I always perform a urine test one to two weeks prior to the biopsy to make sure that the patient does not have an infection. Even in the absence of infection, I start patients on an antibiotic the night before the biopsy—a practice I find dramatically reduces infection rate after the procedure.

The first part of the biopsy is the insertion of the ultrasound probe into the rectum. Although initially this may be somewhat uncomfortable, there is little pain, and within a few minutes the muscles and rectal sphincter relax and sensations of pressure from the ultrasound probe dissipate. At this point, I insert a small amount of a local anesthetic. This can be administered right through the ultrasound probe, and several milliliters of lidocaine can be injected around both sides of the prostate. By doing a "prostate block," I numb the prostate nerves, rendering the rest of the biopsy process relatively pain-free.

Once the local anesthesia is in, the prostate size or volume can be determined. In addition, cysts, calcifications, seminal vesicle abnormalities, and the presence of areas in the gland suspicious for prostate cancer can be detected by the ultrasound.

The number of prostate cores—thin, conical samples of tissue—taken during a biopsy has risen over the past few years. When I was a urology resident, we took six cores. Recent research

Color Doppler Imaging: A New, High-Tech Test

Some investigators use a new technique during ultrasound testing that involves the use of color Doppler imaging with microbubble contrast so that physicians are better able to determine the presence and exact location of a mass within the prostate, even if it is small. Doppler imaging can sense differences in velocity (i.e., blood flow versus solid tissue) and transmits these differences through different color pixels to create a picture on a screen. Microbubbles are tiny bubbles of gas that can permeate through small blood vessels without creating any harm. The microbubbles further enhance imaging by increasing the intensity of backscatter signal. Since blood vessels and blood flow are more prevalent in cancerous tissues than regular tissues, microbubbles tend to concentrate in the cancer, which is revealed on the created picture. This allows physicians to more accurately locate where biopsies should be taken.

Researchers from France recently conducted a clinical study to determine the effectiveness of the contrast-enhanced microbubble technique in determining biopsy sites in men suspected of having prostate cancer. This trial included 85 men who underwent conventional Doppler and microbubble-enhanced color Doppler during the biopsy procedure. The results between the two were directly compared based on biopsy results. Contrast-enhanced color Doppler had a 93 percent detection rate of prostate cancer, compared with only 54 percent for un-enhanced color Doppler. Biopsies from areas of the prostate that did not contain cancer occurred in 21 percent of biopsies under Doppler that was not enhanced, compared with only 11 percent of biopsies under contrast-enhanced Doppler—dramatic improvements in detection and accuracy that could be used to reduce unnecessary biopsies in comparison to color Doppler that is not enhanced.

Patients suspected of having prostate cancer may wish to speak with their physician about the risks and benefits of microbubble-enhanced color Doppler in endorectal ultrasound for biopsy placement—or the participation in a clinical trial evaluating other novel screening approaches. It's still controversial, but research over the next few years at Columbia and elsewhere may establish it as mainstream practice.

has shown, not surprisingly, that the more tissues we sample, the more cancers we find. So, it has become almost the standard to take at least 12 biopsies: 6 on the right and 6 on the left. We take even more if we have found a nodule during the rectal exam or a suspicious area on ultrasound.

These cores of tissue can be placed in separate containers and labeled. When the pathologist reads the biopsies, the analysis will be interpreted for each core. If prostate cancer is found, your doctor can tell you where it is located in the prostate.

It is important to realize that even with 12 or more biopsy sites, there is still a chance that the biopsy can miss an area of cancer. The biopsy is performed with a skinny needle, and if the cancer is small, it could be missed on biopsy. By taking more samples, we aim to reduce this false negative risk, and so I think that it is important that your doctor sample the gland well, and do at least the 12 biopsies.

If your exam and test results seem to be due to problems other than cancer, you will be treated accordingly (or advised to watchfully wait). If cancer is found, the pathologist grades the tumor to give us information on how aggressive it is and how quickly it is likely to grow. The lower the score, the less aggressive the cancer.

STAGING

Staging of cancer is performed to determine the extent of the cancer, and to give us all the information we need to make treatment decisions. Further blood tests and imaging tests may be needed to accurately designate the stage of the disease. As I mentioned earlier, one of the main advantages that has come out of PSA screening is a down-staging of prostate cancer over the past decade. Today the majority of patients diagnosed with prostate cancer are considered to be early stage, and staging evaluations to determine the spread of cancer may not be needed. For patients with low risk features (PSA less than 10 ng/ml, Gleason score of 6 or less, small-volume cancers with normal rectal exams) the likelihood of finding disease in the bones or lymph nodes is so low that most urologists and oncologists have stopped recommending a CT scan or bone scan in these situations. However, in the higher-risk patients (PSA over 10 ng/ml, Gleason score 7 or greater), baseline CT scan and bone scan should be performed prior to treatment.

In certain cases where there may be concern that the prostate capsule or seminal vesicles are involved with cancer, an *endorectal coil MRI* may be helpful. I would recommend this test, especially if you are considering radical surgery, as the results of this test may help your doctor decide whether you would be a candidate for a nerve-sparing procedure. If the MRI reveals cancer in the neurovascular bundle on one side, this may need to be sacrificed during the surgery, reducing but not eliminating the chances for spontaneous erections after surgery.

If you have been diagnosed with prostate cancer, your doctor will likely tell you what stage of cancer you have based on his findings:

Stage T1—The cancer isn't palpable by rectal exam; usually, stage 1 cancer is discovered during surgery for BPH. Tumors may be found in more than one part of the prostate, but there is no spreading of cancerous cells beyond the gland.

Stage T2—The tumor is felt in a rectal exam or detected by a blood test, and has not spread beyond the prostate.

Stage T3—The cancer has spread to tissues near the prostate.

Stage T4—The cancer has metastasized to the rectum or bladder neck (T4a) or to the pelvis or levator ani muscles (T4b).

Gleason grading. When you were first conceived, you were a small blob of cells, all of which did pretty much the same things. The process of growth and development from that point relies heavily on proper cellular *differentiation*—the process where different cells' genetic codes are "turned on" in different ways so that they can become a working part of different organs and tissues. Cancer cells turn this process backwards, becoming *less* differentiated, and less able to do the work they once did in the body.

Gleason grading is a measure of the cancer cells' differentiation—the extent to which the cells still resemble the cells of the organ in which they are growing. The more differentiated the cells, the better your prognosis. Well-differentiated cancers have a Gleason score of 2 to 4; moderately well-differentiated cancers have a moderate Gleason score of 5 or 6; and poorly differentiated cancers have Gleason scores of 7, 8, 9, or 10.

These scores directly correlate to patient outcomes, and can be used to predict whether a patient will have a recurrence.

TREATING PROSTATE CANCER

The treatment options for prostate cancer are many, and trying to make the right choice can be hard under the best of circumstances. In this section, I'll do my best to keep things simple so you can work with your doctor (or doctors; it's best to have at least two medical opinions) to make the best possible decisions about your treatment.

Surgical Options

Radical prostatectomy. Surgery is the preferred route for early-stage cancer that appears to be local to the prostate, if the patient is young (under 65) and otherwise healthy. Prostatectomy is tried and true, and has high, long-lasting cure rates in patients with disease that is confined to the prostate.

The goal of the surgery is to remove the prostate gland, seminal vesicles, and pelvic lymph nodes. Two versions of this surgery are performed: *retropubic* prostatectomy, where the prostate and adjacent lymph nodes are removed through an abdominal incision; and *perineal* prostatectomy, where the gland is removed through an incision made between the anus and the scrotum. In the latter procedure, the surgeon may also remove lymph nodes through an additional incision in the abdomen, or laparoscopically (using a probe with a very small camera attached, allowing the surgeon to perform the procedure with a minimal incision). If cancer cells are found in the lymph nodes by the pathologist, we know that the cancer has spread and we may need to do some additional treatments. Otherwise, chances are good that prostatectomy will cure the disease.

Prostatectomy requires a hospital stay. It is major surgery that can have significant side effects, such as impotence (in a high percentage of patients), incontinence (in a small percent-

Questions to Ask At Least Two Urologists Before Choosing a Treatment

- What is the stage of my disease?
- What is the grade of my disease?
- What are my treatment choices, and which do you recommend for me?
- How will I benefit from each treatment?
- What are the risks and side effects of each treatment?
- Will my sex life be affected?
- How probable is it that I will have urinary problems after the treatment?
- Do you know of any new treatments being studied in clinical trials that might help me?

Write down each doctor's answers, or bring a voice recorder to your appointment. The shock and stress of a cancer diagnosis, and hearing about the treatments, is enough to make even the steadiest person a bit forgetful, and you'll be glad you recorded some information to help you review and consider your options. Use them along with this book to make your treatment decisions. And be sure to have your biopsy reviewed by an independent pathology laboratory.

age), and urethral narrowing. Over the past decade there have been some major advances in the surgical technique of radical prostatectomy, reducing the incidence of these side effects.

Laparoscopic and robotic prostatectomy. The use of laparoscopic techniques makes prostatectomy safer, significantly reducing the likelihood of excessive bleeding during surgery and of incontinence or impotence afterwards. Laparoscopy also shortens recovery time in comparison with traditional prostatectomy; instead of four to six weeks, recovery time may be only a matter of days. If all goes well and the man is in overall good health, he may only need to stay in the hospital for one night following the procedure.

In a laparoscopic procedure—which takes three to five hours, longer than traditional surgery—we give general anesthesia and insert a probe with a tiny camera on its end through a small incision in the abdomen. Other very small incisions (smaller than a dime) are used to insert instruments with which we do the actual procedure.

During the operation, carbon dioxide gas is used to inflate the abdomen. The pressure of the gas compresses the veins of the pelvis, and this reduces bleeding during surgery.

Robotic prostatectomy is, basically, robot-assisted laparoscopic prostatectomy. The incisions are still small, and the same technique is used, but a robot—the da Vinci Surgical System—assists the surgeon. This robotic system works as an extension of the surgeon's hands, enhancing his or her precision and range of motion. The camera used gives three-dimensional images of the area being operated on. Definitely the state of the art in radical prostatectomy, this procedure so far appears to be the best for preserving nerves vital to sexual and urinary function when in the hands of a skilled urological surgeon. Incidence of both minor and major surgical complications are one-fourth that of traditional open prostatectomy.

Study Suggests Advantages of Immediate Prostate Removal for Early Prostate Cancer

The medical world is in a bind when it comes to overtreatment versus undertreatment. We don't want to withhold potentially helpful treatments, and in the current environment—where a lot of doctors worry about getting sued if they don't try every possible therapy—medicine tends to take a more aggressive approach. On the other hand, treatments usually involve side effects that can impair quality of life. Weighing the risks and benefits of a treatment like radical prostatectomy, which can lead to incontinence and impotency but can be lifesaving, is a formidable job.

A study published in the May 12, 2005 issue of the *New England Journal of Medicine* further complicates the issue of watchful waiting in early prostate cancer. Over a 10-year period, a Swedish research team found a significant survival advantage in men who had their prostates removed completely over those who watchfully waited. Specifically, 50 of 348 men in the watchful waiting group died of prostate cancer during follow-up, while 30 of the men who underwent radical prostatectomy died from the disease. In men who were under 65 years of age at the conclusion of the 10-year follow-up period, the advantage of surgery was greater, with 19 percent of the watchful waiters dying of prostate cancer, compared with 11 percent of the men who had prostatectomy.

This surgery—which entails complete removal of the prostate and the surrounding lymph nodes—also had effects on disease spread. In the group that had surgery, 19.2 percent experienced local disease progression, and 15.2 percent had distant progression. In the watchful waiting group, 44.3 percent had local progression and 25.4 percent had distant progression. The men with the most to gain from immediate surgery appear to be those under 65.

If the men in the watchful waiting group had also used targeted chemoprevention and lifestyle changes, my guess is that the outcomes between the two groups would have been more similar. As it stands, this study gives us useful information for helping men to make treatment decisions.

We have a surgeon here at Columbia, Dr. David Samadi, who has been using the da Vinci system with terrific success. To date, Dr. Samadi has performed over 100 robotic prostatectomies. His cancer results parallel those of the open surgical technique (margin positive rates are very similar), and most of his patients are continent and have full control by six weeks post-surgery.

Cryotherapy/cryoablation. Basically, what we do with cryosurgery is freeze cancer cells to death, immediately and with pinpoint accuracy. We use ultrasound to guide the placement of several probes or cryoneedles into the prostate, and use argon gas to rapidly cool cancerous areas. After the tissue is frozen, helium gas is run through the same needles to thaw the tissue.

Targeted cryoablation of the prostate is a promising, minimally invasive therapy for localized prostate cancer. In seven- to eight-year studies, it has an 89 to 92 percent success rate as a primary treatment for localized or locally advanced disease (T1 to T3). I have also used cryosurgery to treat patients who have a recurrence when radiation has failed. I have had excellent long-term results with these patients—97 percent of them survived for at least 10 years after the procedure. In men treated with radiation therapy, 38 percent eventually have a positive biopsy (recurrence), while only 12 percent of men who received cryotherapy have a positive biopsy after treatment.

For men whose cancers are likely to have grown just beyond the prostate, or those who have aggressive (Gleason score at or above 7) tumors, this procedure is very effective. It is also a good alternative for men who cannot have surgery or radiation, or don't want to have either of these therapies. The FDA has approved it and Medicare covers it. In my experience, for patients who fail radiation therapy, the advantages of cryosurgery over radical prostatectomy are outstanding.

Cryosurgery: What to Expect

Modern-day cryosurgery is performed in the hospital, under either general or spinal (epidural) anesthesia. Before your procedure, you may be advised to take drugs to block the action of hormones on your prostate, to help shrink the gland.

Most procedures are done in an hour and a half or less. We use ultrasound to guide the placement of thin cryoneedles through the perineum, which is located under the scrotum. In two or more freeze-thaw cycles, we freeze cancer cells to death, protecting healthy tissues from damage with thermocouples and a urethral warming device. You can go home the same day or the next day if all goes well. For a week following, you'll need to use a urethral catheter, which will drain into a bag worn on one thigh.

Here's a case study that will help you see how we make treatment decisions with prostate cancer patients.
A 61-year-old African American man was diagnosed with prostate cancer. The biopsy revealed adenocarcinoma of Gleason score 6; PSA was 18.6. He complained of urinary urgency, decreased force of stream, and needing to rise at night often to urinate. The patient had decreased sexual potency that did not respond well to medication.

The patient had history of congestive heart failure and related cardiovascular conditions, including a heart attack. He was on multiple medications. After a bone scan and a CT scan, we knew that his disease was confined to the prostate.

Due to his medical history, the patient was a poor candidate for a radical prostatectomy. An invasive operation, such as a prostatectomy, is not considered feasible for a patient with serious cardiac conditions. The alternative treatments included external beam radiation therapy (EBRT), internal radioactive seed implantation, and cryosurgical ablation of the prostate (CSAP). All of these procedures are described as "minimally invasive alternatives to a radical prostatectomy." The challenge was to find the best alternative for

In order to ensure the destruction of all cancer cells, we freeze tissue beyond the prostate, and this can affect nerve bundles associated with erection. These nerves can regenerate, however, and potency may return, depending upon potency prior to cryotherapy. A recent study found that at three years following cryosurgery, patients' self-reported quality of life was not worse than for men treated with radiotherapy, radical prostatectomy, brachytherapy, or watchful waiting; the cryotherapy patients were more likely to have erectile dysfunction, but this improved with the passage of time and with medical help. Nerve-sparing techniques are being developed, and the technology continues to improve.

Patients who undergo cryotherapy may also have incontinence, although with modern-day technology, this is very rare,

this particular patient. To do so, we assessed the patient's risk of experiencing a recurrence of cancer following the chosen treatment procedure.

According to the standards outlined in a study by Dr. John P. Long at Tufts University, the patient was at a high risk of biochemical recurrence due to his high PSA of 18.6, a Gleason score of 6, and T3 stage adenocarcinoma. This ground-breaking study compiled data on recurrence rates in men with prostate cancer who underwent either EBRT or CSAP. We determined that our patient's risk of recurrence would be less with the cryoablation procedure than with the radiation therapy. Furthermore, unlike radiation therapy, cryosurgical ablation can be repeated if the cancer recurs or the patient has a positive biopsy. After consultation with his urology and cardiology teams on this and other matters, the patient consented to cryosurgical ablation.

He experienced no post-operative complications and was discharged the day following the procedure. The patient's postoperative digital rectal exam revealed no problems, and his PSA was undetectable! He also reported improvement with urinary continence and sexual function.

even in patients that have failed previous radiation therapy. There may be also a period of time, around six weeks, where there is some blood in the urine. Mild urinary urgency and scrotal swelling may also occur, but will resolve in a few weeks' time. Most men recover normal bowel and bladder function.

Alternative and Pharmaceutical Treatments for Surgical Side Effects

Following surgery, your doctors will give you medication for pain. Be sure to speak out if your pain is not being adequately managed; the science of pain control is quite advanced now, and we can do a lot to ease this kind of discomfort while you are recovering.

You will probably feel weak or tired for at least a week after your operation. The amount of time it takes to feel energetic again will vary from person to person.

Impotence is a major concern for most men who undergo prostate surgery for cancer. Surgery can damage the nerve bundles that run along the outside of the prostate, and this can lead to impotency. Today, more than ever before, we can identify those nerves in the operating room. We know their anatomy, and we can work with a technology called CaverMap—a nerve stimulator that helps us to positively identify nerve pathways— to preserve crucial nerve bundles.

The chance of surgery-related impotence is much greater with prostate cancer that has spread beyond the prostate. It's important to work with a surgeon with plenty of experience and skill. If you are under 60 and you have decent erections, your likelihood of having them post-surgery is quite high (over 70 percent, according to some studies). But it depends on a number of factors, including:

The quality of your erections before the operation. Your erections will not improve after surgery from your baseline. That much is clear. But if you were able to have normal erections before the surgery without using any oral agents, such as Viagra, then you have a greater chance of retaining your erections after surgery than men who needed those aids before surgery. Men who go into treatment with poor-quality erections will likely suffer the most in this area, and need some assistance after surgery—either with oral medications, injections, or a penile implant.

Your age. Most of the studies show a clear relationship between the age of a man undergoing surgery and the likelihood of being potent post-operatively. This is likely due to nerve and blood supply to the penis. Younger men overall have less cholesterol deposits in their arteries, and can get more blood into the penis. If there are other pre-existing medical conditions, such as diabetes, this may affect the nerve conduction and prevent erections. Overall, men under the age of 60 are much more likely to regain and recover normal erections than men over the age of 70.

Nerve-Sparing Surgery

If your cancer is located to one side of the gland and the disease is still considered to be early stage (T1c), your surgeon may discuss with you an approach called *nerve-sparing radical prostatectomy*. The goal of this technique is to remove the prostate gland completely, yet at the same time prevent any damage to the nerve bundles that are necessary for erection.

The nerves that conduct energy for erections are known as the cavernosus nerves. There is a bundle on each side of the prostate, and these bundles lie very close to the capsule of the gland. Men can still have an erection if only one nerve bundle is removed; however, potency rates are highest for men who have bilateral nerve sparing—both groups of nerves intact after surgery.

The downside of preserving the bundles is that the cancer may have extended out of the prostate into the bundles, and there is a concern that performing nerve-sparing surgery may leave cancerous cells behind.

In the hands of an experienced surgeon who spares both nerve bundles while operating on a patient under 60, the patient's likelihood of being potent without medical help is around 75 percent. Of the remaining 25 percent of patients, about half of these will be able to have satisfactory erections with the use of oral agents like Viagra, Levitra, or Cialis. If the same type of patient has only one of the two bundles of nerves after surgery, the chances of non-drug-assisted potency drops to around 40 percent.

VIAGRA USE AFTER PROSTATE SURGERY

For those who don't have great erections before surgery and who have impotency complaints afterwards, we often try Viagra at a dose of 50 to 100 mg, not more than three times per week. Some studies have looked at daily low-dose Viagra given for a few weeks, and the results are promising.

I believe that it is necessary to start men early on Viagra or another oral agent to improve potency rates. In the past, we would wait six months to a year before any therapy. I think that is a mistake. As the saying goes, "if you don't use it, you lose it." I routinely start my patients on medications to aid erectile function within two to three weeks after the procedure, assuming they want to have sexual relations. The oral medications facilitate erection by opening up blood vessels in the penis.

Men with heart disease, especially those who use nitrate drugs, cannot use Viagra or related drugs, and they may have to turn to other alternatives for impotence, such as the penile vacuum erection device, penile injections, or a penile implant. See the next sections for more on these treatments.

A man who has had a complete prostatectomy will no longer produce semen, and will have dry orgasms. But in an increasing number of men, with new surgical techniques, impotence and urinary incontinence are often only a temporary problem following surgery.

MEDICAL OPTIONS FOR
POST-SURGICAL IMPOTENCY

One of my colleagues at Columbia University, Ridwan Shabsigh, M.D., heads the New York Center for Human Sexuality at the New York Presbyterian Hospital. He oversees the care of thousands of patients with erectile dysfunction (ED) and other sexual dysfunctions, and is one of the forces behind research into daily low-dose Viagra. He is one of the world's leading experts on ED treatments. I highly recommend his

---

Self-Diagnostic Questionnaire for Erectile Dysfunction

This questionnaire can be found on page 20 of Dr. Shabsigh's book, and in the Massachusetts Male Aging Study, performed at the New England Research Institute.

How would you describe your ability to get and keep an erection that is rigid enough for satisfactory sexual activity?

A. *No ED*
Always able to get and keep an erection good enough for sexual intercourse.

B. *Minimal ED*
Usually able to get and keep an erection good enough for sexual intercourse.

C. *Moderate ED*
Sometimes able to get and keep an erection good enough for sexual intercourse.

D. *Complete ED*
Never able to get and keep an erection good enough for sexual intercourse.

If you fit the criteria in B through D, visit a urologist or ED specialist. They can help you to return to healthy sexual intimacy.

book, *Back to Great Sex: Overcome ED and Reclaim Lost Intimacy* (Kensington Books, 2002). The information below about ED treatment is adapted, in large part, from Dr. Shabsigh's book.

If you visit a urologist or ED specialist to be evaluated, your doctor will, of course, first determine whether you have ED or not.

He will ask you a lot of questions about your sex life, and you may find yourself squirming with embarrassment. Don't worry—we've heard everything under the sun! It's important to work through your embarrassment, in order to honestly reveal your issues and get the best possible treatment. It is a good idea to bring your partner along for this evaluation. If the two of you have sexual issues that have little to do with physically based ED, you may be referred to a marriage counselor or sex therapist.

Some men require a more advanced battery of tests to figure out why they are not able to achieve or maintain erections. If circulatory problems are suspected, these tests may include a *nocturnal penile tumescence and rigidity test* (NPTR). This test employs a mechanical device that you bring home and wear overnight on your penis. It measures the frequency and strength of your nighttime erections.

You may also be given an *intracavernosal injection test* to rule out circulatory problems in the penis and to see whether you are a good candidate for injectable ED drugs. The doctor will give you an alprostadil injection and check the strength and duration of the resulting erection. Or, you may have *penile ultrasound* or *cavernosometry*, tests that check blood flow and blood pressure in the penis. *Penile arteriography* and *cavernosography*, involving the injection of dyes into the penis so that any arterial blockage or venous leakage can be seen with x-rays, may also (rarely) be used.

If nerve damage is suspected—as it often is following prostate surgery—you may have other tests to determine the location and extent of the injury. And we may do some endocrinologic testing, to see whether your pituitary gland is making enough of its hormones and to measure total and free testosterone levels. (Low testosterone can cause ED.)

TREATMENTS FOR ED

- Viagra, Cialis, and Levitra are oral medications designed to bring on a hard erection in response to stimulation. Cialis is a longer-acting version, known in Europe as "the weekender." Not all men can use these drugs; men with heart disease shouldn't use them, and if they are taken with nitrate drugs (given for angina), they can cause death. But for men who can use them, they are safe and have about a 70 percent success rate. Some men experience side effects, including headache, flushing, stuffy nose, indigestion, or altered vision.
- The vacuum constriction device (VCD) is a bit cumbersome, but can work well for men who can't or don't wish to use medications to treat ED. It consists of a chamber placed over the well-lubricated penis, and a pumping device that pulls a vacuum inside the chamber and brings blood into the penis. An elastic band placed at the base of the penis maintains the erection. Bruising and numbness in the penis are common side effects.
- Injectable or intraurethral (inserted into the penis with a thin, disposable plastic applicator) alprostadil brings on an erection that lasts for 45 minutes to an hour. Injection therapy is more often effective than intraurethral therapy; the success rate of injections is 73 to 94 percent, while the success rate of intraurethral therapy is only about 43 percent. The intraurethral method for delivering the drug isn't nearly as uncomfortable as it sounds; the injection is virtually painless. Your doctor will probably have you try injecting or inserting the medication two or three times in his office, and will use these trial runs to ensure that you have the proper

dosage. (Too much medication can cause *priapism*, a long-lasting and potentially harmful erection that requires medical attention. **If you ever have an erection that lasts for more than four hours, consider this a medical emergency and head for the emergency room!**) This therapy can be used once per day, two or three times a week.

- Penile implants are reliable and safe. Modern devices are invisible from the outside and easy to use. Some implants consist of rods implanted in the penis that become erect when the penis is manually placed in the erect position. Others use pumps filled with water, implanted in the abdomen; the user releases the water into the implants with a mechanism hidden in the scrotum, bringing on an erection. The process is reversed when sexual activity is over. These pumps are a sure thing for men who end up using them, but they should be considered permanent. Removal will probably lead to scar tissue and further erectile problems.

For more details on these therapies and all other aspects of ED treatment, please check out Dr. Shabsigh's book. It's the best one on the subject.

BIOFEEDBACK AND PELVIC MUSCLE TRAINING FOR POST-SURGICAL INCONTINENCE

Several studies have been done on a technique called PMT (pelvic muscle training) for the restoration of urinary continence after prostate cancer surgery. Some practitioners also use biofeedback, a technique used to train people to influence autonomic (automatic) bodily functions by exerting the will and the power of the mind.

RADIATION AND CHEMOTHERAPY

Radiation therapy. This may be used instead of surgery or following surgery to get rid of any cancerous cells that have spread beyond the prostate. Some patients whose cancer is high risk, and who are not surgical candidates, may be advised to have radiation treatments along with hormonal therapy. In patients with metastatic disease, radiation therapy is used to relieve pain or other problems caused when cancer has spread to the bones. Also known as radiotherapy, this treatment entails directing high-energy rays in a targeted manner to damage and thwart the growth of cancer cells. It affects cells only in the areas treated.

We can either direct beams of radiation from an external source (external radiation) or from a small capsule of radioactive material (a "seed") that we implant directly into or near the tumor (*internal radiation*, also called *brachytherapy*). We may use both internal and external radiation in some patients.

External radiation therapy is performed in an outpatient clinic. We spread the doses of radiation out over five days a week for about six weeks. The final treatments may include a radiation "boost" aimed at the area from which the tumor initially arose. Typical external radiation therapies include x-rays and Cobalt-60 gamma rays. You may have the option of conformal/proton beam therapy, a type of radiation that makes it possible to shape the beam in three dimensions to adhere to the shape of the tumor. Conformal/proton beam therapy may help avoid damage to surrounding normal tissues.

The newest type of radiation therapy that is available is the proton-beam. This is similar to the conformal radiation except that protons are used to generate the radiation. Protons are microscopic particles that produce energy in the form of a radiation beam. The proton beams can pass through healthy tissues without damaging them, yet still can be aimed at cancer tissue to destroy these cancerous cells. This type of therapy can precisely target the tumor while sparing surrounding tissues. It is believed to be associated with fewer side effects. In a recent study of proton-beam therapy in 1,200 men with early-stage localized prostate cancer, 75 percent were disease-free five years later. If you are considering this proton-beam therapy, you should know that it will require at least 40 treatments over two months.

Intensity modulated radiation therapy (IMRT) is another form of external beam radiation. In this approach, a CT scan is used to generate a 3-D picture of the prostate gland and surrounding organs. IMRT is more precise than other forms of external beam radiation. Because it uses thinner beams to target the gland, the prostate receives a higher total dose of radiation, and the surrounding tissues (rectum and bladder) receive less. IMRT is given in short sessions, five times a week, for seven to eight weeks.

If you have a radiation implant, expect a brief hospital stay for implantation. The implant may be removed after a period of time (at which point it will no longer be radioactive), or it may be left in the body permanently. You will be cautioned to avoid close contact with others for a while following the implantation—just to be on the safe side. Internal radiation with compounds like radioactive strontium, injected directly into bone, may be used to relieve pain in patients with metastasized cancer that no longer responds to hormone therapy.

Radiation therapy can cure early-stage prostate cancer, and can significantly extend life if the cancer is advanced. Urinary symptoms and impotence are less common with radiation than with surgery, at least in the short term. Unfortunately, it's virtually impossible to avoid killing at least a few healthy cells around the area being targeted, and this can lead to side effects.

Side effects you might experience due to radiation therapy:
- Fatigue
- Skin reactions in treated areas
- Frequent, painful urination
- Upset stomach
- Diarrhea

- Rectal bleeding or irritation
- Later development of impotence (in some patients who have external radiation)
- Decreased white blood cell and platelet counts (signs of decreased immune system function)

ALTERNATIVE MEDICINE FOR
RADIATION THERAPY SIDE EFFECTS

Typically, patients who undergo radiation therapy become very tired, and they may have bothersome side effects, such as diarrhea or frequent, painful urination. Those who receive external radiation will also probably experience redness, tenderness, and dryness on the skin where the beam enters the body. There can be nerve damage that leads to impotence—more often with external radiation than with internal radiation. Pubic hair may fall out, and may not grow back in some people.

One recent paper published in the *Journal of Clinical Oncology* has confirmed earlier evidence that an ointment made from the herb *calendula*, from marigold flowers, is an effective therapy for radiation-induced dermatitis (which may involve pain, redness, itching, cracking, and blistering). French researchers divided just over 250 breast cancer patients into two groups; one got a drug called trolamine that is customarily used to prevent radiation dermatitis, and the other used a calendula cream. Of the trolamine users, 63 percent ended up with radiation dermatitis. Of the calendula users, only 41 percent developed this side effect.

An amino acid called *glutamine* has been found to help patients get through radiation therapy and chemotherapy with fewer problems. A review of studies on glutamine and cancer therapies, published in *Cancer Treatment Reviews* in 2003, indicates that glutamine has protective effects against common gastrointestinal, neurological, and cardiac complications of cancer therapy. It also appears to enhance the effects of those therapies against tumor cells, increasing their sensitivity to radiation and chemo.

CHEMOTHERAPY

The use of highly toxic drugs, such as estramustine phosphate (EmCyt) to try to eradicate cancer cells—without killing off too many healthy cells—is chemotherapy. We use drugs that target rapidly growing cells. Our main challenge with chemo is to make it specific enough to attack cancer cells while doing a minimum of harm to healthy tissues.

Some cancers are treated with chemotherapy in their early stages; with prostate cancer, we use it only for patients with advanced cancer (Stage M+) that has become resistant to hormonal therapy. Basically, chemotherapy's use for prostate cancer is to relieve the symptoms of advanced prostate cancer by slowing the growth of tumors that may impinge on surrounding tissues.

The side effects of chemotherapy are many. Chemotherapy drugs are made to target rapidly dividing cells, because that's what cancer is. Unfortunately, so are hair follicles, the lining of the gastrointestinal tract, and blood component-producing cells in bone marrow. The drugs often attack these tissues, and this is why patients may experience hair loss, vomiting, nausea, diarrhea, reduced blood-clotting ability, reduced numbers of white and red blood cells (white are for immunity, red carry oxygen throughout the body), and a higher risk of contracting infections.

Recent studies by Daniel Petrylak, M.D., one of my colleagues at Columbia, suggest that a combination of the drugs paclitaxel (Taxol) or docetaxel (Taxotere, a synthetic compound similar to Taxol) with EmCyt may be a good option for men who have advanced, hormone-refractory prostate cancer.

So far, we have seen significant decreases in PSA with this treatment, and we have seen a lengthening of average survival time in study subjects on such a regimen. Talk with your urological oncology team to see whether this might be a good approach for you.

VACCINE THERAPIES

In the past, immunotherapy has played a limited role for patients with advanced prostate cancer. Recently, however, several small studies have shown great promise in this area. One particular compound that has gained publicity is known as Provenge. Although still under investigation and not FDA-approved, this compound appears to prolong survival in prostate cancer patients.

In a recent study at the University of California in San Francisco, three times as many patients on Provenge were alive as compared to those on placebo. This trial included 127 men with metastatic prostate cancer who had previously been treated with hormones and failed. The side effects appeared to be minimal and included flu-like symptoms. This could be a new area of hope for men with advanced prostate cancer. Further long-term investigations are underway.

ALTERNATIVE AND ALLOPATHIC MEDICINE FOR CHEMOTHERAPY SIDE EFFECTS

Under the direction of Jillian Capodice, the Center for Holistic Urology has established an acupuncture program. We are evaluating the role of acupuncture in helping:

- alleviate hot flashes in men undergoing hormonal therapy for prostate cancer;
- relieve pain for men experiencing discomfort from prostatitis;
- reduce pain in men and women who have metastatic cancers.

We have been impressed with the positive progress of those in our program.

One particularly interesting study, published in the *Journal of the American Medical Association*, found that electroacupuncture treatments—mild electrical current is passed into ultra-thin needles at anti-vomiting points on the wrists and legs—may reduce vomiting in patients receiving high-dose chemotherapy. The study was performed on 104 women with breast cancer who were in the hospital undergoing high-dose chemo for five days. All of the women got the same antiemetic drugs and chemotherapy agents. A third of the group had electroacupuncture treatments, another third had minimal needling (acupuncture in sites other than the vomiting sites, without electrical current), and the final third got no acupuncture. The group that got electroacupuncture had an average of 5 vomiting episodes; the minimal needling group, 10 episodes; and the women who got no acupuncture treatment at all vomited an average of 15 times. Women in the electroacupuncture group were more likely to have vomiting-free days.

Another of the alternative therapies that is often suggested for people undergoing chemo is *alkylglycerols*, a substance found in bone marrow and shark liver oil. Alkylglycerols help the bone marrow to produce white cells, protecting against systemic infection (sepsis)—a common problem in patients undergoing aggressive cancer treatment.

SYSTEMIC (HORMONAL) THERAPIES

Prostate cancer growth can be slowed down—at least temporarily—by cutting off its supply of hormones. We may use hormonal therapies for localized cancer, in conjunction with radiation, or for the treatment of advanced disease. By reducing testosterone levels in the body, we can forestall cancer growth for anywhere from six months to over 10 years.

Hormonal therapies work longer in men with less advanced cancers, less aggressive cancers, or cancers that contain a higher proportion of hormone-sensitive cells.

The control of the testosterone level in the body is under the control of another hormone, located in the brain. Leutinizing hormone (LH) is made in the pituitary gland in the brain and controls the release of testosterone, which is made in the testicles. By lowering LH, we can lower testosterone. If we lower testosterone, we can reduce prostate cancer cells, lower PSA, and in some cases, prolong survival.

In a study of 206 men who started out with localized prostate cancer, researchers employed two treatments. One group got radiation only, and the other got radiation plus short-term hormone treatment. The radiation treatments were given daily for about seven weeks, and the medication treatments began along with the radiation but went on for a total of six months. Six men in the radiation-only group died from prostate cancer during five years of follow-up; none of the men in the radiation plus hormones group died.

Therapies like these do not cure advanced prostate cancer, but they do extend life and relieve symptoms. When cancer has spread beyond the pelvic area (Stage T3 or T4), we may advise men to undergo some form of hormonal therapy. (Removing the prostate isn't a common course of action once cancer is advanced.) We can cut off the cancer's hormone supply either surgically or pharmacologically.

Metastatic prostate cancer can be controlled for several years with hormone therapy. Unfortunately, some prostate cancers develop the ability to grow without help from male hormones, and enter a hormone-refractory state.

Orchiectomy. Orchiectomy is the surgical removal of the testicles. When we remove the testicles, we remove the source of 95 percent of the body's testosterone. This slows the growth of the cancer.

For obvious reasons, orchiectomy is generally reserved for advanced cancers that haven't been slowed by other, less invasive treatments. But for men with advanced cancer, it's a relatively simple procedure, and can be done using local anesthetic. The patient may be allowed to go home the same day, or may have to be hospitalized, depending on his overall condition.

Antiandrogen therapy. Prostate cancer may be treated with drugs that interfere with the ability of the androgen to interact with the target cell (cancer cell, usually) at the cell's receptor. We use one of three drugs: bicalutamide (Casodex), flutamide (Eulexin), or nilutamide (Nilandron).

Antiandrogen therapy may be used in conjunction with LHRH analogues or estrogen therapy (see below) to block the action of the minor (but possibly still significant) production of testosterone in the adrenal glands. When we do this, we are administering *total androgen blockade* (TAB) or *maximal androgen blockade* (MAB). At this point, studies suggest that MAB improves survival time over LHRH therapy alone.

In addition to the effect on the adrenals, these agents may have a direct effect on the cancer cells. The antiandrogens compete with the androgens for the receptor site on the cell. By interfering with this binding, the drugs cause prostate cancer cells to die. Although these agents are not FDA-approved to be used alone in treating prostate cancer, there is some promising data from Europe that 150 mg a day of Casodex may be effective by itself. The main use of antiandrogens is in combination with the LHRH analogues (maximal androgen deprivation, or MAD). Numerous clinical studies have investigated the role of MAD versus LHRH analogues alone. Most of the studies do not show any major significant survival difference between the two groups.

You may have unpleasant side effects, including breast enlargement, breast tenderness, hot flashes, diarrhea, vomiting, liver problems, and loss of libido.

Estrogen therapy. Administering this "female" hormone (men's bodies do make some estrogen) reduces testicular production of testosterone. Most commonly, the estrogen DES (diethylstilbestrol) is used. Men who choose this route simply take an estrogen pill each day. Side effects may include breast growth and tenderness, water retention, upset stomach, nausea, and vomiting.

Estrogens significantly raise risk of circulatory problems, including heart attacks and blood clots. Men with a history of heart disease should not take them. Due to their many side effects, estrogens are rarely used today.

LHRH-analogue therapy. LHRH stands for *luteinizing hormone-releasing hormone*, which is made in the body and stimulates the testicles to make testosterone. When we raise LHRH levels in the body by injecting this look-alike molecule, the testicles stop producing testosterone. It is just as effective as orchiectomy and does not have the side effects of estrogen therapy.

We use either goserelin acetate (Zoladex) or leuprolide acetate (Lupron) for LHRH therapy. Expect an injection every 28 days or every 12 weeks. This therapy will probably eliminate sex drive and cause impotence. It can cause osteoporotic bone changes, hot flashes, and weight gain in the long term. There are new medications today, such as Zometa (zoledronic acid), which prevent osteoporosis caused by hormone-blocking drugs.

Dealing with Hormone Therapy Side Effects

Orchiectomy, LHRH agonists, and estrogen often cause side effects, such as loss of sexual desire, impotence, and hot flashes. When first taken, an LHRH agonist tends to increase testosterone and may make the patient's symptoms worse. This temporary problem is called "tumor flare." Gradually, however, the drug causes a man's testosterone level to fall. Without testosterone, tumor growth slows down and the patient's condition improves. Prostate cancer patients who receive estrogen or an antiandrogen may have nausea, vomiting, or tenderness and swelling of the breasts.

Ketoconazole. This antifungal drug suppresses testosterone production. It may be added to a hormone ablation regimen if other drugs fail to completely block hormone production. I have had success with this medication in the cases where the PSA rises and hormone therapy (LHRH and antiandrogen therapy) is no longer working. It is important that when taking this medication, liver function tests are ordered. This medication is best absorbed in an acidic environment, and I have my patients drink cola or take vitamin C with the pills.

Watchful waiting. Men whose cancer grows slowly and has been found at an early stage may be advised to hold off on treatment. Men who are of an advanced age or who have other serious medical issues may also go on surveillance instead of immediate treatment. You will be closely followed by your medical team, given periodic DRE and PSA tests, and treated for any symptoms that turn up, and may eventually undergo additional treatments if the benefits come to outweigh the risks.

MORE ON SECOND OPINIONS

Don't forgo a second expert opinion out of fear that you're losing valuable time. A second opinion will give you a better grasp of what you're facing. The week or two it will take to consider all of your options will be worthwhile in the long run.

Check with your insurance company before you get your second opinion; some actually require you to get one, and others might not cover the cost of a second consultation if you do not ask them to.

Ask your urologist or general practitioner to recommend a colleague he or she thinks highly of. You might benefit most from seeing a doctor in another of the specialties that focuses on prostate cancer treatment—a radiation oncologist or a medical oncologist, for example. Check with local hospitals or medical schools. Look in your public library for the *Directory of Medical Specialists*. Do an online search for urologists, medical oncologists, or radiation oncologists in your area. Or you can call the Cancer Information Service (1-800-4-CANCER) to learn about National Cancer Institute-supported treatment facilities and cancer centers near you.

Your treatment plan should be designed with your age, your overall health, your feelings about the various treatments, your concern about side effects, the stage of the disease, and the grade of the tumor (how fast it is likely to grow or spread) in mind.

Work in a partnership with your medical team. Learn all you can about your disease and your treatment choices. When it comes time to undergo treatment, it makes sense to ask your doctor what to expect. Find out whether you will be able to continue working and playing in a relatively normal way while you are under treatment. Ask whether you can expect to be in pain or suffer debilitating side effects. When you know what to expect, you and your loved ones will be better prepared to cope with this difficult process.

CLINICAL TRIALS

Taking part in a clinical trial—a study conducted by doctors to test the effectiveness and learn about the side effects of new treatments—is one way to benefit from treatments that are still in the research pipeline, and to make a contribution to medical science in the process. Studies may give the same treatment to all patients, or may have an experimental group (which receives the new treatment) and a placebo group that receives an inactive treatment. Or, they may compare a known, standard treatment to a newer one by giving some patients the old therapy and others the new one.

To find out about current cancer studies, go to the National Cancer Institute's clinical trials database on their website at http://cancernet.nci.nih.gov.

FOLLOW-UP CARE FOR
MEN WITH PROSTATE CANCER

Aside from using chemopreventive strategies to stave off a cancer recurrence, it is important for men who have had this disease to have regular follow-up exams. Your doctor will suggest an appropriate follow-up schedule, and will examine you to be sure that the disease has not returned or progressed. If other medical care is needed, your doctor will make sure you get it. Follow-up exams may include x-rays, scans, and laboratory tests, including the PSA blood test.

SUPPORT FOR CANCER PATIENTS

The challenges of living with prostate cancer can seem overwhelming, both to the patient and to those who care about him. Problems and challenges come up at every turn. Take advantage of information on the Internet and in books like this one, and, if you feel so inclined, seek out a support group. You can start by visiting Us TOO at www.ustoo.com, and the National Cancer Institute website at http://cancernet.nci.nih.gov/cancertopics.

One of the best things about support groups is finding others who have had experiences similar to your own. You get a chance to talk about your disease and your treatment and to help others cope by telling them about your own choices. Keep in mind, however, that treatments and ways of dealing with cancer that work for one person may not be right for another, even if they both have the same kind of cancer. Discuss any advice you are given, especially advice you are considering following, with your doctor.

Discuss your worries about keeping up with work, family, and daily activities with your health care team. Ask them any questions you have about tests, treatments, hospital stays, and medical bills; there are no stupid questions when it comes to these issues. You and your partner may have questions about sexual intimacy and how it will be affected by your disease and its treatment. A social worker, counselor, or member of the clergy may be helpful when you are feeling overwhelmed by feelings and concerns.

Meditation, yoga, and guided imagery can help you cope with fears and frustrations. Gentle yoga is a good alternative to more vigorous exercise when you are feeling ill or weak, and training in the use of guided imagery can help you activate your immune system and relieve stress.

What is guided imagery? It is a way of focusing the mind on images that help the body heal. Belleruth Naparstek, author and host of the website HealthJourneys, says that guided imagery can be used to imagine "the busy, focused buzz of thousands of loyal immune cells, scooting out of the thymus gland on a search-and-destroy mission to wipe out unsuspecting cancer cells." She goes on to say that guided imagery "acts like a depth charge dropped beneath the surface of the body-mind." It sounds like mumbo-jumbo to a lot of people, but its effectiveness is backed by more than two-and-a-half decades of scientific research. Just 10 minutes of guided imagery can heighten immune cell activity or diminish pain.

YOU'RE IN REMISSION…NOW WHAT?

It's natural for you and your loved ones to be concerned about what the future holds. Prognosis is often stated in terms of statistics, and you may lean heavily on those statistics to figure out your chances of a cure. Keep in mind that statistics are based on large numbers of patients with wide variations in the course of their disease and big differences in how they respond to treatments. No two patients are alike.

The most reliable source of information on your prognosis is your medical team. Don't be alarmed when they use the term *remission* instead of cure. This does not mean your cancer will definitely return; it means that it may. Chemopreventive measures and careful monitoring are the best ways to proactively maintain your health once you are in remission. But, also, natural health measures support your healing and recovery.

Chapter 6

Chemoprevention and Holistic Treatments for Prostate Cancer

DESPITE THE PROGRESS we've made in surgical and radiation therapies for prostate cancer, the sad truth is that a certain percentage of men who undergo treatment for this disease will have a recurrence. It's crushing for a man who has gone through prostate cancer treatment and has enjoyed some time in remission to find that his PSA is once again on the rise.

Powerful evidence exists that we can prevent or put off prostate cancer recurrences with nutritional intervention. Based on this evidence, our Center and others are focusing our efforts on determining which dietary modifications can (a) prevent prostate cancer in the first place, particularly in men in high-risk groups; or, (b) alter the course of the disease.

Chemoprevention is defined as the administration of agents to prevent the induction of, inhibit, or prevent the progression of cancers. Prostate cancer's high incidence and long *latency—* it grows slowly and may be present for many years before it is detected or causes symptoms—make it a good candidate for chemoprevention strategies. From the research I and others have done, I can conclude that if every man who was told to "watchfully wait" entered into a focused chemoprevention program, we would see a major shift in their health (prostatic and otherwise) in the ensuing years.

Chemoprevention involves the use of nutritional supplements and herbs, but it also involves dietary changes.

COMMON DENOMINATORS

Doctors can end up overfocused on high-tech treatments that only address one aspect of a disease process while failing to address the big picture—in this case, the factors that collaborate to create the disease in the first place.

Complementary medicine is all about seeing that big picture. As holistic urology gets better at seeing the forest, we have identified two major factors that appear to be common denominators that set up an ideal environment for prostate cancer formation: *oxidation* and *inflammation*.

A good deal of current holistic urological research is focusing on modifying these common denominators, seeking out nutritional, herbal, and other natural interventions that will modify a whole spectrum of risk factors for prostate cancer— and, usually, other diseases, too, such as heart disease and osteoarthritis. These interventions improve overall health. And

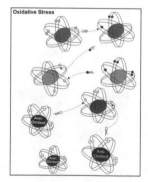

they will, most likely, help men to avoid severe BPH and prostatitis.

OXIDATIVE STRESS

A *free radical* is an atom or group of atoms that contains at least one unpaired electron. Free radicals are formed in the normal process of metabolism (the transformation of food to energy at the cellular level). When free radicals "grab" electrons from other atoms or groups of atoms to try to find a mate for their unpaired electron(s), they are engaging in the process of *oxidation*.

An oxidized atom or group of atoms then becomes a free radical, and can oxidize other atoms, continuing a chain reaction. Oxidation of DNA, the cells' genetic code, is one known causative factor in cancer initiation. The overall amount of electron-grabbing going on in the body at any given time is its level of *oxidative stress*.

The body has some resources to deal with oxidation; they are called antioxidants. Antioxidants donate electrons to free radicals, stopping chain reactions and helping to protect cells against DNA damage. We make antioxidants in our bodies, but we also need to get them from the foods we eat. Unfortunately, most people living in Westernized parts of the world have high oxidative stress (from eating poor diets, being stressed out, and coming into contact with pollutants that cause free radicals to form in the body) and low intake of antioxidant nutrients. Oxidative stress has been identified as a plausible link between diet and prostate cancer, and researchers have found that measurements of oxidation are significantly higher in cancerous prostate than in non-cancerous prostate.

INFLAMMATION

Inflammation and oxidative stress go hand in hand. The inflammatory action of immune cells creates free radicals. Some of the best minds in urological research are making a compelling case that chronic inflammation is a precursor of prostate cancer, as well as of a pre-cancerous prostate condition called *prostatic intraepithelial neoplasia* (PIN). If this is indeed the case—and I think that it is, based on available evidence—we can target that inflammation very effectively in a chemoprevention program.

The inflammatory process—most basically, where immune cells are called into infected or damaged tissues to eliminate pathogens, and to break down and eliminate damaged tissues—can be either acute or chronic. In a healthy body, acute inflammation sets in quickly to deal with threats, does its

The PIN Conundrum

PIN stands for *prostatic intraepithelial neoplasia*. It isn't cancer, but it is a harbinger of the disease. In medical circles, we sometimes refer to PIN as *dysplasia*—abnormal cells that are likely to turn cancerous at some point in the future.

Prostate cancer begins with very small changes in the size and shape of the prostate gland cells. These changed cells then proliferate throughout the prostate, but unlike cancer, PIN alone has no apparent influence on serum prostate-specific antigen (PSA) concentration. PIN isn't cancer yet. But not doing something to treat PIN is like letting children play with matches.

We can't discover PIN by measuring PSA, with radar scans or other laboratory tests, or by palpating the gland. We only find it when we do a biopsy. Why does PIN deserve the attention of a holistic urologist like myself—and your attention as well? Consider these facts:

- In the United States, the frequency of PIN in prostates with cancer is significantly higher than in prostates without cancer, appearing up to 10 years before diagnosable cancer.
- PIN coexists with cancer in more than 85 percent of cases.
- In a series of 249 autopsy cases, 77 percent of prostates with high-grade (severe) PIN harbored invasive adenocarcinoma, compared to only 24 percent without high-grade PIN.

PIN is a very early warning that prostate cancer is a possibility, but we don't currently have a method to detect it in apparently healthy men. Even when we do detect it, allopathy has no treatment for it, and usually the recommendation is "watchful waiting."

What we *can* do, knowing what we know today, is use nutrients and herbs to decrease the inflammation that spurs PIN on and that may in the end turn PIN to full-blown cancer.

dirty work, and subsides. A less healthy organism doesn't use inflammation so efficiently.

When you catch a bad bug and have a high fever, cough, vomiting, diarrhea, and a runny nose, this is your body's healthy inflammatory response to an infection. It is killing off the offending organisms and flushing them out. Some people's bodies don't do this very well, however, and their immune systems instead heave into a "slow burn" of chronic inflammation. We aren't sure what puts some people at greater risk of chronic inflammation, but it's likely that an interplay between genetics and diet explains most of it.

In the days before antibiotics, many people died from acute inflammation. Today, this is rare, but chronic inflammation is increasingly common. Allergies, asthma, autoimmune diseases (including chronic inflammatory bowel disease, rheumatoid arthritis, lupus, some forms of nonbacterial prostatitis, and psoriasis) are examples of chronic inflammation. It's notoriously hard to treat through allopathic medical means alone; the most allopathy has done for chronic inflammation is use drugs to try and minimize symptoms. Nutrition and holistic therapies should be used in these disorders, along with allopathic medicines, to treat chronic inflammation.

THE INFLAMMATORY CASCADE: COX, LO, AND THE PROSTATE

The inflammatory process is mediated by hormone-like substances called *eicosanoids*, a class of substances that includes the *prostaglandins* and *leukotrienes*— both of which are major players in chronic inflammation. Eico-

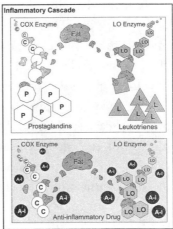

sanoids are created in the body from the fats we eat, through a cascade of biochemical reactions that involve the action of specific enzymes. The COX (cyclooxygenase) enzymes mediate prostaglandin production, and the LO (lipoxygenase) enzymes mediate leukotriene production. When we take an anti-inflammatory drug, it works by affecting those enzymes, suppressing their production so that the pro-inflammatory eicosanoids don't get produced.

Unhealthy diet and lifestyle choices can affect the action of the COX and LO enzymes, predisposing the body to overreacting to any insult that causes inflammation. Some research suggests that certain people are genetically susceptible to this kind of overreaction.

BPH, nonbacterial prostatitis, prostate cancer, and PIN have all been linked with a heightened state of inflammation. (So have many other disease processes, notably heart disease.) Research is ongoing to test drugs that inhibit COX and LO for the relief or prevention of these conditions. You can also use natural COX and LO inhibitors to tame inflammation.

When inflammation is chronic, there is a general and persistent increase in oxidative stress. It follows that people with localized chronic inflammation are at greater risk of developing cancerous growths in the area where that inflammation takes place. Women who have been infected with a chronic wart virus on the cervix are at much greater risk of developing cervical cancer; people who have had Crohn's disease (a chronic inflammation of the colon) are at greater risk of colon cancer. Men and women who have chronic inflammation of the bladder may develop squamous cell cancer in that organ. This relationship between free-radical stress, inflammation, and cancer is believed to have an impact on prostate cancer risk as well, and is particularly important in the treatment of PIN.

So, let's refer back to some of the risk factors for prostate cancer, and think about how they might relate to inflammation and oxidation:

- *Age:* The older you get, the more your body is susceptible to chronic inflammation and excessive oxidation. Antioxidant production falls.
- *Race:* Different races have differing susceptibility to pathological or chronic inflammatory conditions. They may also have differing levels of endogenous (made in the body) antioxidant enzymes; variations in how their bodies absorb and utilize antioxidants and fats from foods; and culturally based variations in the foods they choose to eat.
- *High-animal fat diet:* Diets high in arachidonic acid, an omega-6 fat, raise the activity of inflammatory COX and LO enzymes and increase oxidation.
- *Obesity:* Fat cells make inflammatory substances; simply being overweight has been found to increase overall inflammation in the body.
- *History of venereal disease:* May cause excessive inflammation of the genitourinary tract, increasing a man's vulnerability to DNA changes that lead to cancer. History of prostatitis or BPH may also indicate inflammatory or oxidative activity that can lead to cancerous changes or accelerate the growth of existing cancers.
- *Presence of PIN*, linked with heightened inflammation.

By controlling the key enzymes that spur excess and chronic inflammation, we can take a holistic "big picture" approach to chemoprevention. And we can do this with herbs and nutrients, as long as they are in a form that is useful to the body.

COX-2 INHIBITION:
NEW WEAPON AGAINST CANCER?

Controlling chronic inflammation might be one way to prevent prostate cancer or slow its growth. The COX-2 enzyme is a key player in this picture.

The COX-2 enzyme is essential for conversion of arachidonic acid—a fatty acid that is both made in the body and consumed in the diet, particularly in the typical high-fat Western diet—into prostaglandins, which are key inflammatory molecules. In cancerous prostate tissues, COX-2 and other inflammatory markers are measurably more active than in non-cancerous tissues.

The latest developments in anti-inflammatory drugs are the COX-2 inhibitors—drugs like Celebrex (celecoxib) and Vioxx (rofecoxib). A recent series of studies has addressed the chemo-preventive and therapeutic effects of COX-2 inhibitors against virtually all forms of cancer.

One way COX-2 inhibitors reduce cancer risk is by stifling the growth of the blood vessels that bring nutrients into the tumor. Animal research suggests that this may make COX-2 inhibition a valid therapy for already established tumors.

Unfortunately, the kind of highly specific inhibition of the COX-2 enzyme that is created by pharmaceutical COX-2 inhibitor drugs has turned out to have a dark and dangerous side.

COX-2 Dangers—And Safe, Natural Alternatives

Greater specificity doesn't appear to be the way to avoid drug side effects. Case in point: the voluntary withdrawal of Vioxx from the market by its manufacturer, Merck & Co. In a study of over one million HMO members, it was found that a dose of Vioxx above 25 mg increased the risk of a serious cardiac event or stroke more than three times. Smaller increase in risk was seen with lower doses. Vioxx had great specificity, inhibiting the COX-2 isoform, but in the end this sent the other inflammatory "flames" higher. The result was increased risk of cardiovascular disease.

Aspirin, ibuprofen, naproxen, rofecoxib (Vioxx), celecoxib (Celebrex), valdecoxib (Bextra)—all belong to a class of drugs called *nonsteroidal anti-inflammatory drugs* (NSAIDs). Holy basil, ginger, turmeric, green tea, oregano, and rosemary—all substances that you might expect to find in your pantry, not on a drugstore shelf—also happen to have anti-inflammatory activity. Why should you choose the herbal anti-inflammatories over the pharmaceutical versions?

About Arachidonic Acid

Arachidonic acid is an omega-6 fatty acid that can be made in the body from other fats. It is abundant in the typical Western diet—too abundant, especially in relation to intake of health-promoting omega-3 fats.

Excessively high quantities of omega-6 fatty acids are found in foods like meat, corn, dairy, eggs and peanuts. The types of omega-6 fatty acids found in these foods are readily converted into arachidonic acid. This starts the pro-inflammatory and pro-carcinogenic cascade that ultimately leads to increased 5-HETE levels and prostate cancer cell proliferation. In a physiologic sense, this cascade constitutes one of the leading causes of death among men.

The average diet today is as overloaded with the less desirable omega-6 fatty acids as it is depleted of omega-3 fatty acids. In Japan, where prostate cancer mortality is lower than in Western nations, the traditional diet consists of more omega-3-rich foods, and their levels of omega-6 fatty acids are much lower, reducing the ratio of omega-6 to omega-3 fatty acids to 2:1—a ratio that nutritional researchers believe to be close to ideal, and what we'd have if we were eating a truly healthful diet. In America, the levels are an astonishing 40:1. The evidence suggests that this is one reason why the American male is at an increased risk for invasive prostate cancer.

NSAIDs work great for aches, pains, and swelling, but they do so at a price in many people. Most of the drugs in this class pose significant risk in the form of possible intestinal ulceration and bleeding—a problem that could land you in the hospital, or even in the funeral home if it isn't promptly diagnosed and treated. GI bleeding from NSAID use is implicated in around 10,000 deaths and over 100,000 hospitalizations each year.

Drug makers met the challenge of NSAID-induced side effects with new drugs called COX-2 inhibitors. They did so because there was strong evidence that the ulcerative effects of aspirin and other NSAIDs were due to their inhibition of the activity of both COX-1 and COX-2 enzymes. COX-1 is an enzyme that does a lot of "housekeeping" in the body, including the protection and maintenance of a strong and well-lubricated mucous membrane along the inner stomach and intestinal wall. By selectively inhibiting COX-2 and letting COX-1 do its work, drug makers expected to cut down the number of patients with intestinal bleeding by a dramatic margin.

Here's the problem with selective inhibitors like Vioxx, Bextra, and Celebrex, all aggressively marketed as the next best thing in medical science. Imagine that the COX enzymes are matches. When ignited, they set fire to the fuel supply in the body known as arachidonic acid. The lipoxygenases, too, are matches, at the ready to ignite that same fuel. Picture them all lined up, at the ready to ignite that fuel and create various types of flames.

COX-2 creates eicosanoids, such as the prostaglandins—its "flames." Certain lipoxygenases create their own "flames," the leukotrienes. Each of these expressions of inflammation is associated with different cancers and other medical conditions (including heart disease, osteoarthritis, and autoimmune diseases).

When we snuff out just one of these matches with a selective inhibitor, we very well may reduce that one inflammatory flame. But the fuel depot is still there. Other matches are still there, ready to ignite arachidonic acid. The research is just beginning to show that COX-2 inhibition will reduce one fire, but it will also dynamically increase other types of inflammation.

In a study on this subject, performed at the MD Anderson Cancer Center, authors Robert Newman, Ph.D., and colleagues write that "...we demonstrate [here] for the first time...that inhibition of the COX pathway by celecoxib resulted in a time-dependent activation of the LO pathway. Specifically, the production of multiple LO-metabolites...increased as the PGE2 [prostaglandin E2, one of the inflammatory eicosanoids inhibited by COX-2 inhibiting drugs] level declined...with celecoxib at one microgram, a concentration that is easily achieved in patients." Blowing out one match does not reduce the net inflammation; it only changes the expression or character of the fires.

It's something like putting out a fire in one room of a house by sucking away its oxygen—and directing the oxygen into another room, which also happens to be on fire. You might save that one room, but the rest of the house will burn down more quickly.

The recent withdrawal of Vioxx and Bextra and concerns about Celebrex are due to the very specificity for which they were designed. When an NSAID doesn't tone down COX-1, it fails to decrease cardiovascular risk in the ways that older NSAIDs appear to. In lowering one risk of these drugs (gastrointestinal bleeding), drug developers ended up increasing another risk (cardiovascular events) so much that risk exceeded benefit—at least, in the case of Vioxx and Bextra.

Greater drug selectivity all too often leads us into new and potentially more problematic imbalances than those with which we began. Highly selective inhibition doesn't make sense when you look at the laws of nature, at the inherent balance that our bodies want to cultivate. A holistic approach requires that we take this balance into account when we look for preventive and curative options.

Herbal anti-inflammatories, unlike the selective inhibitors, effectively—not selectively—inhibit the activity of the COX and LO pathways. Aspirin does, too, but it and other less-selective NSAIDs are still more specific and targeted than herbs, and thus there is risk of gastrointestinal bleeding. Many cancers are driven by LO metabolites, including prostate cancer. We know that inhibiting 5-LO metabolites caused rapid, massive die-off of prostate cancer cells in test tube studies.

Still, the research has indicated that COX-2 inhibition may help to prevent cancers of the colon, esophagus, skin, and bladder. Over 40 studies of long-term, high-dose COX-2 inhibitors for prevention or treatment of cancers of the colon, prostate, and lung were sponsored by the National Institutes of Health, and most were suspended because of concerns about the risks of these drugs. Overall, however, the trials have demonstrated that the anticancer properties of COX-2 inhibitors are deserving of further investigation.

Can we justify risking heart disease and stroke in order to prevent cancers and Alzheimer's disease? These are tough calls to make. The good news is that there may be another way—a way that not only improves your chances of avoiding prostate cancer, but that also will *improve* the health of your cardiovascular system at the same time: herbs and other nutrients that effect a milder, more across-the-board inhibition of COX and LO.

5-LO AND 5-HETE

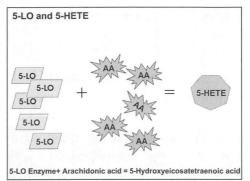

The activity of the 5-LO enzyme—one of the class of leukotrienes—is also turning out to be important to our understanding of the interaction between inflammation and prostate cancer. Drugs that inhibit COX-2 don't address this enzyme at all, but many herbs and nutrients do—another reason why natural anti-inflammatory substances are a promising chemopreventive strategy.

Substantial research evidence tells us that by suppressing 5-LO and reducing its collaboration with arachidonic acid to form 5-hydroxyeicosatetraenoic acid (5-HETE), we can slow or stop prostate cancer growth.

In fact, 5-HETE is absolutely essential to the survival of prostate cancer cells. Inhibit production of 5-HETE and we can literally starve the tumor.

By inhibiting the 5-LO inflammatory cascade, we can cause formerly immortal cancer cells to enter into orderly programmed cell death; prevent the development of blood vessels to feed the tumor; and inhibit the ability of cancer cells to spread.

We also know now that benign prostatic hyperplasia (enlarged prostate) is linked with excess inflammatory mediators, such as 5-LO. So by inhibiting the 5-LO cascade, we may reduce symptoms of BPH and risk for recurrence.

How can we do this? We have some promising nutritional tools for shifting both 5-LO and COX-2 away from chronic inflammation.

Aside from adopting a way of eating that improves your omega-6 to omega-3 ratio—which you'll learn how to do in

Chapter 7—you can use a prostate health supplement that inhibits the 5-LO cascade.

Supplements That Inhibit 5-LO Activity

Pharmaceutical companies are scrambling to test and bring to market synthetic drugs to inhibit the lipoxygenase pathway that creates 5-HETE and inflammation. Much research is being done with these compounds for cancer prevention and control. Fortunately, there are several natural, potent 5-LO inhibitors you can use to control these factors today. I've already discussed a few, including ginger, green tea, and rosemary. Saw palmetto, nettle, pumpkin seed oil, and olive oil also have documented inhibitory activity over 5-LO; this may explain why they help to shrink swollen prostate tissues in men with BPH. Frankincense, also known as *Boswellia serrata*, has proven 5-LO inhibitory activity as well.

Millions of people, over thousands of years, have used all of these herbs and obtained beneficial results with a strong degree of safety. Today we have the advantage of being able to study them in depth and figure out how best to use them synergistically to treat prostate conditions, including cancer.

The mortality rate from prostate cancer in cultures that regularly consume ginger and other 5-LO inhibitors is only one-fifth that of the West. We can include many of these foods in our diets, but you may also decide to add supplements containing these herbs and oils, to enhance their positive effects on the health of your prostate.

You can try New Chapter's Prostate 5LX formula, which contains most of the previously mentioned 5-LO-inhibiting substances. New Chapter uses a supercritical fluid extraction method to obtain high concentrations of the 5-LO inhibitors in these herbs. They don't use chemical solvents or heat, which can damage the herb's active constituents. In addition, current clinical trials are showing some amazing reversals of precancerous conditions in the prostate biopsies of men participating in a clinical trial at our Center.

INFLAMMATION CONTROL WITH
A UNIQUE NUTRITIONAL SUPPLEMENT

Two well-known herbal researchers, Tom Newmark and Paul Schulick, of New Chapter in Brattleboro, Vermont, have developed an herbal combination containing ginger and other herbs and nutrients that calm inflammation, positively affecting the 5-LO and COX-2 pathways—a natural nonsteroidal anti-inflammatory they call Zyflamend®.

When I first discovered Zyflamend, I decided to do some studies to evaluate its effects on prostatic inflammation and cancer. The results have been striking.

Zyflamend inhibits COX-2 about as well as the potent COX-2 inhibitor drugs. It does so in a different way, but the

Zyflamend Inhibits Cyclooxygenase Activity

	Percent Inhibition	
	COX-1	COX-2
Zyflamend (0.90 µl/ml)	73.8 ± 1.83	85.7 ± 5.60
Zyflamend (0.45 µl/ml)	36.5 ± 10.46	80.9 ± 12.00
NS-398 (0.15 µM)	N.D.	52.5 ± 21.26
Indomethacin (6 µM)	45.0 ± 23.32	58.0 ± 13.18

Zyflamend inhibits COX-1 and COX-2 enzyme activity, as determined using purified ovine COX-1 and COX-2 colorimetric screening assay (Cayman Chemical, MI).

NS-398 = specific COX-2 inhibitor (IC50 = 0.15 µM)
Indomethacin = non-specific COX inhibitor (COX-1 IC50 = 6 µM)
Findings are reported as means and SEM, n=3 for all data points.
N.D. = not determined.

end result is the same: control of inflammation. In our test-tube studies, Zyflamend doubled the apoptosis rate and significantly slowed the growth of prostate cancer cells.

Research suggests that inflammatory mediators (eicosanoids) play a significant role in prostate cancer, PIN, and possibly in BPH. Most men have some prostate cancer cells by the time they reach their late twenties. The key is that they are kept in check—particularly when our inflammatory levels, as mediated by the COX-2 and 5-LO enzymes, are maintained at low-normal values.

At Columbia, I have received approval for a clinical trial to give Zyflamend to men at high risk of prostate cancer to see whether it can reverse or halt PIN. We are tracking men who take Zyflamend daily, and we are assessing disease status every six months with biopsies. Preliminary results have been very encouraging.

At this writing, the final results of this study are not yet available. But there is so little chance of harm and so much evidence of benefit with this kind of herbal anti-inflammatory therapy that I'd make this recommendation: If you have had a diagnosis of PIN, you should strongly consider making Zyflamend or something like it a part of your nutritional supplement program.

Anti-Inflammatory Herbs

Here are the ingredients of Zyflamend and the research support for including them in a natural anti-inflammatory. Other companies have made products that combine some of the herbs in Zyflamend, but at Columbia, we've only researched this formulation. Based on our results, coupled with New Chapter's supercritical extraction techniques—which create a highly concentrated, pure product—I'm comfortable recommending this supplement to anyone looking for a natural anti-inflammatory.

* *Holy basil (Ocimum sanctum):* Contains ursolic acid, a known inhibitor of COX-2. The ancient medical art of Ayurveda regards holy basil—which, in Sanskrit, is known as tulsi—as one of the most powerful medicinal plants, claiming that it promotes perfect health, long life, and enlightenment. This non-culinary form of basil is loaded with antioxidant, anti-inflammatory substances, including eugenol, rosmarinic acid, apigenin, and ursolic acid.

Preliminary Results of Zyflamend PIN Study Promising

My team at Columbia is conducting a study to see if Zyflamend could have an impact on the progression or regression of PIN. We have enrolled 16 men with biopsy-proven PIN and put them on a Zyflamend protocol, which includes three capsules per day of Zyflamend and other select food supplements. The study's protocol involves doing repeat biopsies at 6, 12, and 18 months. We are analyzing their PSAs and other blood parameters throughout.

As you may know, clinical studies are very carefully monitored and overseen by hospital review boards. As an industry standard, review boards discourage doctors from publishing specific results before a clinical trial is completed, no matter how good the news might be. As we go to press, our final results won't be ready for another 9 months.

So, at this date, I can't tell you all the good news; all I can tell you is that the news is good. Very good. We have performed our first and second biopsies and it's fair to say that we are extremely encouraged by what we've seen so far. We need to enroll more patients to complete the study, and we'll have more definitive data early in 2006.

Clinical trials like this are important to prove that these combinations of herbs not only work, but are safe. When my patients ask me about Zyflamend, I feel confident recommending it at three capsules per day.

- *Ginger:* Ginger has long been used to treat motion sickness and nausea; it's more effective than a lot of the antiemetic drugs available for these purposes. Ginger has also traditionally been used to treat nasal and sinus congestion when brewed as a tea. More recently, it has been found to have significant anti-inflammatory properties. Researchers have found that that ginger contains 22 molecules that are effective inhibitors of 5-LO and COX-2, the enzymes that are markedly detected in PIN and cancerous prostate cells.

- *Turmeric (Curcuma longa):* This root, traditionally used in Indian foods, has been shown to inhibit COX-2 in several studies, including those performed at the University of California at San Diego, the University of Arizona, the University of Illinois at Chicago, and the University of Pennsylvania Medical Center. Turmeric has also been the subject of intense study for its antioxidant effects and its usefulness as a cancer preventative. Curcumin, one of turmeric's active ingredients, is an anti-inflammatory that has been described as half as strong as cortisone—a steroid that is one of modern medicine's most powerful anti-inflammatories (and that has some of the most problematic side effects of any drug around, none of which have ever been associated with curcumin). In our own research at Columbia, we have found that curcumin modulates proteins that suppress apoptosis and interferes with growth factors that promote cancer progression, in addition to suppressing *angiogenesis*, the growth of blood vessels to supply a tumor with blood and nutrients.

- *Green tea:* In a *Journal of Nutrition* report, researchers observed that the equivalent of six cups of green tea daily "significantly inhibits [prostate cancer] development and metastasis." Since few of us consume six cups daily, and because the research on this is so compelling, my opinion is that supplementation is not only appropriate but critical. This ancient beverage contains the most antioxidants in any food: 51 anti-inflammatory phytonutrients, according to major university databases. The effects of green tea on prostate cancer have been researched in laboratory experiments, animal models, and in large-scale population studies. In cultures where green tea is consumed often, incidence of and mortality from prostate cancer is significantly lower. Chemicals found in green tea—*polyphenols*—have been found to downregulate an enzyme called ornithine decarboxylase, which is overexpressed in prostate cancer patients. Another green tea chemical with documented activity against prostate cancer is *epigallocatechin-3-gallate* (EGCG), a substance that has inhibited prostate cancer growth (both androgen-sensitive and androgen-insensitive) in animal studies. One recent study published in the *International Journal of Cancer* found that EGCG selectively inhibits COX-2 in both hormone-sensitive and hormone-refractory prostate cancer cells.

- *Oregano:* The herb that gives red sauce its aromatic odor also happens to be a source of antioxidants and as many as 31 anti-inflammatory compounds.
- *Rosemary:* The most important constituents of rosemary are betulinic acid and caffeic acid and its derivatives, such as rosmarinic acid and carnosic acid, which have antioxidant properties. Since 1992, researchers from Libya, Sweden, France and the United States have published research that reveals rosemary's COX-2 inhibiting properties.
- *Hu zhang (Polygonum cuspidatum):* This herb is a rich source of *resveratrol*, a phytochemical best known as the heart-protective, cancer-preventative component of red wine. Resveratrol has documented antioxidant and anti-inflammatory effects.

- *Chinese goldthread and barberry:* This herbal combination is rich in a phytonutrient called berberine, which has documented anti-inflammatory effects.
- *Scutellaria baicalensis:* A traditional Chinese herbal medicine that modern science has researched for its anti-inflammatory properties. It has been found to inhibit chronic inflammation in several animal models. Recent research has found that baicalin and baicalein, flavonoid phytochemicals unique to this herb, directly interfere with the biochemical process of inflammation.

In December of 2002, my research team at Columbia released its findings on Zyflamend at a meeting for the Society of Urologic Oncology at the National Institutes of Health in Bethesda, Maryland. The 10-herb formula suppressed the growth of prostate cancer cells and caused many more to commit cellular suicide (apoptosis). More recently in the journal *Nutrition and Cancer* in 2005, our research team, led by Dr. D.L. Bemis, demonstrated that Zyflamend inhibits prostate cancer cells that lack COX-2 expression, indicating an enhanced prostate cancer inhibition.

Zyflamend Inhibits LNCaP Cell Growth

Growth inhibition of LNCaP cells following exposure to Zyflamend. Cells were seeded at a density of 38,000 cells/well in 12-well plates and treated with various concentrations of Zyflamend or vehicle control (0.1% DMSO). Five separate counts/well were obtained at 24, 48, and 72 hrs. Data is reported as mean and SEM, *p $\leq$ 0.0001 as determined by Student's *t* test. The experiment was repeated in quadruplicate.

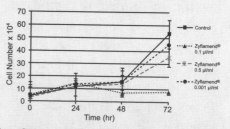

COLUMBIA UNIVERSITY
Center for Holistic Urology

Zyflamend-PIN Prevention Protocol

Participatory and reader interest in our clinical study of prostatic intraepithelial neoplasia (PIN) at Columbia University's Center for Holistic Urology is intense. The presence of PIN in the prostate often signals precancerous changes; experts believe that reversing PIN is the first defense against prostate cancer.

Men in the Columbia University Center for Holistic Urology PIN study are given a specific protocol of dietary supplements from New Chapter, of Brattleboro, Vermont, that they are told to take daily to help maintain healthy inflammation levels and provide antioxidant and nutritional support. Because of the early interest in our study, I have detailed the complete daily nutritional supplement protocol.

The Zyflamend Protocol

SUPPLEMENT	DOSAGE
Zyflamend®	1 capsule with each meal (3 total)
Supercritical DHA100™	1 capsule with lunch
Supercritical Holy Basil™	1 capsule with lunch
Turmericforce™	1 capsule with lunch
Baikal Skullcap	1 capsule with lunch
Green & White Tea Extract	1 capsule with lunch
Anti-Aging Formula™ Probiotic with a Purpose	1 capsule with breakfast
Every Man® One Daily Multivitamin	1 tablet with breakfast

OTHER HOLISTIC THERAPIES
FOR MEN WITH PROSTATE CANCER

The use of unconventional herbal therapies (phytotherapies) for prostate cancer as well as for other malignancies has been dramatically rising in the last few years in the United States. A survey conducted in 1990, focusing on the use of alternative treatments for cancer, estimated that there were 425 million visits to providers of unconventional therapies during the previous year, and that the expenditures associated with this use amounted to approximately $13.7 billion. It is likely that these numbers have increased since that time. Here, I intend to help you to avail yourself of the best that these unconventional therapies have to offer, should you be in the unfortunate position of needing them.

You can use substances from nature to support your immune system, increase energy levels, improve your body's native ability to squash cancer cells, and control side effects from treatment. If you are fortunate enough to have a small, slow-growing cancer that is being watched carefully without being treated, you are a perfect candidate for holistic therapy. And if you do not have prostate cancer but wish to hedge your bets against ever having it, many of the herbs and nutrients we recommend at the Center will be useful to you. In this section, I'll talk about medicinal mushrooms, curcumin, lycopene, antioxidants, IP$_6$ and soy for prostate cancer patients. You will also learn about more supplements for reducing inflammation, a key player in prostate cancer progression, and about the usefulness of acupuncture and support groups for men with this disease.

Frankincense (Boswellia serrata)

This herb, derived from the gummy sap of the boswellia tree, has been used in Ayurvedic medicine for centuries, primarily to treat illnesses related to excess inflammation (arthritis, ulcerative colitis, Crohn's disease, asthma). Modern research has traced its medicinal effects to active constituents called *boswellic acids.*

Boswellia studies show that this herb powerfully inhibits 5-LO activity and that it blocks the formation of both 5 HETE and leukotriene B4.

If you would like to try boswellia, take 200 to 400 mg, three times daily, of a standardized extract that contains between 37.5 and 65 percent boswellic acids.

Medicinal Mushrooms

Mushrooms contain a wide variety of unique *polysaccharides,* complex carbohydrate molecules that have notable antitumor and immunostimulant properties. They appear to be useful not only in oncology—for their apoptosis-inducing, tumor-shrinking, anti-inflammatory, and side effect-reducing properties—but in other fields of medicine, as well. They improve immune function, cardiovascular health, liver function, and blood sugar balance, and have been used to enhance energy levels and even sexual performance.

Medicinal mushroom compounds have clear value for the prevention and treatment of many of the health conditions that have stumped modern medicine. Active Hexose Correlated Compound (AHCC) and Genistein Combined Polysaccharide (GCP), both derived from medicinal mushrooms, are currently the subject of much research attention.

Active Hexose Correlated Compound (AHCC)

This compound is derived from cultivation and enzymatic modification of several species of mushroom mycelia, including shiitakes. In Japan, AHCC is considered to be a "superfood," and the research into its application to cancer therapy is promising—

particularly when it is used in combination with GCP. Its effects on breast cancer and liver cancer growth have been the most researched up to this point.

Studies suggest that AHCC works against cancer growth in a number of ways. It appears to increase the activity of natural killer (NK) cells and macrophages, and it also may improve liver function and act as an antioxidant. AHCC also shows promise as an adjuvant therapy for patients undergoing chemotherapy, helping to reduce nausea, pain, vomiting, loss of appetite, liver damage, and immune suppression. It is likely that further research will show AHCC to be a valuable adjunctive therapy for prostate cancer.

Genistein Combined Polysaccharide (GCP): Combining Soy with Mushroom Phytochemicals

Research into GCP has suggested that this supplement fights prostate cancer by reducing blood flow to the tumor (antiangiogenic effects); by enhancing apoptosis of cancerous prostate cells; and by increasing tolerance to chemotherapy and radiation. It is antiangiogenic both *in vitro* and *in vivo*. And lab experiments have shown GCP to have greater activity than genistein alone. Test tube studies at Columbia and elsewhere have shown growth inhibitory effects on prostate and breast cancer cells with GCP.

Epidemiological reports (large-scale studies that compare disease incidence in various populations and search for possible reasons for those differences, such as differences in diet) suggest that Asians consuming a diet high in soy have a low incidence of prostate cancer. Soy and one of its principal constituents, *genistein*, have been demonstrated to suppress the development of prostate cancer in experimental studies.

Overall, the research suggests that genistein is nontoxic and that it strongly protects against prostate cancer, primarily via inhibition of a signaling pathway required by cancerous cells to proliferate. Numerous studies have shown that soy isoflavones (including genistein and daidzein) inhibit the growth of prostate cancer in mice, and consistently alter measurements and markers associated with prostate cancer growth—including angiogenesis, the growth of blood vessels to feed the tumor.

Genistein Combined Polysaccharide (GCP; Amino Up Chemical Co., Sapporo, Japan) is sold as a nutritional supplement in Japan, the United States, and other countries. It is prepared by fermenting soy extract with mushroom mycelia. This process increases the bioavailability of soy isoflavones, the compounds believed to be responsible for the chemopreventive effects of soybeans and soy-containing foods.

Our laboratory has published data showing GCP has a dose-dependent growth inhibitory effect on prostate and bladder cancer cell growth *in vitro*. In fact, we found that GCP was more effective in inhibiting cancer cell growth than pure genistein, the major soy isoflavone.

The manufacturers report a study where two grams per day of GCP were given in pill form to 27 healthy human volunteers for 28 days. Blood tests were done before the trial began and on days 14 and 28 (liver enzymes, blood sugars, cholesterol, triglycerides, nitrogen levels, and other blood measurements used to discern whether a drug is toxic), and all were within normal limits. In our experience at Columbia, the most common complaint in those who use this supplement is flatulence.

At Columbia, we wrote up a case study for the *Journal of Alternative and Complementary Medicine* about a patient who had significant regression of his prostate cancer following the use of GCP. The patient was enrolled in a study where he received GCP for six weeks prior to radical prostatectomy. After 44 days of low-dose GCP, the patient's PSA fell from 19.7 to 4.2. More strikingly, after the radical prostatectomy was performed, there was no identifiable cancer in the gland. The patient complained of no side effects.

More research is forthcoming. We instruct patients on a watchful waiting protocol to take five grams of GCP daily. Unfortunately, GCP is very expensive, in the range of $275 to $600 for a month's supply.

Vitamin D for Metastatic Prostate Cancer

Several studies show a link between sun exposure—more specifically, exposure to UVB rays and the vitamin D formation that is stimulated in skin by those rays—and reduced risk of and mortality from prostate cancer. Men with genetic variations that decrease their vitamin D levels are at increased risk of developing the disease. This could help to explain why African Americans, whose dark skin does not absorb as much UVB radiation, are at increased risk compared to Caucasians. Men who live in colder climates and get less sun are also at increased risk.

The mechanism is still being studied, but it appears to have something to do with the influence of vitamin D levels on a substance called *insulin-like growth factor 1* (IGF-1).

Patients with advanced, hormone-refractory prostate cancer often develop a deficiency of vitamin D. In a study published in the *Journal of Urology*, researchers evaluated the effects of 2,000 IU of vitamin D per day, administered to men with metastatic, hormone-refractory prostate cancer for 12 weeks. At each four-week increment, patients filled out questionnaires designed to evaluate pain and muscle strength, and had their blood calcium and vitamin D levels measured. Of those treated with vitamin D, four patients (25 percent) had improved pain scores; six (37 percent) had improvements in muscle strength. Vitamin D may turn out to be a valuable natural therapy to help men with advanced disease to control pain, maintain strength, and improve their quality of life. More research still needs to be done to find the optimal dosage, and to find out whether vitamin D supplements might help men who are in earlier stages of prostate cancer.

Getting extra vitamin D by drinking milk may not be the best plan. Research from the Harvard School of Public Health shows that men who consume more milk (more than four glasses a day) have lowered vitamin D levels. Dietary calcium "uses up" vitamin D. Although vitamin D is added to milk, it is not enough to make up for its high calcium content.

Get extra vitamin D through regular exposure to sunlight (15 to 30 minutes, three times a week, if possible), without sunscreen. If you live in a climate where this is not possible, use a multivitamin that contains up to 400 IU per day of vitamin D.

Still More Nutrients for Prostate Cancer Prevention

Lycopene. This is a carotenoid nutrient that lends red color to fruits and vegetables. It is most often associated with tomato products, because 80 percent of the lycopene consumed by the average person comes from foods like tomatoes, tomato sauce, and ketchup. In studies of populations with varying amounts of lycopene in their diets, an association has been found between high lycopene consumption and low risk of prostate cancer. Men with prostate cancer have lower levels of this nutrient in their bodies. Taking lycopene supplements has been found to slow the growth of tumors and lower PSA scores in men with prostate cancer. Cooked tomato products contain more bioavailable lycopene. It appears that tomatoes cooked with oil are the best source of this nutrient.

Vitamin E. In a study of mice implanted with human prostate tumors, it was found that the growth-promoting effects of a high-fat diet were curbed by vitamin E. In one large Finnish study, reported in the *New England Journal of Medicine,* vitamin E was shown to be highly protective against prostate cancer.

All men should take a minimum of 240 IU of vitamin E daily. New research suggests that more vitamin E is not better; an analysis of studies on this nutrient found increased heart failure in people who took high doses (above 400 IU per day). Choose a version that contains the d-alpha tocopherol succinate form of vitamin E.

Selenium. This trace mineral is essential for life. It works as an antioxidant alongside vitamin E, cooling the fires of excess oxidation. The amount obtained in the diet can vary widely due to variations in selenium content of soil in different parts of the world where food is grown. Population studies consistently show that men with higher intake of selenium have lower risk of cancer of the prostate, and that men with prostate cancer have lower selenium levels than men without it.

The protective effects of selenium against cancer—and not just cancer of the prostate—are remarkable. One study at the Arizona Cancer Center at the University of Arizona in Tucson was designed to measure the effects of 200 mcg per day selenium supplementation versus placebo on cancer risk. Here's what they found:

- There was a slight reduction in risk of death from all causes in the selenium group: 108 deaths in the selenium group and 129 in the control group.
- There were highly significant* reductions in deaths from cancer. The selenium group had 29 deaths from cancer during the follow-up, and the control group had 57.

---

* This means that there is a statistical probability that the difference in cancer incidence between the selenium group and the control group could have been due to chance rather than to the supplement. When the results of a study are said to be significant, we mean that the results were most probably not due to chance—that they were caused by the intervention.

- The selenium group had 77 cancers, and the control group had 119 cancers. The risk of prostate cancer was decreased by nearly 60 percent.

These results were so promising that the control arm of the trial was stopped early, to give the control subjects a chance to take advantage of this powerful nutritional therapy.

It's important to note that the University of Arizona researchers used a special form of selenium derived from fermented yeast. Fermentation is achieved by adding a yeast called *Saccharomyces cerevisiae* to selenium salt. The yeast biotransforms the selenium, making it more biologically active and exerting enhanced anticancer activity. At this writing, the Arizona researchers were well into a second series of studies on selenium.

The SELECT (selenium and vitamin E chemoprevention trial) study, which is currently underway, builds on previous evidence that supplementing men with these two nutrients over several years' time will cut their risk of prostate cancer substantially. The 12-year, government-sponsored study involves 32,400 men at about 300 research centers in the United States and Canada. It will be the largest prevention trial ever undertaken using a drug or nutrient.

In one study published in the *British Journal of Cancer,* the authors concluded that the selenium treatment was associated with a 63 percent reduction in prostate cancer recurrence in 974 men with a history of the disease.

Vitamin C. Several studies have found an inverse relationship between blood vitamin C levels and cancer; in other words, the higher the vitamin C levels, the less likely the person is to have cancer. One study found that vitamin C slowed cell division and cell growth in two androgen-independent prostate cancer cell lines. A study by another research group found that men who had higher dietary vitamin C intakes had better odds for survival when they developed prostate cancer.

IP₆ with inositol. Inositol hexaphosphate (IP_6 with inositol) is a nutrient found in soy, rice, sesame, legumes, beans, corn, and whole grains. IP_6 with inositol has shown strong inhibitory action against prostate cancer.

In 1995, University of Maryland researchers investigated the effects of inositol hexaphosphate on growth inhibition and differentiation of human prostate cancer cells PC-3 *in vitro.* When cells begin to differentiate again, it is a sign of a return to normal. A significant dose- and time-dependent growth inhibition was observed. A marker for prostatic cell differentiation, prostate acid phosphatase, was significantly increased after 48 hours of treatment. The compound "strongly inhibits growth and induces differentiation in human prostate cancer cells," said the researchers.

Antioxidants May Prevent Progression of PIN

Mitchell C. Benson, M.D., Ihor S. Sawczuk, M.D., urology resident David R. Knowles, M.D., and I recently evaluated the effects of selenium, lycopene, and vitamin E on the progression of PIN to prostate cancer. We followed 60 patients diagnosed with PIN from May 1993 through July 2000. The patients were advised to start a daily antioxidant therapy regimen, including 400 IU of vitamin E, 200 micrograms of selenium, and 20 mg of lycopene. Thirty-nine of the 60 patients—65 percent of the subjects—have, at this writing, undergone at least one repeat biopsy. Prior to each set of biopsies, free and total PSA was measured and PSA velocity calculated.

Of the 39 re-biopsied patients, only 11 (28.2 percent) were diagnosed with prostate cancer. The average time to diagnosis of prostate cancer from the first PIN diagnosis was 14.9 months. The average follow-up for patients from first PIN biopsy to last benign biopsy was 21.1 months. These findings to me suggest that these antioxidants are working in the prostate gland to prevent the development of cancer, and should also be included in your daily regimen if you have a diagnosis of PIN.

IP$_6$ enhances natural killer (NK) cell activity. NK cells are immune cells produced in the bone marrow. Once released into the bloodstream, they recognize and destroy both viral and cancer cells. In investigations of the effect of IP$_6$ on experimental NK cell activity, researchers found that a colon carcinogen called DMH depressed NK cell activity, but that treating the cell culture with IP$_6$ reversed the NK cell depression. IP$_6$ also enhanced the potency of the NK cells, with higher doses of the nutrient bringing about greater cancer cell-killing activity.

More recent research on IP$_6$, performed at the Department of Pharmaceutical Sciences at the University of Colorado Cancer Center, involved mice inoculated with hormone-refractory prostate cancer cells that were then given either plain drinking water or water containing 1 or 2 percent IP$_6$ for 12 weeks. The volume of tumor growth was suppressed in the animals given IP$_6$, in the mice who got the higher dose of the nutrient, by 66 percent. In mice who got only 1 percent IP$_6$ in their water, tumor volume was reduced by 40 percent compared to the mice who got plain water. When the tumors were examined, the researchers found increased apoptosis in those from IP$_6$-fed mice, and decreased markers of uncontrolled, undifferentiated cellular growth and markers of angiogenesis.

IP$_6$ with inositol is a formula that every American should consider because it has such a wide spectrum of action against cancer. The formulas that have been clinically validated and conform to the actual research studies are Cell Forté® with IP-6 and Inositol from Enzymatic Therapy (available at health food stores or natural product supermarkets) or Cellular Forté® with IP-6 and Inositol from PhytoPharmica (available at pharmacies and from health professionals).

Saw palmetto. In a recent clinical study, saw palmetto was found to inhibit conversion of testosterone into the toxic metabolite dihydrotestosterone (DHT) and to lower levels of epidermal growth factor (EGF), a key driver of cancerous cell growth, while enhancing men's levels of beneficial free testosterone. High levels of both DHT and EGF have been suggested to play a role in prostate cancer.

Beta-sitosterol. Phytosterols like beta-sitosterol are used widely in Europe to treat enlarged prostate (BPH). Beta-sitosterol is a minor component of saw palmetto and pygeum, both herbs that support prostate health.

Nutrition researchers at the University at Buffalo have provided the first evidence that this phytosterol appears to play a role in inhibiting the growth of human prostate-cancer cells, according to Atif Awad, Ph.D., head of the University of Buffalo's Nutrition Program, in a presentation on October 25 at the Sixth International Conference of Anti-Cancer Research in Kallithea, Greece. They found that the phytosterol B-sitosterol, a fat abundant in vegetarian diets, enhances an intracellular signaling system that tells cells not to divide. The study showed a 28 percent inhibition of prostate-cancer cell growth after being exposed to B-sitosterol for only five days. The authors write, "If cell proliferation can be stopped before it becomes uncontrolled, cancer can be contained. When we treated prostate-cancer cells with phytosterols, cell proliferation was inhibited."

The work of Awad and colleagues is grounded in epidemiologic studies showing that prostate cancer is less common in Asian countries, where diets are primarily vegetarian, and that rates increase when these people migrate to Western societies where rates are higher and diets are primarily animal-based.

Lignans for Chemoprevention

We all know dietary fiber is a good thing. Adequate fiber helps with what is delicately referred to as "regularity," and we all know that a little regularity in the morning can make a big difference in the way your day goes. Soluble fiber, a type of fiber that is absorbed into the bloodstream through the intestinal wall, is known to help reduce "bad" LDL cholesterol levels in the body—one reason why you might have been inspired to start eating Cheerios again after a long hiatus. And chances are good that if your diet is fiber-rich, it's also rich in other good things like vegetables, whole grains, fruit, and legumes.

There is yet another health-promoting aspect to increasing your fiber intake. I'm referring to a specific type of fiber that has some other intriguing qualities that make it an ideal addition to a prostate cancer chemoprevention program: *lignans*.

The richest food source of lignans is flaxseed, although many other plant foods (seeds, whole grains, legumes, fruits, and vegetables) contain small amounts. The research suggests that at least some of the benefits of including flax in your diet have to do with the way these lignans act once they've entered your body.

Flaxseed is transformed by "friendly" bacteria in the intestines, turning substances in those seeds—known as *lignan precursors*— into natural chemicals called *enterodiol* and *enterolactone*. Enterodiol and enterolactone are phytoestrogens, like the genistein found in soy. They have the ability to bind to estrogen receptors throughout the body, blocking the binding of stronger estrogens to those sites.

When you're a young buck, testosterone rides herd over estrogen; but as you age, testosterone production wanes and estrogen production (through aromatization, a process where testosterone is transformed into estrogens in fat cells) doesn't. That excess estrogen has been implicated in both BPH and prostate cancer. Increasing lignans in the diet increases levels of phytoestrogens in the body, which, in turn, blocks the binding of excess estrogens to receptors in the prostate. Additionally, lignans may help to block the action of aromatase, the enzyme that transforms testosterone into estrogen, and of the enzyme that transforms testosterone into that enemy of the prostate gland (and the hairline), DHT.

At this writing, much research into the chemopreventive potential of lignans is going on. In a 1997 article published in the *Journal of Progressive Drug Research*, the authors write that lignans "have now been shown to influence not only sex hormone metabolism and biological activity, but also intracellular enzymes, protein synthesis, growth factor action, malignant cell proliferation, differentiation, and angiogenesis, making them strong candidates as natural chemopreventive compounds." Let's talk about some of the research that backs up these promising applications for lignans.

Populations with high-lignan diets may have lower rates of hormone-dependent cancers. In a study performed in Sweden, subjects with the lowest blood levels of enterolactone had increased risk of prostate cancer. Diets high in lignan-rich foods have been repeatedly associated with decreased risk of prostate cancer.

Other research has suggested that high intake of lignans correlates with lower incidence of breast, ovarian, and uterine cancers.

Flax supplementation slows the growth of prostate cancer between diagnosis and surgery. In a study from Duke University Medical Center, researchers added flax to a low-fat diet prescribed to 25 patients scheduled for prostatectomy. The diet was 20 percent fat and supplemented with 30 grams of flaxseed a day.

The results were remarkable. Men who adhered to the diet for an average of 34 days (actual adherence ranged from 21 to 77 days) saw their total cholesterol drop an average of 25 points. Their testosterone and free androgen levels fell—a good thing when you're trying to control prostate cancer growth. More importantly, proliferation rate and apoptosis, in addition to other markers of cancer growth, were favorably altered by the low-fat/flax intervention.

Other studies have come to similar conclusions, with flaxseed helping to slow cancer growth in patients with prostate and breast cancers.

Test-tube studies and animal studies show that lignans have anticancer effects. In lab studies, lignans and their metabolites (enterodiol and enterolactone) have been found to increase apoptosis, downregulate the expression of sex steroid receptors (translation: reduce the cancer growth-enhancing effects of sex hormones in the prostate), and inhibit the growth of both androgen-dependent and androgen-independent prostate cancer cell lines. In animals with prostate cancer that has been experimentally caused, lignan supplementation slowed cancer growth. Lignans have been found to inhibit angiogenesis, the growth of extra blood vessels to feed hungry tumors.

Lignans have antioxidant activity; they limit the activity of an enzyme associated with retroviral cancer-causing genes; and they inhibit the binding of estrogens to alpha-fetoprotein, a protein that is associated with cancer development.

Increasing Your Lignan Intake

The evidence in favor of lignans supports adding ground flax to your diet. Purchase the whole seeds and keep a coffee grinder for flaxseeds only. Grind a tablespoon and add it to your yogurt, smoothie, or hot cereal; stir a tablespoon into soup or stew; add it to nut butters or other spreads. Aim for three tablespoons a day. You can also purchase a quality, pre-ground flaxseed product, such as Forti-Flax from Barlean's. And eat plenty of other nuts, seeds, vegetables, and legumes.

Supplement companies are developing lignan supplements, containing purified lignans from flax, that are a safe way to add chemopreventive levels of flax lignans to your diet. One company called Lignan Research L.L.C. has recently come out with a high-quality product called Provail®. Be sure to choose a product that is made from whole flaxseeds and standardized, not a flax oil that has had lignans added back in.

Prostabel

In addition to the Zyflamend combination, our group at Columbia has found two other herbs that are effective against prostate cancer cells in the laboratory. Directly inspired by Mirko Beljanski's 50 years of research in biochemistry and molecular biology, Prostabel® is an innovative, all-natural blend of *Pao pereira* and *Rauwolfia vomitoria* extracts—350 mg total per capsule—that specifically promotes the health of prostate cells.

For centuries, South American Indian tribes have used the bark of *Pao pereira*, a tree from the Amazonian rain forest, to enhance immune function. We are about to initiate a clinical trial at our Center using this herb to prevent PSA from rising in men with a negative prostate biopsy. In the laboratory, our researchers have been very impressed with the ability of the pao extracts to slow the growth of prostate cancer cells and interfere with the cancer cell cycle. If you would like to try Prostabel, take two capsules with a full glass of water up to five times per day.

Chapter 7

Nutrition—
Diet, Whole Foods
and Supplements

RECENTLY I SAW a television commercial that said everything there is to say about the stereotypical American male's attitude towards diet. The ad, for "Hungry Man" frozen dinners, involves a child's birthday party, with adult family and friends sitting around the table—including two men, both of whom are overweight.

One man asks the other what he had for dinner, and he replies, "Quiche." The birthday girl then blows her candles out, and the strength of her exhalation sends the "lightweight" quiche-eater flying into the shelving unit behind him. Then, the ad makes a pitch for its filled-to-the-brim plastic plate loaded down with fried chicken, with a heap of mashed potatoes on the side. Not a green vegetable in sight.

The message is clear: Real men eat lots of meat, some of it fried. And because real men don't cook, they should buy their prefab, mega-meat meals from the freezer department at the supermarket, and just pop that plastic plate into the microwave or the oven for a hearty (and heavy) repast.

The problem with this image of macho men who eat fried meat with gusto is that this kind of diet kills. It kills by making you fat—a condition that, in and of itself, has been found to dramatically increase your risk of cancer of the prostate. It kills by clogging your arteries; by thickening your blood; by increasing oxidation (free-radical production) in your body; and by exposing you to unacceptably high levels of carcinogens.

Cancer-causing chemicals are found in the meat itself, put there by modern factory farming practices that are heavy on the use of estrogenic drugs to fatten livestock, and that feed their animals on diets rich in carcinogenic pesticides and herbicides. Additionally, the extent to which potentially harmful estrogenic chemicals in plastic food packaging can migrate into the food it contains is also now being explored.

This kind of diet is rich in "bad" fats—the omega-6 fatty acids—and when not balanced out by more health-promoting versions, these fats set up an inflammatory state in the body that promotes the production of growth factors and other biochemical messengers that lead to cancer of the prostate, or to other cancers.

And the typical American diet, heavy on fried food, sugar, and simple starches, is conspicuously bad in what it does not contain. A belly filled to bursting with meat and potatoes doesn't have much room for deeply colored vegetables, fatty fish, whole grains, fruit, or soy foods. (It also merits mentioning that quiche, a combination of eggs, heavy cream, and usually some kind of cheese, with a butter-laden, white-flour crust, isn't exactly health food.)

SOME OF THE WAYS A HEALTHY
DIET PROTECTS YOUR PROSTATE

Hippocrates said, "Make your food your medicine, and your medicine your food." What would Hippocrates say about that

Hungry Man feast? About pepperoni pizza? Cheez Doodles? Not only are they not good medicine—some of them aren't even really food. They've been so processed, so adulterated, that your body barely knows what to do with them. They are loaded with ingredients that are outright toxic or that have no nutritional value aside from providing calories, something that most of us get too many of. Processed, adulterated foods don't heal you. They don't promote good health.

You can increase your risk of prostate cancer by eating too much; by eating too much of the wrong kinds of fats; by taking in too many contaminants in those fats; or by taking in contaminants through your drinking water or by eating foods from cans that are lined with materials that leak carcinogens. Let's take a closer look at how diet reduces or increases your risk of developing cancer of the prostate.

In this chapter, I'm going to give you a lot of practical hints on how to incorporate healthful, prostate-protective, cancer-preventative foods into your diet. (I'm a doctor, not a chef; I got most of these ideas from nutritionists and other staff members and colleagues who help people make healthier dietary choices.) If you don't do the cooking at your home, now might be the time to make some copies of the relevant pages for whomever you are fortunate enough to have preparing meals for you. Your household chef might resist some of these changes, but in the end—hopefully—she (or he) will care more about your prostate health than about getting her (or his) money's worth out of the deep-fat fryer.

THE EFFECT OF OBESITY

Excess body fat alters the production patterns of certain hormones, especially the sex hormones estrogen and testosterone. A study by UCLA researchers found that when 27 obese men were put on a very low-fat (less than 10 percent of calories from

Mad Cow, Schmad Cow: Brits on "U.S. Farmers' Hideous Pursuit of Profit"

The next time you feel lucky that you can go into the supermarket and buy a huge slab of red meat or pork, or a gallon of milk, for so little, think about what an article published in the June 12, 1999 issue of the *London Daily Mail* had to say about U.S. livestock farming and dairy farming methods—the methods that make these foods so abundant and cheap, but that also load most non-organic American beef, pork, and dairy products with hormone-altering chemicals:

...{T}housands of cattle had been corralled into a series of steel pens, called feedlots, around 200 to each. There was no shade, no shelter and no grass on the ground, only dust. On one side of each feedlot was a trough containing herbicide-soaked grain.

All of the cattle were enormous—the result of the grain diet and a series of steroid hormone implants inserted under the skin behind their ears. At least one of the hormones is feared to cause cancer in humans.

Because the cattle were carrying so much weight, and because their digestive systems are designed for grass, not grain, some of the cattle's internal organs had fallen out. And because it would be too expensive to call a vet out to treat these problems, a couple of sweating, panting farm hands in cowboy hats were going from cow to cow, prising their organs back inside and stitching up the cows...

Next Tuesday the European Union will impose a new ban on all imports of American beef, believing that even stocks labeled steroid-free are frequently full of hormones...

The statistics are indeed terrifying. At least one in six farmers injects his cows with genetically engineered growth hormone. Around 90 percent of the 29 billion pounds of beef consumed by Americans each year comes from cattle which have been fattened by hormone implants. For pork, the figure is almost 100 percent.

fat), high-fiber diet and exercise program, those who had started out with high PSA levels (over 2.5 ng/ml) all saw their PSA values decline. Their levels of *sex hormone-binding globulin* (SHBG) rose, causing the men's free testosterone levels to drop—possibly decreasing growth-promoting effects on the prostate.

The diet also significantly decreased the men's circulating insulin levels. A large body of current research shows that hyperinsulinemia, or high insulin levels, promotes the development of cancer. Overweight and the kind of diet that promotes overweight are known causes of *hyperinsulinemia*. Interestingly, in the Health Professionals Follow-Up Study, researchers found a strong association between childhood obesity and adult risk of prostate cancer.

THE EFFECT OF DIETARY FAT

A number of epidemiologic studies have suggested that dietary fat intake and prostate cancer incidence are intimately related. Men whose diets consist of 30 to 40 percent fat—about average for the average American male, possibly below average for those who embrace the low-carb lifestyle or who subsist on burgers, fries, and pizza—are at higher risk for developing prostate cancer than those who eat a diet composed of less than 30 percent fat.

A research team at the University of California, San Francisco, found that even in populations with low overall risk of prostate cancer, such as Chinese men, the percentage of fat in the diet was significantly higher in men who ultimately developed prostate cancer than in men who did not. Another study, this one from the Northern California Cancer Center, found an especially strong relationship between a high-fat diet and risk of aggressive prostate cancers in older men.

Not all fats are created equal. All fats have basic similarities, but some are primarily *saturated* and some are primarily *unsat-*

urated.* Saturated fats are solid at room temperature (think butter, lard, bacon fat), while unsaturated fats are liquid (think olive oil, canola oil, peanut oil). Fats do more than go into your body, make energy, or get packed away into fat cells for storage; they affect hormone levels and activity and the balance of hormone-like, inflammation-mediating eicosanoids. So far, the research suggests that excessive saturated fat, especially animal fat, in the diet works to promote the development of prostate cancer. This could be one reason why prostate cancer risk is elevated in African American men; the studies show that by and large, the traditional African American diet is heavy on animal fat.

Saturated fats from non-organic animal sources contain more organochlorines and other xenoestrogens (environmental estrogens) than vegetable fats. They become concentrated in the fat of livestock, and these known carcinogens can then affect a man's hormone balance in ways that promote prostate cancer development. Damage to the prostate by environmental estrogens is believed to begin *in utero*, during the development of the male reproductive tract. Animal studies show that tiny amounts of these chemicals in the mother's body can alter the cellular function and microstructure of the prostate. Bovine growth hormones given to dairy cows have been linked with increases in human levels of a growth factor called IGF-1, which has, in turn, been linked with increased cancer risk.

It also appears that not all unsaturated fats are created equal, either. The omega-3 and omega-6 fatty acids are unsaturated,

---

* Actually, fats are made up of mixtures of fatty acids with varying levels of saturation. A fat that is solid at room temperature does contain saturated fatty acids, but it also contains unsaturated ones—generally, a lot of arachidonic acid (AA). This is especially true of animals, such as cattle and chicken, which are fed steady diets of grain. Grass-fed animals yield meat and milk that is lower in AA. Remember that arachidonic acid serves as the fuel depot for the fires of COX and LO.

but the omega-3 fats appear to protect the prostate, while the omega-6 fats have been shown to have either no effect or a disease-promoting effect.

Greater intake of fish has been associated with significantly lower risk of prostate cancer. A recent study published in the journal *Cancer Epidemiology, Biomarkers and Prevention* followed 47,882 men who were participating in the Health Professionals' Follow-Up Study. Their dietary intake was assessed with a food frequency questionnaire in 1986, 1990, and 1994; during 12 years of follow-up, 2,482 cases of prostate cancer were diagnosed. Metastatic cancers were found in 278 of these men. It turned out that men who ate fish more than three times a week had a bit more than half the risk of metastatic prostate cancer than men who ate fish less than twice a month. The researchers write: "Each additional daily intake of 0.5 g of marine fatty acid from food was associated with a 24 percent decreased risk of metastatic cancer."

IMPROVING YOUR OMEGA-6/
OMEGA-3 RATIO: AT A GLANCE

- Eat more fatty, deep-water fish, such as salmon, sardines, and cod.
- One word: sushi.
- Consume fruits and vegetables—particularly antioxidant-rich blueberries and members of the crucifer family.
- Add milled flaxseed, walnuts, and pumpkin seeds to your diet. Keep whole flaxseeds in your pantry and grind them as needed in a coffee grinder, adding them to yogurt, salads, or hot cereal. Or, buy them pre-ground (such as Barlean's Forti-Flax) and keep them in the freezer. Although flax oil contains no fiber, a high-quality oil like Barlean's Highest Lignan Content Flax Oil is an excellent source of omega-3s.

- Avoid excess amounts of saturated fats (meats, dairy, butter). Try eating at least one vegetarian meal a day, then work your way down to eating meat (beef, pork) only once a day, then only two or three times a week. Replace those foods with fish, soy, and vegetables. Keep portion sizes of meats to the size of a deck of cards. If you like cheese, use it, but try using half the amount you normally would. When you eat two eggs, try removing one of the yolks.
- Do not eat foods made with hydrogenated fats. Choose extra-virgin olive oil or canola oil over oils made from seeds and nuts.
- Avoid processed flour and sugar. Both shift COX and LO enzyme activity towards inflammation.
- Consume fermented soy-based foods, such as tempeh and miso.

HOW ABOUT OLIVE OIL?

The benefits of olive oil are well known. It is a staple of the Mediterranean diet, which is now understood to be one of the planet's most healthful. Research has linked low prostate cancer rates in southern Italy and Spain with olive oil consumption there.

Olive oil is a rich source of monounsaturated fat, a type of fatty acid that seems to have no stimulatory effect on cancer rates. Canola, high oleic sunflower, and safflower oils are also high in monounsaturates, but the research is unclear on whether these highly processed oils match up to olive oil for prostate protection. Of all of these oils, olive oil is the least processed—especially if you buy extra-virgin oil, which comes from the first pressing of the olives. If you choose to use the other oils, choose expeller-pressed oils that have not been extracted with solvents.

If you love bread, try eating it (in moderation, and whole grain, please) dipped in a little dish of good olive oil. Add a little chopped garlic and some kalamata olives if you're in the mood. Cooking olive oil at high temperatures appears to alter its content in ways that may reduce its protective powers.

Any time you buy oil, avoid plastic bottles. Plasticizers love to migrate into fats and oils. Choose glass packaging instead.

MORE ON THE ROLE OF
DIETARY CONTAMINANTS

Research evidence collected over more than five decades make a consistent argument that dietary fat, in and of itself, is not really the problem. *It's what's in the fat.* There are studies involving animals and humans, as well as those performed on wildlife and in test tubes, and they all suggest that contaminants in fat are the wild card when it comes to elevating cancer risk. If our food was clean, if it wasn't riddled with toxic industrial waste and factory-farming chemicals, we could probably eat all the fat we wanted without ever increasing our prostate cancer risk.

The pollutants found in the fat of meat and dairy products are persistent (they don't break down); they just concentrate in the fat of animals, and further concentrate in the fat of those of us who are above those animals on the food chain. Humans, in their cozy spot at the apex of that food chain, are turning into chemical repositories, and those chemicals are making us sick. Tissues like the prostate and the breast are especially good at concentrating these chemicals. Prostate tissues often have levels of these pollutants that are thousands of times greater than levels in the foods we eat. The editor of the *Journal of Pesticide Reform*, Caroline Cox, recently published a list of 16 pesticides that are currently used in food crops that have been linked with cancer of the prostate.

How do you protect yourself against these chemicals? Well, they are probably already in your body in high concentrations, but there's good evidence that by shifting to a cleaner, less-contaminated diet, you can minimize their effects and reduce your cancer risk.

Contaminants are found in their greatest concentrations in fatty flesh foods, such as beef, lamb, chicken, dairy products, and fatty freshwater fish. It follows that your best chances of avoiding those contaminants is to eat a diet that is largely organic and vegetarian, and that goes very light on the dairy. Whenever you can, eat organic foods, which are raised (as in livestock), grown (as in crops), or produced (as in products made from milk) without the use of chemical pesticides, hormones, or drugs.

Note, before clutching your chest in dismay that you have to give up cheeseburgers, that you don't have to go totally vegetarian. You can have occasional treats of a burger (grass-fed, organic beef) or a small scoop of ice cream (organic, if possible). There are lots of acceptable choices when it comes to flesh foods and dairy. You can put a little bit of butter on your food once in a while. The important thing is to avoid making less healthful foods daily indulgences. Start thinking of meat not as a main course, but as a side dish or a condiment—a flavorful accompaniment for a plate filled mostly with vegetables and whole grains.

You will probably be surprised at the cost of organic foods compared to that of conventional foods. Believe me: It's a worthwhile way to spend your food dollars. If you end up eating less food, well, that's probably a good thing, too. Lower caloric intake from day to day is one of the best ways to prolong your life and to stay healthy and energetic for more of it.

Here are some specifics to help you figure out what to put in your shopping cart. Some of it might seem impossibly exotic and difficult to procure, but with the Internet, you can get a lot of these foods sent right to your doorstep.

FOOD	BEST SOURCES	AVOID
Meats (including red meat, poultry, pork)	Range-raised, grass-fed beef Organic beef raised without hormones and given pesticide-free feed Buffalo, antelope, venison, other wild game Turkey Organically raised chicken Rabbit Quail Pheasant	Commercial, non-organic beef and chicken Non-organic pork and pork products Cured meats (e.g., lunch meats, bacon, jerky, salami, hot dogs) Meat that is charred over an open flame (creates carcinogenic chemicals)
Dairy products	Low-fat or non-fat plain organic yogurt Organic and low-fat sour cream and cheeses Non-fat salad dressings and toppings Organic low-fat milk Goat's milk Soy, rice, almond milk or other non-dairy milk substitutes Soy, rice, almond cheese	Non-organic dairy products High-fat dairy products Milk from cows treated with bovine growth hormone (bGH) Ice cream or sweetened yogurts (okay once a week or so, in moderate serving sizes!)
Grains	Most are free from carcinogenic contaminants and pseudoestrogens	Buying organic is still more environmentally sound; growing non-organic grains requires intensive use of herbicides, which contaminate drinking water resources

continued on next page

FOOD	BEST SOURCES	AVOID
Seafood	Deep-sea species, including Arctic char, halibut, orange roughy, red snapper, sea bass Fresh tuna Non-albacore canned tuna Wild-caught salmon Wild shrimp Lobsters from California, Mexico, Australia, New Zealand Sardines Anchovies Farmed trout	Farmed fish (high in contaminants) Fish from inland lakes and rivers (e.g., Great Lakes) Bluefish Striped bass Farm-raised catfish Maine lobster Massachusetts lobster Swordfish Shark Fish from major European inland areas Deep-fried fish, fish sticks (loaded with omega-6 fats)
Fruits	Organic! Safest non-organic (on which the fewest chemicals are used): avocadoes, bananas, dates, figs, guava, lemons, tangerines, tangelos, watermelon	Non-organics other than those listed here; if you do buy non-organics, wash very thoroughly or peel before eating
Vegetables	Organic! Safest non-organic: artichokes, tofu, corn, eggplant, escarole, garbanzo beans, green beans, kidney beans, kohlrabi, mature lima beans, mushrooms, navy beans, okra, green onions, dried peas, pinto beans, red beans, rhubarb, swiss chard, turnips, watercress, yams	Non-organics other than those listed here; if you do buy non-organics, wash very thoroughly or peel before eating

FOOD	BEST SOURCES	AVOID
Drinking water	Request a water-quality report from your municipality or local supplier, or have your drinking water tested for contaminants	Water straight from the tap is generally not your best bet; it can be contaminated with any number of chemicals
	Choose a water filtration/treatment system that uses both activated carbon and reverse osmosis; use a filter mounted under the kitchen sink, or buy a larger system to filter the water used in the whole house	Water bottled in plastic leaches xenoestrogens into the water; choose glass bottles if possible
		To find a high-quality bottled water, contact the National Sanitation Foundation or the Quality Bottled Water Association, both of which certify bottled waters according to quality
Coffee	From organic beans	Non-organic beans
	Organic Swiss Water® Process decaffeinated; other decaffeination processes use methylene chloride, which causes prostate cancer	High-sugar, high-calorie coffee drinks
		Try replacing coffee with tea—especially green tea

Produce raised organically is not treated with mineral waxes, preservatives, or fungicides. You will also have to handle it more carefully, because it bruises more easily.

Finally: *Never* cook food or beverages in plastic wrap, styrofoam, or other packaging. This causes carcinogens to migrate directly into the food. Remove food from packaging and put it into glass cookware before cooking.

THE EFFECT OF FIBER

There is no fiber whatsoever in meat or dairy products. This indigestible food component is found in whole grains, beans, seeds, vegetables, and fruit.

Dietary fiber is best known for its protective effects against cancer of the colon, but it also protects against other cancers by helping to move carcinogens out of the body. Fiber passes through your gut and is excreted in the stool. Along the way, it binds to carcinogenic compounds. It also increases stool bulk (by holding water in the bowel) and decreases *transit time*. In other words, more fiber causes the food you eat to pass through your digestive tract more quickly. This gives the body less time to absorb potentially carcinogenic substances into the walls of the large intestine—a major route for the absorption of hormone-disrupting chemicals. Fiber-rich grains are also your most important dietary source of selenium.

Research has shown an inverse relationship between prostate cancer incidence and intake of dietary fiber. The higher a man's intake of fiber, the lower his plasma testosterone and estradiol (a kind of estrogen) levels—both hormones that have been found to contribute to the development and progression of prostate cancer.

The fiber in milled flaxseeds, called *lignans*, appears to have particularly protective effects against cancer of the prostate. I advise all of my patients to consume flax every day.

Increasing Your Fiber Intake

Don't try to raise your fiber intake with gritty fiber supplements made from oat bran. These can actually cause constipation. Your best bet is to get fiber from foods that are naturally rich in it. Instead:

- Eat one big green salad a day. Mix lettuces, greens like arugula, and chopped raw seasonal vegetables. Sprinkle sprouts on top, or try lightly steamed broccoli. Use an olive oil-based vinaigrette, and toss the lettuces in a couple of tablespoons of dressing rather than pouring gobs of it on top. Top with shredded chicken, thinly sliced beef, or baked or fried tofu or tempeh.

- Eat a bowl of steel-cut or slow-cooked oats for breakfast, with one to one-and-a-half tablespoons of ground flaxseeds mixed in and a dollop of plain yogurt on top. Stir in a tablespoon of maple syrup or honey for sweetness, cook dried or fresh fruit in the oatmeal, or try a dash of stevia, a naturally sweet herb that has no effect on insulin or blood-sugar levels.

- One day a week, eat nothing but vegetables and fruit.

- Switch from white to brown rice; from white bread to whole-grain or sprouted-grain bread; and skip the pasta altogether (I have yet to try a whole-grain pasta with an agreeable taste or texture). Or, if you love pasta, consciously limit the amount you eat, and double up on the veggies you put in the sauce.

Try to get 25 to 35 grams of fiber per day.

THE EFFECT OF ANTIOXIDANTS IN THE DIET

Free-radical damage to DNA has been linked to many cancers, and prostate cancer is no exception. Studies indicate that a diet low in antioxidant nutrients—the nutrients that protect cells against free radicals—increases a man's risk of developing prostate cancer.

It isn't easy to get enough antioxidant nutrients in the diet. Dark, leafy greens (such as spinach, chard, kale, parsley, and arugula) and cruciferous vegetables (such as broccoli, brussels sprouts, cauliflower, and red and green cabbage) tend not to be high on the average American man's list of foods to eat while watching the Super Bowl—or at any other time, for that matter. But he ignores these foods at his own peril.

Indole-3-Carbinol

Indole-3-carbinol (I-3-C) is a phytochemical produced when your body digests cruciferous vegetables. Research shows that it can inhibit the growth of prostate cancer cells. Within the body, I-3-C is converted to another compound called 3,3"-diindolylmethane (DIM) during digestion. DIM acts as a powerful antiandrogen that inhibits the spread of androgen-dependent human prostate cancer cells in test tube studies. Recent research has uncovered some of I-3-C and DIM's protective mechanisms: they appear to act as both inhibitors of carcinogens, apoptosis inducers, and enhancers of the liver's detoxification enzymes. They also have been found to chemosensitize chemoresistant cancer cells—in other words, they alter cancer cells in ways that make them more vulnerable to chemotherapy.

Leafy greens and cruciferous vegetables are being increasingly recognized as important sources of a wide array of synergistic antioxidant nutrients—combinations of natural antioxidant phytochemicals, vitamins, and minerals. Most antioxidant supplements are made with lab-created USP (United States Pharmacopoeia) nutrients, or nutrients that have been isolated from foods, and it is turning out that these kinds of supplements don't have the same powerful protective effects as the foods themselves. Studies of isolated antioxidant nutrients don't indicate the same health-promoting effects as the foods that are naturally abundant in those antioxidant nutrients in their natural setting.

Current research also strongly suggests that deeply colored fruits are important sources of antioxidant nutrition. Particularly good: blueberries and cranberries, papaya, pomegranate, and grapes. Organic apples are a good source of the anti-inflammatory flavonoid *quercetin*. Herbs also provide unique combinations of antioxidant nutrients—ginger, cinnamon, and turmeric are among the best.

These foods are rich in more than antioxidant nutrition. Leafy greens are excellent sources of vitamin K, which plays a critical role in calcium regulation and bone formation; they are also extremely rich in folic acid, a B vitamin that promotes circulatory, reproductive, and nervous system health. And these superfoods protect far more than the prostate; they have been linked to decreased risk of virtually every chronic disease process known to us today, including heart disease, macular degeneration (an age-related blinding eye disease), and osteoporosis. Both are abundant in nutrients that reduce inflammation and oxidative stress.

Crucifers are highly protective. There are many to choose from: bok choy, kale, broccoli, broccoli sprouts, kohlrabi, brussels sprouts, mustard greens, cabbage, radishes, cauliflower, rutabaga, collards, turnips, horseradish, watercress. These foods hang onto their healthful properties even when cooked, but don't cook them into mush. Lightly steam or stir-fry to preserve the foods' indole-3-carbinol.

Crucifers are also our best source of chemicals called isothiocyanates, which activate enzymes in the body that detoxify carcinogens. For example, broccoli sprouts have been shown to contain substantial quantities of these strong enzyme inducers. It may be that up-regulation of these enzyme systems has a protective effect against cancer.

It isn't hard for most people to find ways to eat berries or papaya a few times a week. Stir them into yogurt; try organic grape or pomegranate juices; make berry smoothies; or just enjoy them plain right from the farmer's market. Red wine is a good source of antioxidants, but keep it to one to two glasses a day.

Some may find greens and cruciferous vegetables far less tasty, and more challenging to include on a regular basis.

Some Suggestions for Incorporating
Greens and Crucifers into Your Diet

- Before scrambling eggs, lightly sauté a handful of spinach leaves or finely chopped broccoli florets in the pan with a small amount of butter or spray oil, then add the eggs.

- Add raw chopped or baby spinach to hot soup or pasta sauce just before eating.

- Or, make your own quick vegetable soup with store-bought chicken or vegetable broth. First, chop an onion and sauté it in olive oil. Add some chopped celery and garlic if you like. Then, when those vegetables start to look thoroughly sautéed, pour in three to four cups of chicken or vegetable broth; bring to a simmer and add a variety of chopped vegetables. Add tofu cubes or beans for extra protein. You can stir in a couple of tablespoons of miso (soybean paste) at the very end. (Miso should never be boiled, so be sure not to add at the beginning.) For Thai flavor, try adding some minced ginger at the beginning, when cooking the onions and garlic, and then pour in a can of coconut milk at the end; warm through.

Foolproof Stir-Fry

Use a regular frying pan, not a wok; they aren't made to use on a regular stovetop.

Chop any combination of vegetables up in small pieces. Get the pan so hot that you can't hold your hand three inches above it for more than a couple of seconds.

Drizzle some dry sherry and low-sodium soy sauce on small cubes of raw meat, chicken, fish, or tofu. Stir-fry in a tablespoon of oil. Remove them, then add another tablespoon of oil to the pan.

When it starts to sizzle and sputter, toss in the greens, along with some minced ginger and garlic. Within a minute or two, your food will be done. Stir in a store-bought Chinese or Japanese sauce if you like, or just sprinkle on some low-sodium soy sauce. Serve with brown rice.

- When you get a few leaves of greens on your plate as garnish in a restaurant, *eat them*. It's probably kale, and it may be a tad bitter, and your lunch mates might laugh at you, but your prostate will laugh last.
- If you despise broccoli, try broccoli sprouts on sandwiches and in salads. Broccoli sprouts are an ideal source of cancer-fighting phytochemicals.
- More hardy greens like chard, kale, and collards, as well as any of the cruciferous vegetables, can be stir-fried, boiled, or steamed. Season them with plenty of garlic, salt, and pepper.
- Split a baked potato or yam down the middle and pile in a combination of steamed broccoli and cauliflower, with other vegetables if you like. Sprinkle over it a small amount of really flavorful cheese. Add some ButterBuds, baked tofu, beans, soy sauce, salsa or herbs that you like.

THE EFFECT OF SOY FOODS

Estrogens found in plants are known as phytoestrogens (the Greek *phyto* means "plant"). They are members of the flavonoid family, a group of nutrients responsible for the vivid colors of flower petals. One kind of phytoestrogen, a class of compounds called isoflavones, provides raw materials that are acted upon by intestinal bacteria to create estrogens. Probably the richest dietary source of these isoflavones is soy, a staple of diets in Asian countries. In epidemiological studies, an inverse relationship has been found between soy consumption and deaths from prostate cancer. The more soy men ate, the less likely they were to die from this disease.

How could a man possibly benefit from eating foods that create a feminizing hormone in his body? How would this protect his prostate? The theory is that these plant estrogens block the effects of far more potent, growth-promoting synthetic estrogens, to which men are exposed starting with their time in their mothers' bellies. There is no mistaking one thing: that men who eat more soy appear to gain significant protection against BPH and prostate cancer.

Research has revealed evidence of a number of cancer-fighting ingredients in soy. Many of these ingredients are hard for the body to access unless the soy is *predigested* through a process called *fermentation*. Tofu, miso, and tempeh are all fermented forms of soy, from which these nutrients are readily bioavailable.

Some of soy's cancer-fighting ingredients:

- *Protease inhibitors:* These biochemicals are protective against radiation and oxidation, two of the most likely culprits in cancer initiation.
- *Saponins:* Also protect cells against free-radical and radiation damage.
- *Phytates:* Enhance immunity and prevent free-radical formation.
- *Phytoestrogens:* The abundance of specific varieties of these plant chemicals in soy is what sets this food apart from all others. Phytoestrogens are one hundred-thousandth as potent as the endogenous estrogens naturally made in the body. A plethora of studies have shown that genistein inhibits the growth of prostate cancer cells, both androgen-dependent and androgen-independent. Some of this research indicates that genistein has the ability to cause cancerous cells to differentiate and turn back into normal cells. It inhibits *tyrosine kinases*, enzymes instrumental to cancer development, and some studies show that highly concentrated genistein can inhibit angiogenesis. Increased serum isoflavone levels in men have been associated with decreased risk of prostate cancer.

Men can help keep their prostate glands cancer-free by eating a diet rich in soy products or using genistein supplements.

While genistein and daidzein supplements are widely available, most of the evidence supporting the health-promoting effects of soy come from research that involves whole soy foods, not isolated isoflavone supplements. Isoflavones are readily absorbed from soy in the diet, and are measurable in both urine and blood; higher measurements of these plant chemicals are associated with decreased cancer risk. So if you've always thought that tofu was for sissies, think again. It's time to try it.

Consume soy-rich foods, such as miso, tempeh, and cultured soy yogurts. Here are some suggestions for how to add these and other soy foods to your diet.

Adding Soy Foods to the Typical American Male Diet

If you can get past the tofu-eater jokes, you will learn that soybeans and foods made from them are not only excellent sources of isoflavones—they can be quite tasty, too. Many also are rich in fiber (exceptions: soy milk and tofu), calcium, and B vitamins.

- Cheese, hot dogs, veggie burgers, and "meats" made from tofu or soy protein are widely available.
- Try soy milk as a substitute for regular milk. (FYI: Soy milk is made by grinding hulled soybeans, mixing them with water, then cooking, filtering, and sweetening it.) Use in cereal, for making cream sauces or salad dressings, or in recipes for muffins, pancakes, or waffles.
- Many protein-shake mixes and bars are made with soy protein. You can also use soy protein powder to thicken sauces or as a replacement for part of the flour in a recipe.
- Try edamame, green soybean pods that are boiled before serving. Scrape the pod between your teeth, and the beans pop into your mouth. Truly delicious.
- Tempeh is a soybean patty that makes a great substitute for ground meat. It is made by cooking and hulling soybeans,

then adding a culture to it that binds the beans together. It can be grilled, broiled, or baked after marinating in your favorite BBQ sauce; chunks can be added to sauces or salads; or it can be cut into thin slices and used to make sandwiches.

BBQ Tempeh Recipe

Cut 16 ounces of tempeh into chunks. Steam it over boiling water for 15 minutes; meanwhile, thinly slice a large onion. Once tempeh is steamed, place it and the onions into a deep dish and pour two cups of prepared barbecue sauce over both. Heat up the grill while the tempeh marinates for at least an hour, then grill until browned and heated through, basting often. Or you can bake the tempeh in a 350 degree oven, covered, for a half-hour. Serve on whole-grain buns or over cornbread with beans.

- Use firm or extra-firm tofu as you would meat or hard cheese; use soft tofu to blend into dressings or sauces, or to replace cream, yogurt, or egg in recipes. Tofu should be stored in water and used by its expiration date. It can also be frozen for up to five months.

Tofu is bland on its own, but it soaks up the flavors of other foods quite well—so it's easy to add to dishes without changing the flavor.

- Mix chunks of tofu into casseroles, soups, lasagna, or sauces.
- Add some soft tofu to scrambled eggs.
- Replace some chicken or tuna with tofu when you make chicken or tuna salad.
- Add soup mixes or seasoning packets to silken or soft tofu to create a non-dairy dip.
- Bake tofu in the oven. Either of the following two variations makes a great sandwich filler. Slice the tofu into half-inch slices and place on a non-stick baking sheet. Pour over the marinade (6 tbsp soy sauce, 2 tsp honey, 2 tsp balsamic vinegar, 1 1/2 tbsp grated ginger, 1 tsp minced garlic) and

bake at 400 degrees for a half hour. Or, a simpler version: Cut a block of tofu into quarter- to third-inch slices, then press them (sandwich them between two cutting boards over the sink for a half-hour to squeeze extra water out; this gives it a meatier texture and helps it to absorb more flavor from the marinade). Marinate in soy sauce for two hours to overnight, then bake the tofu at 350 degrees until lightly browned and chewy.

If you are concerned about prostate cancer or trying to prevent a recurrence, consider taking a soy supplement such as the GCP I mentioned earlier. **Do not take any soy genistein product 10 days prior to, during, or three weeks after any form of radiation therapy.** Genistein may protect cancer cells against radiation-induced death.

TRY SOME SEAWEED

You know that wonderful clean feeling you get after taking a dip in the ocean? It appears that you can bring the ocean's cleansing power into your body by eating seaweed. A brown kelp called laminaria, also known as kombu, is rich in a substance called *algin*. Algin binds heavy metals and toxins in the body. Kelp is also a rich source of minerals and immune-stimulating complex polysaccharides.

I'm not suggesting that you swim out into the ocean and graze like a manatee. Seaweed is a staple of traditional Japanese diets, and you can find ways to use it in virtually every meal. Visit a Japanese market and have a look around. Try *nori*, flat sheets of pressed seaweed, for making homemade sushi or in commercially available rice crackers. Pick up some seaweed noodles to mix into your soup. You can add dried kombu, nori, or wakame to soups. Use a strip of kombu when cooking beans to soften them. Try Japanese sea vegetable "candy" made from nori and kombu. When you eat miso soup, you're getting a healthy dose of soy in addition to the kombu that is used to make the broth. While you're there, you might want to pick up some dried shiitake mushrooms!

DON'T FORGET THE GARLIC AND ONIONS

Eat plenty of garlic, which is rich in protective, sulfur-rich amino acids. Over 350 research studies and articles attest to its preventative and growth-slowing effects on a wide variety of cancers. Selenium-enriched garlic is especially good—you can buy it as a supplement. Include fresh garlic in your diet whenever you can, eaten raw or lightly cooked.

Onions are rich in the bioflavonoid quercetin, which has antioxidant and anti-inflammatory effects. Use them cooked and raw.

WHAT ABOUT SUPPLEMENTS?

With the popularity of vitamin and mineral supplements, and the many other nutritional supplements now available, many people think that they can eat the way they've always eaten and take their supplements and come out even. It doesn't work that way.

This is not to say that nutritional supplements are not valuable. They simply must be used in concert with a healthful diet. They don't replace a healthy diet, and they aren't magic bullets that cancel out the effects of poor dietary choices. You will see as you read on that the best nutritional supplements are really *food*—they contain high concentrations of healing and disease-preventing nutrients, but those nutrients are not isolated from the ingredients that work with them in a synergistic fashion within the body.

Different brands of the same nutritional supplement can be as different as wheat berries from white bread. Let's put aside the fact that many manufacturers don't accurately state what they are putting into their supplements, and the fact that the supplement industry's veracity when it comes to ingredients is not strictly monitored by the government, the way drug makers are. When a supplemental nutrient or herb is shown to have benefits or protective effects in a study, the researchers have usually used a standardized or pharmaceutical-grade version of the nutrient in question. Unethical supplement makers can advertise that they offer the product that has been shown to be beneficial, but they aren't bound by any law to match the standards of whatever was used by the research team.

Once we've put those issues aside, there is an additional issue with nutritional supplements—an issue that likely explains why lots of research can demonstrate that a specific food is protective, but a nutrient isolated from that food can fail to provide protection against disease, or may even promote disease.

In my experience as a researcher, I have found that the truer a nutritional supplement is to its natural source, the more effective it is. Many supplements are a conglomeration of laboratory-produced, isolated vitamins and minerals. So-called "whole-food" supplements are derived from (you guessed it) whole food—usually, nutrient-packed "superfoods" like deep leafy greens, chlorella, spirulina, wheatgrass, berries, soy, seaweed, or mineral-rich yeasts.

Some supplement makers further improve on the whole-food approach by using a natural process called *fermentation* to, in essence, partially digest the superfood ingredients. Fermentation makes the nutrients more bioavailable, and leads to the production of novel compounds that have potent anticancer and otherwise protective properties. It involves the addition of specific "friendly" bacteria (probiotics) to nutrients—a step that turns a vitamin, mineral, or herbal supplement into "living food."

According to the Food and Agricultural Organization of the United Nations, "[f]ermentation is the oldest known form of food biotechnology...The traditional fermentation of food serves several functions, [including] enrichment of food substrates biologically with protein, essential amino acids, essential fatty acids, and vitamins."

Fermentation, also known as *culturing*, is a sort of nutritional alchemy that has been around for millennia. Miso is cultured soy. Yogurt is cultured milk. The evidence that these foods are powerfully health-promoting is all over the nutritional research

How One Company Makes Its Living Nutritional Supplements

New Chapter—the company in Brattleboro, Vermont that makes Zyflamend and Prostate 5LX, two supplements I have researched in my lab at Columbia—makes what they call Probiotic Nutrient formulas. They start with purified water and soymilk from non-GMO soybeans, and they add appropriate fruits and vegetables (these vary depending upon which nutrient supplement they are making), and a very small amount of the USP (United States Pharmacopoeia, the pure, gold standard pharmaceutical grade version) vitamin or mineral they are culturing. This "soup" is then inoculated with a nutritional yeast called *Saccharomyces cerevisiae*, which you may know as brewer's yeast. During the second stage of fermentation, they add friendly bacteria from the lactobacillus family: *L. acidophilus*, *L. rhamnosus*, and *L. bifidus*.

The yeast and bacteria literally eat the soup, culturing everything in the broth and yielding a nutrient-dense, easily digestible product. Supplements made this way are really living food complexes, not the mass-marketed isolated vitamins and minerals found on most drugstore shelves. Tom Newmark and Paul Schulick of New Chapter, along with physician Richard Sarnat, M.D., are so convinced that fermentation is the best way to make vitamins that they have published a fascinating little book on the subject called *The Life Bridge: The Way to Longevity with Probiotic Nutrients*. It is available at Amazon.com.

journals. The process of making wine and beer also involves fermentation, and the health benefits of these beverages (when imbibed with moderation) are likely due to the effects of this process on the nutrients they contain. Fermentation of grapes dramatically increases their content of the antioxidant resveratrol, which is well-established as an anticarcinogen.

By culturing USP nutrients with friendly bacteria and yeasts, we turn these isolated, dead chemicals back into living food. We transform inorganic molecules to organic complexes that are infused with life energy. Supplements like these are more bioavailable, active, and potent in the body.

Unique Products of Nutrient Fermentation

The fermentation of isolated nutrients with appropriate probiotics and whole foods yields bioavailable and desireable nutrients, antioxidants, enzymes, and:

- *Bacteriocins:* natural antibacterial agents
- *Beta-glucans:* natural immune stimulants that have been found to have anticancer, antiviral, antibacterial, and antifungal effects and to help lower cholesterol; a main therapeutic component of medicinal mushrooms
- *Phenolic acids:* antioxidant, antiproliferative, pro-apoptotic breakdown products of polyphenols in foods
- *Short-chain fatty acids:* a product of bacterial fermentation of dietary carbohydrates in the large intestine; increasingly recognized for protective role against colon cancer and inflammatory bowel disease, and as an important part of the diet
- *Butyrate:* when we culture soluble food fibers, such as those from apples, or the prebiotic *inulin* (a favorite food of the friendly bacteria that live in the human gastrointestinal tract), we create this powerful cancer-fighting compound; inhibits an enzyme called beta-glucuronidase, which is theorized to play a part in liver cancer

General Guidelines for Nutritional Supplementation

Aside from the specific nutrients, herbs, and herbal combinations already recommended in this book, you can give yourself a solid nutritional base by using a complete multivitamin and mineral supplement. Other supplements can be added to round out your program.

Doing this won't take you off the hook of needing to eat a healthful diet, but it will help back you up on the days when you just can't seem to get enough vegetables and fruit, or when you indulge in something that isn't exactly health food. On days when you've been good, your multivitamin and other supplements will still provide you with insurance—helping to guard your body against toxins and stressors.

There is so much controversy over vitamins and how much to take; it really depends on your own diet and lifestyle. But here's a tip: When choosing a multivitamin, or any supplement for that matter, look for a reputable company (such as New Chapter's Every Man, or supplements from Enzymatic Therapy, Rainbow Light, Source Naturals, Jarrow or Life Extensions) to ensure that you're getting what the label says you're getting. Look for a men's multi that includes superfoods like chlorella, kelp, and wheatgrass, and look for herbal extracts like saw palmetto, eleuthero (Siberian ginseng), dandelion, licorice and ginger.

What to Look for in a Multivitamin/Mineral

Overall, I think that the best supplements are cultured, whole-foods versions. Isolated USP nutrients might be better than nothing, but your body will better absorb and utilize the cultured, real-food versions. Some vitamins that use USP nutrients will deliver high doses of these nutrients; when you take them in cultured form, they are more bioavailable, and so megadoses aren't necessary.

GET BY WITH A LITTLE
HELP FROM MORE GREENS

If you have trouble getting enough greens, you may want to experiment with a green drink or some greens in supplement form. There are a number of supplements on the market that are made from dark green leafy vegetables (kale, spinach, parsley, broccoli, brussels sprouts, red cabbage, green cabbage, okra) and organic berries and herbs.

FISH OIL

Overall, the research evidence shows that marine fatty acids are protective against prostate cancer. They're also great for your circulatory system, and help to tip omega-3/omega-6 balance in the right direction.

Here are some guidelines for picking a fish oil supplement that's low in industrial toxins—remember that fish can concentrate these toxins in their flesh and fat—and that contains the right balance of omega-3s. I've adapted these guidelines from a terrific book called *The Omega-3 Connection* by Andrew Stoll, M.D., the director of the Psychopharmacology Research Laboratory at McLean Hospital, Harvard Medical School.

Choose a fish oil supplement that:
- Has a high concentration of omega-3 fatty acids: They are available with concentrations from 30 to 90 percent. Look for one that is closer to 90 percent.
- Has a high concentration of EPA (eicosapentaenoic acid) per capsule (this is the most anti-inflammatory of the omega-3s) and a higher ratio of EPA to DHA (docosahexaenoic acid).
- Has very low or nonexistent concentrations of omega-6s and saturated fats.
- Is labeled "pharmaceutical grade purity."
- Has a mild odor and a clear, light yellow color. Oil that is dark or strongly fishy-smelling is probably rancid.

- Has been molecularly distilled to remove toxins.
- Is taken from small, oily fish from cold water. Fish like anchovies and sardines are lower on the food chain than bigger fish, and so contain fewer toxins. Antarctic waters are an excellent source, because they are the least polluted waters on Earth.
- Contains at least one type of antioxidant. Look for a supplement that has up to 5 IU of tocopherols (vitamin E).

A dosage of 1,000 mg per day of omega-3s should be enough to help balance your omega-3s and omega-6s. Don't take any more than three grams a day. Fish oil thins the blood, and can put you at risk for a life-threatening bleed if you have a bleeding disorder or uncontrolled hypertension, or take anticoagulant drugs.

PROBIOTICS

These "friendly bacteria" are natural residents of the human gastrointestinal tract. Aside from consuming them in the form of cultured nutritional supplements, and in foods like miso, tempeh, and yogurt, you can take them in supplement form.

The first researcher to clue in on the health benefits of these bacteria was Elie Metchnikoff, a nineteenth century Russian Nobel laureate who noticed that certain peasants were living life spans of 100 years or more. As he investigated, he found that these long-lived people had an important commonality: Fermented milk (kefir) was a regular part of their diets. Metchnikoff theorized that these good bacteria helped to prevent chronic disease. Today, based on voluminous research, we know that he theorized correctly.

A long pause in probiotic research coincided with the advent of antibiotic therapy. Modern science believed so strongly in the power of antibiotics that it forgot about the probiotics—our natural defenses against less-friendly, illness-causing bacteria.

Today, we know that antibiotics can be overused, creating antibiotic-resistant bacteria. We know that antibiotics can make us more vulnerable to infection and chronic disease by knocking out our probiotic protectors along with the unfriendly bugs they were sent in to nab. Probiotics—also known as *microflora*—are the natural enemy of "bad" bacteria, and they are beginning to enter the picture again as an alternative to antibiotic therapy.

A healthy human body contains over 400 species of microflora. Most of these "bugs" live in the intestinal tract, with between one hundred million and one hundred billion bacteria residing in the colon alone. It might astonish you to know that probiotic bacteria outnumber the cells that make up the human body by about 10 times, and that they make up about 3.5 pounds of the average adult human's body weight.

Probiotics can help in the treatment of bacterial infections and viral and fungal infections. They support digestive health, enhancing nutrient absorption and helping the body to thoroughly digest, absorb, and detoxify the foods you eat. Probiotic supplements can help reduce intestinal gas and infections that cause diarrhea, bloating, and constipation. They can be an effective treatment for bad breath (halitosis). They help to prevent autoimmune disorders of the colon like Crohn's disease and ulcerative colitis. They even make nutrients in the large intestine—notably, several B vitamins, fatty acids, antioxidants, and vitamin K.

They also boost antibody production and enhance white blood cell activity, aiding the immune system in fighting off infections. Probiotics also help our bodies suppress the initiation and growth of cancer by working diligently to detoxify carcinogens in the gastrointestinal tract. They have been shown to inhibit the activity of enzymes that transform potential carcinogens into carcinogens. Much research points to the importance of a healthy intestinal ecosystem (and the large intestine really is, at root, an ecosystem all its own) at preventing colon cancer. They may also protect against stomach cancer and stomach ulcers by doing battle with the *H. pylori* bacteria, which is now implicated in both diseases of the stomach.

In the natural human state, our bodies maintain healthful probiotic levels all by themselves. Why do we need extra probiotics?

Probiotic populations start out in infancy; a child who is breast-fed is literally inoculated with bacteria from its mother's milk. It follows that a child that is fed formula won't get the benefit of these live bacteria. Infants who are formula-fed have a much less healthful balance of probiotics and tend to have more harmful bacteria in their stool. Being formula-fed is often the beginning of a lifelong imbalance in the intestinal ecosystem.

Over the years, repeated doses of antibiotics and foods that don't support that ecosystem continue to throw it out of balance. Most children don't eat diets that include lots of fermented foods or nutrients; processed junk, refined carbohydrates, sugars, and high-meat diets continue to tip the balance towards unfriendly bacteria in the GI tract. Vegetables and fruit contain fibers (known as prebiotics) that probiotics thrive upon, but most people don't eat nearly enough of these foods to properly nourish these friendly bugs.

Those who take antacids or acid-reducing drugs are also altering the pH of the GI tract in a way that makes it less hospitable to probiotics. Stress, too, can cause probiotic populations to fall.

Convinced that a probiotic is a good idea? Choose a living bacteria supplement that contains two billion or so live cells. Look for of a mixture of *Lactobacillus* (abbreviated as L.) *casei, L. plantarum, L. salivarius, L. acidophilus, L. rhamnosus, Saccharomyces thermophilus,*

Bifidobacterium (abbreviated as B.) *bifidum*, B. *infantis*, B. *longum*, and B. *breve*.

SUMMING UP

In this chapter, I hope I have impressed upon you the enormous impact that your diet has on your overall state of health, and on your risk of developing prostate cancer. The mounds of meat smothered in BBQ sauce, the french fries, the super-sized cola, and the sweet stuff are hard to resist, but the more you know about how they hurt you—and about how replacing them with different foods is likely to help prevent cancer, improve your day-to-day health, and prolong your life—the easier it will be to say no to these foods. And while nutritional supplementation may seem like a big investment of time and energy, the research evidence in its favor is overwhelming.

Chapter 8

Lifestyle, Stress, and Prostate Health

ONE OF THE LEAST PLEASANT ASPECTS of my work is having to tell a man that he has cancer. Even that isn't quite so difficult as telling a man that we've done all we can for him, and that his cancer is probably going to eventually cause his death. Fortunately, with all the advances in urological cancer treatments and with the chemopreventive measures described throughout this book, I expect to have to do this less and less often.

Of course, my stress at having to give a man and his loved ones bad news is nothing compared to the stress of hearing: "You have cancer." The reactions I see are as varied as the personalities of my patients. Some people go completely numb when they get the news, and say virtually nothing. Others fall apart, crying or becoming enraged. Still others shift into "can-do" mode right away, proactively searching out every possible angle on their disease and how it can be treated.

There's no right way to respond to a diagnosis of prostate cancer. You have to go through your own process, and your medical team needs to be respectful of that. But once that initial shock has passed, your attitude, lifestyle, and social support systems become an important aspect of your recovery. You can do a lot to shape these aspects of your life to promote a return to a clean bill of health. There are also impactful changes to be made in your environment—your home, your work—to protect your body against the physical and emotional stressors that can cause your disease to progress more quickly.

Even if you do not have prostate cancer, or if you have other prostate issues, making the kinds of changes I'll recommend in this chapter will help you in many ways. Like most holistic therapies, specific lifestyle changes, relaxation practices, and exercise will do a lot more than protect your prostate. They will help you to avoid other kinds of cancer, as well as heart disease, osteoporosis, musculoskeletal problems, and will even alter immune activity in ways that help prevent infectious disease. You'll feel better, look better, sleep better, and your relationships will improve. All that's required are a few simple changes in your day-to-day routine, and in your way of responding to stress. It's win-win, all the way around.

In this chapter, I'll address the connection between psychological stress and prostate health, and the use of practices like meditation, tai chi, chi kung, and yoga to change your body's reaction to stressful situations. I will also talk about an exercise program that will help you maintain your health. Finally, I'll discuss ways in which you can alter your home environment to reduce its toxicity (yes, most home environments are toxic) and promote relaxation and healing.

REPLACING OLD HABITS WITH NEW
It's hard to imagine any person who does not know that exercise, relaxation, and meditation are good for them. Many might not see exactly how good, or why they are good, but who

doesn't think that 30 minutes of meditation are more health-promoting than 30 minutes of Internet-surfing or football on TV? Who doesn't intuitively know that it makes sense to spend time letting go of stress and tension? And how many people actually do it? Men, in particular, tend to resist doing so, mightily.

Why do so many people neglect to engage in regular exercise, in intentional relaxation or meditation? Why do people not change their lives around in ways that make their environments less toxic and their bodies and minds less tense and stressed?

I think the main obstacle is habit. Especially as we grow older, our habits become ingrained. It's the "old-dog-can't-do-new-tricks" syndrome. We have become comfortable doing things a certain way, in having a certain routine. Disrupting that routine feels wrong. The more you know about the benefits of making big changes, the easier it will feel to make the big leap—or, to continue with the dogs and tricks analogy, to roll over when you used to only know how to stand on your hindquarters and bark. Your treat? A longer life, and more life in your years.

WORKING DEFINITION OF STRESS

Before we get into the ways stress can pave the way for disease, let's define what exactly we mean by *stress*. I like this definition from John W. Travis, M.D., and Regina Sara Ryan's *Wellness Workbook* (3rd ed., Celestial Arts, Berkeley, CA: 2004):

Whether sensing danger from external stressors or from disturbing thoughts within, the body reacts to protect itself. The instinctive response has been called the "fight, flight, or freeze" mechanism. First described by Hans Selye, M.D.,...this mechanism involves a whole range of automatic reactions...{that} serve to energize the body to do battle or to run away...A surge of adrenaline raises blood pressure and increases heart rate, blood flow to muscles, and general metabolism. The rate of breathing becomes faster, more shallow, and arrhythmic [p. 34].

A stressful situation elicits a specific set of physiological responses within the body.

Adrenaline shoots into the bloodstream, raising heart rate, blood pressure, and respiratory rate. Blood flow to the muscles increases as blood flow to the digestive tract decreases—a mechanism designed to divert fuel and oxygen to muscular strength and endurance. The immune system's activity decreases to free up energy for physical action. Longer-term stress causes an increase in the production of a hormone called cortisol, which affects blood pressure, bone metabolism, immunity, and the way the body creates energy from fuel. Long-term oversecretion of cortisol has been linked with abdominal weight gain, decreased immunity, and chronic fatigue. Cancer, hypertension, stroke, osteoporosis, and ulcers have also been linked with chronic oversecretion of cortisol. Other alterations in hormone balance facilitate more energy and physical strength in the moment—at the cost of cellular repair and replacement.

In less civilized times, the physical stress response served a crucial purpose. A man living in prehistoric times needed all the fight or flight he could get when threatened by (let's say) a rampaging mastodon. When he was under the stress of being hungry, his physiology changed in ways that made him a better, more alert, and stronger hunter.

What is the parallel of that situation in modern times? The man who is threatened with the loss of his job, for example, may have all of the same body sensations of his Cro-Magnon counterpart, but he can't *do* anything with them. The man who is late for an appointment and stuck in traffic can't physically do anything to change his situation, and so he is left to boil and stew and long for something to throw or hit. These feelings are deeply ingrained in us, the result of millions of years of evolution, but they come back to bite us when we have no release or methods for coping with them.

To add insult to injury, stress is often unrelenting in modern life. Our mastodon-dodging friend probably had some time to unwind each day without worrying about paying the bills, mowing the lawn, or confronting his rebellious teenaged daughter about her grades. While the stresses we face are not usually life-threatening in the moment, they rarely let up.

SOME WAYS THAT STRESS HARMS US

Stress-induced inflammation may be a major causative factor in heart disease. "Type A" personalities have long been known to be at greater risk of having a heart attack. People who are wound a little tighter than average are also at higher risk of being hypertensive. These are known facts. The question remains: Why? And do the physical changes that increase risk of heart problems also increase risk of other diseases?

Frequent, acute stress or long-term chronic stress causes inflammatory changes throughout the body. Stress causes the levels of certain hormones that lead to increased blood vessel wall tension, making it more vulnerable to damage. Stress also increases levels of an amino acid called homocysteine, which directly damages artery walls. Once this happens, other physiological responses to stress set the stage for inflammation in the areas that have been injured: rising activity of adhesion molecules and mast cells, macrophage activation, and cytokine production. All of these are immune responses that are designed to repair the injured blood vessel wall, but usually end up overshooting the mark and causing excessive inflammation. Chronic stress also causes changes in hormone balance that make blood more viscous and less watery—more likely to throw clots and cause heart attacks and occlusive strokes. It increases the action of free radicals on fats in the blood, a known risk factor for heart disease.

More on inflammation and stress. According to a study published in the November 2002 issue of the journal *Health Psychology*, chronic stress appears to impair the feedback system that tells the body when it's time to turn off the inflammation response. Normally, this system detects rising levels of stress-induced hormones, and when they reach a certain point, their production is tapered off. But something about chronic stress causes the body to, in essence, ignore those signals, allowing inflammation to escalate beyond healthy limits. The good news in this study: Social support counteracted this negative effect of stress.

Remember the evidence that prostate cancer is now believed to be, in part, due to chronic inflammation. It makes good sense to control inflammation to slow or prevent prostate cancer. You can do this with supplements, too, but if you don't also do what is necessary to control the effects of stress on your body, you won't be doing a complete job of fighting or preventing this disease.

Stress amplifies the production of free radicals. You know already that where there is excessive inflammation, there is also excessive free-radical production. Research evidence suggests that this free-radical stress reduces immunity, and that psychologically mediated oxidation may directly damage DNA in ways that increase cancer risk.

Stress hampers the function of the immune system. Research from the 1980s indicated that stress may impede cells' ability to repair damage to DNA—damage that could be the first step towards cancer development.

Israeli psychobiologist Shamgar Ben-Eliyahu has done some fascinating work on the relationship between stress, immunity, and cancer. He has found that stress significantly decreases the function of cancer-fighting immune cells called natural killer (NK) cells. Dr. Ben-Eliyahu forced rats to swim for extended periods, performed surgery on them, and orchestrated tense social situations, and found that the animals' NK cell function fell for between one hour and a day or two. Other research has shown that stressors like these can accelerate tumor growth substantially and promote metastasis.

Think about this for a moment. Surgery decreases NK cell activity. NK cells are one of the immune system's most important weapons against cancer and cancer metastasis. And what do we do, often, to treat prostate cancer? Surgery.

I'm not suggesting that you avoid surgery if you need it. If you do need it, work with your medical team and loved ones to employ stress-reduction techniques before and after your operation (and, if you have a procedure that doesn't require general anesthesia, even *during* your operation). We don't know for sure that this will blunt the effects on NK function, but it certainly won't hurt to try.

Further research from the lab of Emory University researcher Jay Weiss, Ph.D., suggests that a type of white blood cell called a B-lymphocyte plays a role in protecting the lungs against cancer. B-lymphocytes may do this by increasing NK cell activity. This research is still young, and needs more investigation.

Stress has been linked with premature aging. It has long been suspected that chronic stress somehow speeds up the aging process. It may do so by increasing free-radical formation; by reducing immune function; or by its effects on cardiovascular health. In a fascinating study, Dr. Elissa S. Epel of the University of California, San Francisco, may have identified the genetic mechanism by which stress accelerates the aging process.

Within almost all of our body cells lie two sets of *chromosomes*. These contain the genetic material—DNA—that serves as the "blueprint" for the function of those cells. (Every cell contains the same DNA, but different parts of it are activated to create different kinds of cells.) At each end of those chromosomes are "caps" called telomeres. Telomeres are basically chunks of DNA that don't appear to have any role, sort of like spare DNA material. With each division of the cell, the telomeres shorten. Many experts believe that these *telomeres* serve as a sort of biological clock for the cell, triggering apoptosis when the telomeres are gone.

Cancer cells, interestingly, express an enzyme that adds back onto the telomeres, lending those cells the immortality that makes cancer such a difficult foe. So apoptosis is a good thing, right? Not always; it's a matter of balance. We don't want cells that refuse to die (cancer cells), but we also don't want cells that die too soon (premature aging).

Rapid telomere shortening has been linked with premature aging. The purpose of Dr. Epel's study was to find out whether there might be an association between chronic stress and accelerated telomere shortening. She gathered 39 premenopausal women who were primary caregivers for a chronically ill child, and compared them to 19 age-matched controls who were mothers of healthy children. Stress level was measured with a questionnaire, and blood samples were used to measure telomere length. The researchers found that the 14 women with the highest scores on the stress test had telomeres averaging 3,110 units in length, while the 14 with the lowest scores had telomeres averaging 3,660 units in length.

The researchers point out that telomeres shorten by an average of 31 to 63 units each year, meaning that the additional shortening in the group under greater stress amounted to anywhere from 9 to 17 years of additional age. With those years, most likely, comes increased risk of age-related diseases, including prostate disease.

STRESS REDUCTION METHODS THAT WORK

The fields of *psychoneuroimmunology* and *psychoneuroendocrinology* explore the links between thoughts, the nervous system, the hormonal (endocrine) system, and the immune system. These relatively new branches of science seek to describe the ways in which the mind can be used as a tool to heal or otherwise influence the body. Their research has firmly established that stress reduces the effectiveness of the immune system in its jobs of fighting infection and tumor growth. It has also established that meditation is an effective tool for the reduction of stress.

Programs that work the best to rein in the damaging physiological effects of stress—most significantly, the hormonal alterations and immune system downregulation—incorporate relaxation practices, meditation, and gentle yoga, with daily practice at home. Guided imagery has also been shown to be beneficial for patients who are undergoing cancer treatment. (Your oncology team should be able to help you find an expert in guided imagery with whom you can work one-on-one.)

Here are a few exercises you can start with. Try one or more throughout the day.

Progressive Relaxation

Lie in a comfortable position. Tense individual muscle groups one at a time; hold the tension for 5 to 10 seconds; release. You can start at the head and work down, or at the feet and work up. For example: Tense the scalp and face; release. Then, the muscles of the neck. Then, the shoulders. Then, the chest. Then, the arms and hands. Then, the abdomen. Don't forget the back of your body; the upper and lower back and buttocks tend to hold a lot of tension.

Deep Breathing

Sit or lie in a comfortable position. Inhale for a count of four or five; take the same amount of time to exhale. Start with a complete exhalation, feeling your belly hollow slightly. Then, inhale slowly, with the abdomen expanding first, then the chest. Feel the inhalation spread across your upper back and shoulders. Feel your collarbones lifting. Pause briefly at the apex of the breath, then reverse the process to exhale. You can imagine warmth moving in and out of your body as you breathe in and out.

Repeat 20 to 30 times. Count out each breath to help you focus.

Visualization

Focus on a healing, safe, calming, relaxing image. Think of your favorite place in the world, or imagine one you haven't been to yet. For example: Close your eyes and imagine yourself lying in a sunny spot at a tropical beach. Smell the ocean, hear the waves, feel the warm sun on your skin and the sand beneath you, hear the sea birds calling. Take a "mini-vacation."

Meditation

For starters, sit on the floor (lean your back against something if you find it hard to sit up straight) or in a chair, hands in your lap. Relax your shoulders and close your eyes. Begin by focusing on your breath. Breathe in and out for counts of four or five per inhalation and exhalation. If you like, you can verbalize your exhalations with an "oooooooommmmmmm." Or, try your hand at biofeedback by saying with every exhalation, to yourself or out loud, "My hands are feeling warm." As thoughts come and go, observe them in a detached way. Sit for five to ten minutes in this way. To avoid having to watch the clock, use a kitchen timer or buy a special meditation timer and set it beforehand.

You can use soothing music to help you meditate, or purchase a CD or tape that will guide you through your daily relaxation routine. How you do it is less important than making sure you do it every day.

DEFUSING STRESSFUL MOMENTS

You're driving along one day and some jerk cuts you off and nearly causes an accident. Your blood pressure and heart rate soar. You're mad as hell, but the guy's already long gone. What do you do?

First, attend to your breathing. Take a few deep breaths as described above. Then, attend to the tension within your body. Start at the crown of your head and sense spots where the tension of your road rage has begun to grip you. Consciously warm, unknot, and loosen those areas, one at a time. Imagine the tension flooding out with each exhalation.

Another good trick is to switch your focus to something beautiful and pleasant in your immediate environment. This may not be an easy task in a traffic jam, but there is always *something*: that little weed springing up through a crack in the pavement; the pattern of clouds in the sky; the children waiting for the bus on the corner, pelting each other with snowballs. Or, you can keep reminders of what is beautiful and important to you in your car and at your desk and elsewhere you might encounter stressful situations. Photographs, beautiful objects, or mementoes can serve this purpose.

Here's another one: You are in the midst of a heated argument with your spouse. You can feel your stress levels shooting through the roof. Should you walk away and meditate? Perhaps, but there are other things you can do in the moment, without leaving the conversation. Clearly express your thoughts and feelings. Be specific about what you want, think, and feel, speaking in a non-blaming manner. Instead of, "You *always* make me feel like crap when you…" say, "I feel sad when you tell me…" When you speak in "I" statements, there's no arguing with you.

Also try something called *reflective listening*. When your spouse yells, "You never help with the housework!" don't answer, "Well, I work a nine-hour day, and I don't have *time* to do housework," or, worse, "Housework is for women, quit your complaining." Instead, say, "I hear you telling me that you're frustrated when I don't help you with the housework." Instead of escalating the argument, you will assure your spouse that you are hearing her. Then, you can answer her: "It's hard for me to come home after a long day at work and a commute and help you with the housework. Can you tell me exactly what you wish I would help you with?" See the difference? The first answer is argumentative and defensive and doesn't do anything to solve the problem at hand. The second response is constructive and moves towards a solution. You are acknowledging her issue before coming back with your own feelings and thoughts. You don't have to back down and get on your hands and knees and scrub floors after work, either. You can hear her out, and say that you just don't think you can do what she's asking.

And if you don't feel like you can control your anger or stress, tell the person with whom you are having a confrontation that you need a little time to cool off. Then, go do some deep breathing or sit in meditation. Give yourself a quick chest or scalp massage.

GENTLE YOGA

Yoga doesn't have to involve wrapping your legs around your neck or lying on a bed of nails (although, if you're up for it, yoga can involve either or both of these activities). Yoga is, basically, a series of poses that are held and breathed into, increasing flexibility and strength. Many of the poses—most of which are hundreds of years old, a legacy from the original yogis—are purported to have specific healing qualities.

Yoga is a great way to combine movement and relaxation. Gentle yoga is less strenuous and involves more meditation and visualization than hatha yoga. It's best to be introduced to yoga through an experienced instructor. If you are a cancer patient and your cancer center doesn't offer yoga classes, look in the phone book or talk with your doctors about finding a class that suits you. Once you have learned the basics, you will be able to practice on your own or with a video at home.

THE POWER OF HUMOR AND LOVE

In the 1960s, journalist Norman Cousins was struck down by a life-threatening connective tissue disease. Confined to bed and in severe pain, he decided to contribute to his own treatment with two unorthodox practices: high doses of intravenous vitamin C and daily doses of belly laughter. He recovered, despite the skepticism of his medical team. He wrote a classic book about his experience entitled *Anatomy of an Illness*, which was published in 1979. If you are at all doubtful about the healing power of laughter, I recommend that you pick up his book— and then head to the video store to pick out some funny movies.

Researchers at UCLA are currently studying the use of humor to help pediatric patients endure painful procedures. Pain causes a rise in cortisol, blood pressure, and heart rate, and these researchers expect that watching funny videos will blunt these stress-induced physiological changes. Laughter also releases the body's natural opiates into the bloodstream, dulling pain and improving mood.

Dr. Bernie Siegel has also written about the power of humor and love in the healing process. His most famous book is entitled *Love, Medicine, and Miracles*. In 1978, he founded Exceptional Cancer Patients (ECaP), a form of group therapy that incorporates patients' drawings, dreams, and imagery. ECaP helps patients to confront their fears and issues in a safe and ultimately therapeutic way. You can visit his website at http://www.ecap-online.org/.

ORIENTAL HEALING ARTS: TAI CHI AND CHI KUNG

Tai chi is a movement and breath practice that dates at least back to the year 122 BC. Taoist monks began to develop exercises that reflected and promoted the tenets of the *Tao te Ching*, the book of aphorisms upon which Taoism is based. Over the centuries, the practice of tai chi has been expanded and updated, and it continues to be a popular meditative practice throughout the world.

Chi is the Oriental designation for life force or energy. Both tai chi and chi kung are about fostering and directing energy within your body. Tai chi incorporates the elements of yielding, softness, centeredness, slowness, balance, suppleness and rootedness. If you attend a class, you will be taught a slow series of motions, each with its own evocative name (like White Crane Spreads Wings, or Snake Creeps Down, or Wild Horse Leaps the Ravine). You will build on these movements and learn to watch your breath and relax throughout.

Tai chi is excellent for people who are elderly or debilitated. It helps with balance and coordination, and can serve as gentle cardiovascular exercise for those who can't handle anything too strenuous. Check with your local martial arts schools, adult education center, or gym, or call an oriental medicine practitioner for a class recommendation. Or, try using a video at home.

Chi kung is pronounced "chee gong" and may be spelled qi gong. Loosely, it translates as *practice that brings control over internal energy*. According to chi kung master Mark Johnson, any practice that cultivates energy through "the coordination of your mind intent, breathing and postures (moving and still) is a 'Chi Kung,' and there are hundreds of Chi Kungs." Tai chi is actually a form of chi kung. Some types of chi kung are specifically focused on healing through acupuncture points and the meridian system of the body—a sort of needle-less acupuncture. Expect to use the breath and focus the mind on healing if you try any form of chi kung.

HOW ABOUT EXERCISE?

Exercise is, in a way, the flip side of the coin of stress relief. While meditation and relaxation practices give you tools for preventing an over-the-top physical response to stress, exercise gives you tools for blowing off steam. If you like to work out, you know how great it feels to pump iron or go for a run when you are feeling frustrated or angry. Those endogenous opiates (also known as endorphins) kick in, and suddenly, you don't remember what you were so fired up about.

Everyone knows that modern people don't get enough exercise, that they are overweight because they eat too much and don't move enough. What kind of exercise is best for preventing prostate cancer?

Overall, the research suggests that overdoing it is almost as bad as underdoing it. Highly strenuous exercise, particularly when done infrequently, is a setup for injury, increased free-radical stress, and increased stress overall. It also reduces the potency of the immune system. Moderate exercise, on the other hand, increases the body's production of antioxidant substances; mildly increases immune function; and leaves you feeling refreshed and energetic. If you're busting your rear in the gym and hating it, do you think you're reducing your stress, or adding to it? If you dread going back to work out again because your rear was busted last time, do you think that's healthy? It isn't. Exercise should feel good.

Go for a moderate approach. Set the foundation by making your life more active in general. Incorporate more activity into your day-to-day life. Instead of sitting on your hindquarters all day long, then catapulting into motion on the basketball court for a couple of hours once or twice a week—a situation that's likely to get you injured—try to walk, stretch, and move around more often during each day. Take stretching and walking breaks during work. Park farther from your destination and walk. Take the steps instead of the elevator. Dance with your spouse in the family room after you finish the dishes. Laugh a lot, the kind of laughter that gives your abs a workout. Have lots of sex.

Try to fit in three or more actual workouts per week. You can do a brisk walk, jog, or do circuit weight training—anything that gets your heart rate elevated and brings out a bit of a sweat. Even calisthenics will work: good old fashioned pushups, stomach crunches, squats, pull-ups. Stretch following each workout, when your body is warm and your joints are pliable. If you aren't sure how to stretch, check out the classic book *Stretching* by Bob Anderson. It's comprehensive and easy to understand.

If you have any concerns about your heart health, and you are getting ready to start working out again after a long hiatus, consult with your doctor first. He may want to send you for an EKG stress test to rule out any risk of heart problems when you start back into your workout program.

Men undergoing treatment for cancer, BPH, or prostatitis may be better off sticking with very gentle exercise like yoga, tai chi, or chi kung. Check with your medical team to find out what they recommend.

YOUR NONTOXIC, STRESS-REDUCING HOME AND OFFICE

In Chapter 7, you learned how to reduce your exposure to potentially carcinogenic substances in your food and water. That's only part of the job, however. You will also benefit from reducing your use of house and garden products and services that introduce carcinogens into the air you breathe, and through your skin and into the tissues of your body. They sit there, ready to warp DNA and otherwise wreak havoc in ways that can raise your risk of developing cancer of the prostate. An oft quoted EPA scientist once said, "Even downwind from a chemical plant, it's better to open your windows."

Anyone who believes that household chemicals, building materials, and home and garden pesticides and herbicides must be safe because the EPA hasn't banned them is not looking clearly at the facts. Here's a sampling of some of the more alarming of them:

- Federal requirements for warning labels on household products (such as cleansers, disinfectants, and personal care items) are only required if the product is immediately harmful or fatal if swallowed or inhaled—not for hazards from long-term use.

- In our homes and offices, we are exposed to hundreds of potentially toxic man-made chemicals each day. Toxicity testing of individual chemicals is not exactly intensive, and there is little to no testing of these chemicals in combination, which is how most of us are exposed.

- Chemicals in household cleaning products have been linked with cancer, birth defects, and nervous system damage. Many are absorbed right through the skin.

Alternatives: Many nontoxic, all-natural cleaners are commercially available. Or, you can make your own cleaners. See the Resources at the end of this book.

- Many indoor carpets are treated with moth repellants, mold retardants, and pesticides that are toxic to both bugs and humans.

Alternatives: If possible, replace carpets with hardwood floors or ceramic tile, and area rugs made from all-natural materials that have not been treated with synthetic chemical protectants or pesticides. If you like linoleum, avoid synthetics. You can buy all-natural linoleum instead. Those who don't want to give up their carpet can choose natural wool or cotton without chemical additives or latex backings, and have them installed with nontoxic padding and nontoxic adhesives.

- Cooling and heating units, if not cleaned regularly and properly filtered, spew asbestos, cleaning chemicals, pesticides, allergens, cooking gases, and radon into your indoor air.

Alternatives: Invest in a duct and vent cleaning. Make sure that they use nontoxic cleaners. Then, buy electrostatic filters and replace your filters with them. Wash them regularly.

- Do you paint inside or outside of your home? Chemicals from paint and paint products can do more than drive you crazy (think of Van Gogh, who is said to have cleaned out the paint from beneath his fingernails with his teeth). These chemicals enter your body through your lungs, skin, and eyes, and have been correlated with increased risk of cancer, respiratory disease, kidney damage, hypertension, headaches, and other problems. According to federal government reports, 90 percent of Americans have measurable levels of toluene, xylene, styrene, benzene, and ethylbenzene—all chemicals found in paint—stored away in their bodies. Housepainters have a 40 percent higher risk of cancer than the average population, and families with housepainters in them have a greater than average rate of birth defects and leukemia.

Alternatives: Seek out less-toxic, non-latex paints for indoor painting. Only paint when you can throw open windows and keep the area well-ventilated. While painting, wear non-permeable gloves and a respirator that covers your nose and mouth (and wear it while sanding wood, which is also treated with toxic chemicals). Apply nontoxic sealant over paint to prevent outgassing of paint fumes, which happens even after the paint has dried. When it comes time to remove old paint, don't use strippers that contain methylene chloride, and don't sand or burn off old paint. If there is any possibility that your paint contains lead, bring in professionals who know how to safely remove and dispose of it.

- Chlordane, once the pesticide of choice for killing off termites, is associated with cancer and reproductive dysfunction, among other things. It persists for 30 years after a house has been treated. When the chemical companies took it off the market in 1988, they offered Dursban as an alternative—despite evidence that Dursban is toxic to the reproductive system. Also available: methyl bromide, sulfuryl fluoride, and chloropicrin. Methyl bromide is a carcinogen and nervous system toxin. The other two have been linked with other serious health problems.

  Alternatives: Termites? You can hire a contractor to cook the termites to death by raising the heat in your home to 120 degrees. Other contractors will take the opposite tack, freezing the pests with liquid nitrogen. Microwave techniques and electro-guns are also used to eliminate termites without chemicals.

- Of the 34 most commonly used lawn and garden chemicals, 11 are known to cause cancer.

  Alternatives: Do some research into natural pest and plant disease eradication. Most nurseries are now pretty savvy about nontoxic techniques that work with nature instead of against it. For example: You can use microorganisms to get rid of beetles, caterpillars, and mosquitoes; you can release segmented worms called nematodes into your garden to gobble up Japanese beetle grubs; or you can release ladybugs to dine on your aphids. Diatomaceous earth can be dusted over and around plants to get rid of ants and aphids. Weed problems? Just pull them—it's good exercise.

- Pesticides used to eradicate fleas and ticks on pets have been linked with cancer and reproductive dysfunction. In the animals being treated, these chemicals have been linked with bladder cancer.

  Alternatives: Use flea shampoo. Or, try fatty acid soaps from garden nurseries. These work better with dogs than cats, because you need to leave the soap on the pet's fur for a half-hour to suffocate the tiny pests. If you are dealing with an infestation, call Fleabusters at 800-6NO-FLEA (800-666-3532) or visit www.fleabuster.com. They use less-toxic methods.

- Thinking of taking refuge in your swimming pool or hot tub? Chlorine in pools combines with organic material to form a family of carcinogenic chemicals called trihalomethanes.

  Alternatives: Use a pool ozonator or UV light system to kill bacteria in your pool instead of chlorine. If you swim at a sports club or public pool, talk to the people in charge about getting a nontoxic chlorine alternative.

FENG SHUI...GESUNDHEIT!

It can sound like a sneeze, but actually, feng shui (pronounced *fung shwey*) is an effective tool for making your surroundings less stressful and more health-promoting.

Maximizing health and minimizing stress has to include our environment. We are intimately involved with that environment, and it has more power over us than most of us realize. When colors, light, decoration, sounds, objects, and overall design are pleasing to the senses, it's that much easier for us to relax and enjoy ourselves.

The words feng shui actually mean "wind-water." It entails placing objects in your environment in a way that helps to direct the chi (energy) within the space. Bad feng shui leads to energy stagnation, while good feng shui creates an even flow of energy that can move freely.

If you are interested in learning about feng shui yourself, there are a lot of books available on this topic. It has become somewhat trendy in recent years. Or, look for a decorator or feng shui consultant to help you better organize and design your space for maximum serenity.

THE HOLISTIC APPROACH

The changes described in this chapter will have a significant influence on your prostate health, but they should be integrated with the changes described in chapters previous. None of the holistic therapies in this book exist in a vacuum. Most of them won't be easy to implement when you are accustomed to certain foods, certain ways of life, certain ways of coping with stress (or lack of coping mechanisms). But I hope to have convinced you that these difficult changes are well worth your while.

Chapter 9

In Conclusion

WITH MY WORK AND WITH THIS BOOK, my aim is to advance natural healing methods like herbs, nutritional supplements, and acupuncture into the medical mainstream. It is my belief that these two kinds of medicine added together have much more to offer than either one alone.

If you have prostate disease, and your medical team tells you that watchful waiting is your best bet, you can harness the power of natural medicines to strengthen your body's native ability to heal. The research is growing by leaps and bounds, thanks in part to studies done right here at Columbia.

If you have prostate disease that requires treatment, you don't have to go without these potent natural therapies. Work closely with your medical team to integrate the alternative and holistic with the mainstream. Becoming as educated as possible will make you an intelligent participant in your own treatment. Respect what your doctors have to say; they want the best for you, and they know a lot. But if you've read this book, and they haven't, they may not know some of what you do. Share this information and discuss how it can help you return to wellness.

And, if you are a man who has been through prostate cancer treatment, your job now is to do all you can to ward off a recurrence. I hope that I've given you all the information you need to do this.

I've seen the difference that integrative medicine can make in the lives of men with prostate disease. Even if you do not have prostate disease, but want to live a long and healthy life, much of what is in these pages should be helpful to you. The great thing about natural therapies is that they promote health in a general way, strengthening the body's ability to maintain its own ideal balance. Herbs, supplements, balanced diet, environmental toxin avoidance, exercise, and stress-reduction techniques support not only prostate health, but also cardiovascular and nervous system health. They'll improve your energy and your brain power, and they'll keep your digestive tract running more smoothly. A large body of research suggests that the changes described in this book will aid in the prevention of more than one kind of cancer.

For continually updated information on prostate cancer treatments—both alternative and mainstream—I highly recommend you visit the following websites:

Us TOO International, a non-profit support and education organization for prostate cancer patients and their loved ones, can be found on the Internet at www.ustoo.com.

The Prostate Cancer Foundation maintains a website at www.prostatecancerfoundation.org. There, you can find detailed information about treatments, clinical trials, and therapeutics.

The Cancer Cure Coalition website (www.cancercurecoalition.org) is a valuable resource for information on the latest advances in the treatment and prevention of cancer.

Finally, please be sure to visit our Center for Holistic Urology at www.holisticurology.com. We would like to hear your success stories. And we know there will be many!

All my best to you, Aaron Katz, M.D.

Resources

Chapter Three
BPH—THE HOLISTIC APPROACH

National Cancer Institute. Questions and answers about the prostate-specific antigen (PSA) test: http://cis.nci.nih.gov/fact/5_29.htm.

At http://www.topix.net/health/benign-prostatic-hypertrophy you'll find updated information on BPH treatments.

You can also read *Back to Great Sex: Overcome ED and Reclaim Lost Intimacy* (Kensington Books, 2002) by Ridwan Shabsigh, M.D.

A combination nettle, pygeum and pumpkin product is available from Enzymatic Therapy (www.enzy.com).

Chapter Four
PROSTATITIS

The best online resource for men with prostatitis is the site of the Prostatitis Foundation: http://www.prostatitis.org/index.html.

Cernilton® from AB Cernelle is distributed in the U.S. by Cernitin America (www.cernitinamerica.com).

Chapters Five, Six and Seven
PROSTATE CANCER, CHEMOPREVENTION
AND NUTRITION CHAPTERS

Prostate Cancer Foundation: www.prostatecancerfoundation.org.

Call the Cancer Information Service (1-800-4-CANCER) to learn about National Cancer Institute-supported treatment facilities and cancer centers near you.

To find out about current cancer studies and other information, go to the National Cancer Institute's website at http://cancernet.nci.nih.gov.

For the latest information on cancer prevention and treatments, visit the Cancer Cure Coalition at www.cancercurecoalition.org.

The PCRI (Prostate Cancer Research Institute) has an interactive helpline staffed by highly trained personnel to direct you to physicians and centers of excellence as well as offer advice regarding resources. You can reach them at (310) 743-2110 or visit their website at www.pcri.org.

For education and support, visit Us TOO at www.ustoo.com.

Order Prostabel at http://www.natural-source.com/engl/prostabel.html.

If you want to try IP$_6$, try Cell Forté® with IP-6 and Inositol from Enzymatic Therapy (www.enzy.com) or Cellular Forté® with IP-6 and Inositol from PhytoPharmica (www.phytopharmica.com).

In addition to Prostate 5LX®, Zyflamend®, and the Every Man® multivitamin, New Chapter (www.newchapter.info) makes an odorless garlic supplement called Garlicforce™. Kyolic® Garlic 105 with vitamins A, C, E, and selenium is another good choice. You can find this and other state-of-the-art supplements at the Life Extension Foundation website, www.lef.org.

You can buy seaweeds at www.edenfoods.com and dried medicinal mushrooms at http://www.gmushrooms.com.

You can buy fish oil supplements at http://www.vitalchoice. com/shop.cfm. Theirs are from sockeye salmon. Other brands to try: Enzymatic Therapy's Eskimo-3®, Carlson's (www.carlsonlabs. com), or Coromega, whose oil is orange flavored with no hint of fishiness (www.coromega.com).

Shopping for a probiotic? Try Probiotics With A Purpose™, by New Chapter. Other options: Natren, at www.natren.com, calls itself "the probiotic specialist recognized worldwide." Jarrow also makes a good probiotic; try the Jarro-Dophilus EPS™ (www.jarrow.com).

New Chapter also makes a good turmeric supplement (Turmericforce™) and medicinal mushroom supplement (Host Defense®).

For Active Hexose Correlated Compound, AHCC® with Bioperine® (an absorption enhancer from black pepper) can be purchased from Source Naturals, in stores or at www.vitacost.com. American BioSciences also makes an AHCC supplement called ImmPower™, also available at www.vitacost.com.

Genistein Combined Polysaccharide (GCP) from Amino Up is distributed under the name GeniKinoko by Quality of Life Labs. They offer AHCC products as well; visit www.q-o-l.com.

Barlean's makes several flax products, including their Highest Lignan Content Flax Oil and Forti-Flax ground flaxseed (www.barleans.com).

For information on Provail, contact Lignan Research L.L.C. at (888) 503-8300 or visit their website at www.provail.info.

Vitamin Shoppe at www.vitaminshoppe.com is a comprehensive source for many of the nutritional products mentioned in this guide. Speak with a customer support representative by calling (800) 223-1216, fax them at (800) 852-7153 or write them at Vitamin Shoppe, Customer Care Department, 2101 91st Street, North Bergen, NJ 07047. All of the products detailed in the Columbia University-Zyflamend PIN Protocol (see page 149) are available from the Vitamin Shoppe.

Learn more about the benefits of buying organic at www.organic-center.org. The Organic Center for Education and Promotion is a clearinghouse for information for consumers, health care professionals, educators, public officials and government agencies and the media.

Chapter Eight
LIFESTYLE, STRESS AND PROSTATE HEALTH

I highly recommend John W. Travis, M.D. and Regina Sara Ryan's *Wellness Workbook* (3rd ed., Celestial Arts, Berkeley, CA: 2004) for those who need help finding a more healthful lifestyle in every aspect.

You can also visit Dr. Andrew Weil's Self Healing website at http://www.drweilselfhealing.com.

Bernie Siegel's website is http://www.ecap-online.org.

For videos to guide you in both tai chi and chi kung practice, visit http://www.chi-kung.com or http://www.activevideos.com/taichi.htm.

RESOURCES FOR NONTOXIC PRODUCTS FOR YOUR HOME AND OFFICE

Additional Websites
Seventh Generation: http://www.seventhgeneration.com
The Green Guide: http://www.thegreenguide.com/

Books
The Safe Shopper's Bible: A Consumer's Guide to Nontoxic Household Products, by David Steinman and Samuel Epstein
Diet for a Poisoned Planet, by David Steinman
The Naturally Clean Home: 101 Safe and Easy Herbal Formulas for Nontoxic Cleansers, by Karyn Siegel-Maier

Better Basics for the Home: Simple Solutions for Less Toxic Living, by Annie Berthold-Bond
Living Downstream, by Sandra Steingraber

Magazines
E – The Environmental Magazine: www.emagazine.com
Earth Island Journal: www.earthisland.org
Healthy Living: www.freedompressonline.com
Natural Home & Garden: www.naturalhomemagazine.com

References

CHAPTER 1

Lange, P.H. "Is the prostate pill finally here?" *N Engl J Med*, 1992;327(17):1234-1236.

Nickel, J.C. Foreword, *The Prostatitis Manual*. Oxfordshire: Bladon Medical Publishing, 2002.

Whitaker, J. *The Prostate Report: Prevention and Healing.* Potomac, MD: Phillips Publishing, Inc., 1994.

CHAPTER 2

Anonymous. *Marketletter*. March 15, 1993.

Lange, P.H. "Is the prostate pill finally here?" *N Engl J Med*, 1992;327(17):1234-6.

Lepor, H., et al. "The efficacy of terazosin, finasteride or both in benign prostatic hypertrophy. Veterans' Cooperative Studies Benign Prostatic Hyperplasia Study Group." *N Engl J Med*, 1996;335(8):533-9.

McDonald, H. et al. "An economic evaluation of doxazosin, finasteride, and combination therapy in the treatment of benign prostatic hypertrophy." *Can J Urol*, 2004;11(4):2327-40.

Physicians' Desk Reference. Montvale, NJ: Medical Economics Data Production Company, 1994:427-8.

Rittmaster, R.S. "Finasteride." *N Engl J Med*, 1994;330(2):120-5.

United States Department of Health and Human Services. *Benign Prostatic Hyperplasia: Diagnosis and Treatment*. Rockville, MD: United States Department of Health and Human Services, February 1994. AHCPR Publication No. 94-0582.

United States Department of Health and Human Services. *Treating Your Enlarged Prostate*. Rockville, MD: United States Department of Health and Human Services, February 1994. AHCPR Publication 94-0584.

CHAPTER 3

Barlet, A., et al. "Efficacy of *Pygeum africanum* extract in the treatment of micturitional disorders due to benign prostatic hyperplasia. Revaluation of objective and subjective parameters. A multicenter, randomized, double-blind trial." *Wiener klinishce Wochenschrift*, 1990;102(22):667-73.

Bassi, P., et al. "Standardized *Pygeum africanum* extract in the treatment of benign prostatic hypertrophy: a controlled clinical study vs. placebo." *Minerva Urologica e Nefrologica*, 1987;39(1):45-50.

Berges, R.R., et al. "Randomised, placebo-controlled, double-blind clinical trial of beta-sitosterol in patients with benign prostatic hyperplasia." *Lancet*, 1995;345(8964):1529-32.

Breza, J., et al. "Efficacy and acceptability of tadenan (*Pygeum africanum* extract) in the treatment of benign prostatic hyperplasia (BPH): a multicentre trial in central Europe." *Curr Med Res Opin*, 1998;14(3):127-39.

Buck, A.C., et al. "Treatment of outflow tract obstruction due to benign prostate hyperplasia with the pollen extract, Cernilton®." *British Journal of Urology*, 1990;66(4):398-404.

Bush, I.M., et al. "Zinc and the prostate." Presented at the annual meeting of the American Medical Association, Chicago, 1974.

Carani, C., et al. "Urological and sexual evaluation of treatment of benign prostatic disease using *Pygeum africanum* at high dose." *Arch Ital Urol Nefrol Androl*, 1991;63(3):341-5.

Carilla, E., et al. "Binding of Permixon, a new treatment for prostatic benign hyperplasia, to the cytosolic androgen receptor in the rat prostate." *Journal of Steroid Biochemistry*, 1984;20(1):521-3.

Champault, G., et al. "A double-blind trial of an extract of the plant *Serenoa repens* in benign prostatic hyperplasia." *British Journal of Clinical Pharmacology*, 1984;18(3):461-2.

Champault, G., et al. "Medical treatment of prostatic adenoma." *Annals of Urology*, 1984;18(6):407-10.

Chatelain, C., et al. "Comparison of once and twice daily dosage forms of *Pygeum africanum* extract in patients with benign prostatic hyperplasia: a randomized, double-blind study, with long-term open label extension." *Urology*, 1999;54(3):473-8.

Clavert, A., et al. "Effects of an extract of the bark of *Pygeum africanum* on prostatic secretions in the rat and man." *Ann Urol*, 1986;20(5):341-3.

Crimi, A. & Russo, A. "Extract of *Serenoa repens* for the treatment of the functional disturbances of prostatic hypertrophy." *Med Praxis*, 1983;4:47-51.

Damrau, F. "Benign prostatic hypertrophy: amino acid therapy for symptomatic relief." *J Am Geriatr Soc*, 1962;10:426-30.

Di Silverio, F., et al. "Evidence that *Serenoa repens* extract displays an antiestrogenic activity in prostatic tissue of benign prostatic hypertrophy patients." *Eur Urol*, 1992;21(4):309-314.

Dufour, B. "Controlled study of the effects of *Pygeum africanum* extract on the functional symptoms of prostatic adenoma." *Annals of Urology*, 1984;18(3):193-5.

Duke, J.A. *Handbook of Medicinal Herbs*. Boca Raton, FL: CRC Press, 1985: 118.

Emili, E., et al. "Clinical results obtained with a new drug (Permixon) in the treatment of prostatic hypertrophy." *Urologia*, 1983;50:1042-8.

Fahim, M.S., et al. "Zinc treatment for the reduction of hyperplasia of the prostate." *Federal Proceedings*, 1976;35:361.

Gaby, A.R. "Prostate politics part two." *Townsend Letter for Doctors & Patients*, January 1993;114:79.

Goepel, M., et al. "Saw palmetto extracts potently and noncompetitively inhibit human alpha 1-adrenoceptors in vitro." *Prostate*, 1999;38(3):208-15.

Greca, P. & Volpi, R. "Experiments in the use of a new drug in the medical treatment of prostatic adenoma." *Urologia*, 1985;52:532-5.

Hartmann, R.W., et al. "Inhibition of 5 alpha-reductase and aromatase by PHL-00801 (Prostatonin), a combination of PY 102 (*Pygeum africanum*) and UR 102 (*Urtica dioica*)." *Phytomedicine*, 1996;3(2):121-8.

Healthnotes, Inc. "Beta-Sitosterol." http://www.vitacost.com/science/hn/Supp/Beta_Sitosterol.htm.

Indena S.p.A. *Prunus Africana*. Technical Documentation.

Jodai, A., et al. "A long-term therapeutic experience with Cernilton in chronic prostatitis." *Hinyokika Kiyo*, 1988;34(3):561–8.

Klippel, K.F., et al. "A multicentric, placebo-controlled, double-blind clinical trial of ß-sitosterol (phytosterol) for the treatment of benign prostatic hyperplasia." *Br J Urol*, 1997;80(3):427–32.

Krzeski, T., et al. "Combined extracts of *Urtica dioica* and *Pygeum africanum* in the treatment of benign prostatic hyperplasia: double-blind comparison of two doses." *Clin Therapeut*, 1993;15(6):1011-20.

Levin, R.M., et al. "Cellular and molecular aspects of bladder hypertrophy." *Eur Urol*, 1997;32 Suppl 1:15-21.

Lucchetta, G., et al. "Reactivation from the prostatic gland in cases of reduced fertility." *Urol Int*, 1984;39(4):222-4.

Maekuwa, M., et al. "Clinical evaluation of Cernilton on benign prostate hypertrophy—a multiple center double-blind study with Paraprost." *Hinyokika Kiyo*, 1990;36(4):495-516.

Menchini-Fabris, G.F., et al. "New perspectives of treatment of prostate-vesicular pathologies with *Pygeum africanum*." *Arch Int Urol*, 1988;60(3):313-322.

Mowrey, D. "*Pygeum*: natural prostate therapy." *Let's Live*, December 1989: 62-3.

Mowrey, D. *The Scientific Validation of Herbal Medicine.* New Canaan, CT: Keats Publishing, Inc., 1986:111.

Platz, E.A., et al. "Physical activity and benign prostatic hyperplasia." *Arch Intern Med*, 1998;158(21):2349-56.

Riehemann, K., et al. "Plant extracts from stinging nettle (*Urtica dioica*), an antirheumatic remedy, inhibit the proinflammatory transcription factor NF-kappaB." *FEBS Lett*, 1999;442(1):89-94.

Schachter, M.B. *The Natural Way to a Healthy Prostate.* New Canaan, CT: Keats Publishing Inc., 1995.

Sultan, C., et al. "Inhibition of androgen metabolism and binding by a liposterolic extract of *Serenoa repens* B in human foreskin fibroblasts." *Journal of Steroid Biochemistry*, 1984;20(1):515-9.

Suzuki, T., et al. "Clinical effect of Cernilton in chronic prostatitis." *Hinyokika Kiyo*, 1992;38(4):489–94.

Tasca, A., et al. "Treatment of obstructive symptomatology of prostatic adenoma using an extract of *Serenoa repens*: a double-blind clinical study vs. placebo." *Minerva Urol Nefrol*, 1985;37(1):87-91.

Whitaker, J. *The Prostate Report: Prevention and Healing.* Potomac, MD: Phillips Publishing, Inc., 1994.

Yablonsky, F., et al. "Antiproliferative effect of *Pygeum africanum* extract on rat prostatic fibroblasts." *J Urol*, 1997;158(3 Pt 1):889.

Yasumoto, R., et al. "Clinical evaluation of long-term treatment using Cernitin pollen extract in patients with benign prostatic hyperplasia." *Clinical Therapeutics*, 1995;17(1):82-87.

CHAPTER 4

"A headache in the pelvis." Prostatitis Foundation: http://www.prostatitis.org/aheadacheinthepelvis.html.

Bjorling, D.E., et al. "Mast cells mediate the severity of experimental cystitis in mice." *J Urol*, 1999;162(1):231-6.

Buck, A.C., et al. "Therapy of chronic prostatitis and prostatodynia with pollen extract." *Br J Urol*, 1989;64(5):496-9.

Byrnes, Stephen C., PhD, DNT, CNC. "Calming Chamomile." Price Pottenger Nutrition Foundation: http://www.price-pottenger.org/Articles/Chamomile.htm.

Chen, H.J., et al. "Effects of pollen extract EA-10,P5 on chronic prostatitis or infertility with chronic prostatitis." *Acta Pharmacol Sin*, 2002;23(11):1035-9.

Deng, C., et al. "Clinical study of zinc for the treatment of chronic bacterial prostatitis." *Zhonghua Nan Ke Xue*, 2004;10(5):368-70.

"Do bacteria cause chronic prostatitis?" Report on "Current management of prostatitis" from symposium sponsored by *Contemporary Urology*, December 1999. Prostatitis Foundation: http://www.prostatitis.org/bacterialcause.html.

Healthnotes, Inc. "Comfrey." Delicious Living website:
http://www.deliciouslivingmag.com/healthnotes/healthnotes.cfm?org=nh&lang=EN
&ContentID=2073000.

Licking, E. "Getting a grip on bacterial slime." *Business Week*, September 13,
1999:98-100.

Lis-Balchin M., et al. "Buchu (*Agathosma betulina and A. crenulata, Rutaceae*)
essential oils: their pharmacological action on guinea-pig ileum and antimicrobial
activity on microorganisms." *J Pharm Pharmacol*, 2001;53(4):579-82.

Parr, T. "Prostatitis alternative medicine FAQ." Prostatitis Foundation:
http://www.prostatitis.org/altmedfaq.html.

Persson, B.E., et al. "Ameliorative effect of allopurinol on nonbacterial prostatitis:
Parallel double-blind controlled study." *J Urol*,1996;155(3):961-4.

"Prostatitis: Dr. Shoskes FAQ." Prostatitis Foundation:
http://www.prostatitis.org/shoskesfaq.html.

Rugendorff, E.W. "Results of therapy with pollen extract (Cernilton N) in chronic
prostatitis and prostatodynia." *Br J Urol*, 1993;71(4):433-8.

Shoskes, D. Daniel Shoskes Home Page: http://www.dshoskes.com.

Skelly, A. "Urology update: Acupuncture may be prostatitis answer." Medical Post:
http://www.medicalpost.com/mpcontent/article.jsp?content=/
content/EXTRACT/RAWART/3826/13C.html.

Tennant, S. "Is prostatitis related to pelvic muscle dysfunction?" Prostatitis
Foundation: http://www.prostatitis.org/ux2articles.html.

Weiss, E.I., et al. "Inhibiting interspecies coaggregation of plaque bacteria with a
cranberry juice constituent." *J Am Dent Assoc*, 1998;129(12):1719-23.

Yavascaoglu, I., et al. "Role of ejaculate in the therapy of chronic nonbacterial
prostatitis." *Int J Urol*, 1999;6(3):130-4.

CHAPTER 5

American Cancer Society, *Cancer Facts and Figures 2003*. CDC:
http://www.cdc.gov/cancer/prostate/prostate.htm#known.

Bales, G.T., et al. "Effect of preoperative biofeedback/pelvic floor training on
continence in men undergoing radical prostatectomy." *Urology*, 2000;56(4):627-30.

Barrett-Conner, E., et al. "A prospective, population-based study of androstene-
dione, estrogens, and prostatic cancer." *Cancer Res*, 1990;50(1):169-73.

Bill-Axelson, A., et al. "Radical prostatectomy versus watchful waiting in early
prostate cancer." *N Engl J Med*, 2005;352(19):1977-84.

Blair, A., et al. "Cancer among farmers: a review." *Scand J Work Environ Health*,
1985;11(6):397-407.

Bosland, M. "The etiopathogenesis of prostate cancer with special reference to environmental factors." *Adv Canc Res*, 1988;51:1-106.

"Cancer." Online Etymology Dictionary: http://www.etymonline.com/ index.php?search=cancer&searchmode=none.

Dai, W.K., et al., for the MRFIT Research Group. "Cigarette smoking and serum sex hormones in men." *Am J Epidemiol*, 1988;128(4):796-805.

D'Amico, A.V. "6-month androgen suppression plus radiation therapy vs radiation therapy alone for patients with clinically localized prostate cancer: a randomized controlled trial." *JAMA*, 2004;292(7):821-7.

Devesa, S.S., et al. "Cancer incidence and mortality trends among whites in the United States, 1947-84." *J Nat Canc Inst*, 1987;79(4):701-70.

Gargiullo, P., et al. "Number of deaths and death rate among persons with cancer and annual percentage change from 1990 to 1998, by type of cancer, sex, and race/ethnicity." CDC: http://www.cdc.gov/mmwr/preview/mmwrhtml/ mm5103a1.htm#tab1.

Giovannucci, E., et al. "Height, body weight, and risk of prostate cancer." *Cancer Epidemiol Biomarkers Prev*, 1997;6(8):557-63.

Graham, S., et al. "Diet in the epidemiology of carcinoma of the prostate gland." *J Natl Canc Inst*, 1983;70(4):687-92.

"History of Cancer." MedicineWorld.Org: http://medicineworld.org/ cancer/history.html.

"The History of Cancer (Introduction)." Jules Bordet Institute: http:// www.bordet.be/historic/cancer/engl/cancer1.htm.

Honda, G.D., et al. "Vasectomy, cigarette smoking, and age at first sexual intercourse as risk factors for prostate cancer in middle-aged men." *Br J Cancer*, 1988;57(3):326-31.

Howie, B.J. & Schultz, T.D. "Dietary and hormonal interrelationships among vegetarian Seventh Day Adventists and nonvegetarian men." *Am J Clin Nutr*, 1985;42(1):127-34.

Kolonel, L.N., et al. "Diet and prostatic cancer: a case-control study in Hawaii." *Am J Epidemiol*, 1988;127(5):999-1012.

Kovi, J., et al. "Large acinar type atypical hyperplasia and carcinoma of the prostate." *Cancer*, 1988;61(3):555-61.

Kurihara, M., et al, (eds). *Cancer Mortality Statistics in the World, 1950-1985*. Nagoya: University of Nagoya Press, 1989.

Naparstek, B. "What is guided imagery?" Health Journeys: http://www.healthjourneys.com/what_is_guided_imagery.asp.

Nomura, A., et al. "Prediagnostic serum hormones and the risk of prostate cancer." *Cancer Res*, 1988;48(12):3515-17.

Norman, A., et al. "Occupational physical activity and risk for prostate cancer in a nationwide cohort study in Sweden." *Br J Canc*, 2002;86(1):70-5.

"Pesticides linked with prostate cancer," Reuters, Thursday, May 01, 2003.

Petrylak, D.P. "Docetaxel for the treatment of hormone-refractory prostate cancer," *Rev Urol*, 2003;5(Suppl 2):S14-21.

Petrylak, D.P. "Docetaxel (Taxotere) in hormone-refractory prostate cancer." *Semin Oncol*, 2000;27(2 Suppl 3):24-9.

Pommier, P., et al. "Phase III randomized trial of *Calendula officinalis* compared with trolamine for the prevention of acute dermatitis during irradiation for breast cancer." *J Clin Oncol*, 2004,22(8):1447-53.

Reichman, M.E., et al. "Serum vitamin A and subsequent development of prostate cancer in the First Epidemiologic National Health and Nutrition Examination Survey I Followup Study." *Cancer Res*, 1990;50(8):2311-5.

Rose, D.P., et al. "International comparisons of mortality rates for cancer of the breast, ovary, prostate, and colon, and per capita food consumption." *Cancer*, 1986;58(11):2363-71.

Ross, R.K., et al. "5-alpha-reductase activity among Japanese and U.S. white and black males." *Lancet*, 1992;339(8798):887-9.

Ross, R.K., et al. "Case-control studies of prostate cancer in blacks and whites in Southern California." *J Natl Canc Inst*, 1987;78(5):869-74.

Savarese, D.M., et al. "Prevention of chemotherapy and radiation toxicity with glutamine." *Cancer Treat Rev*, 2003;29(6):501-13.

Schwartz, L.M. & Osborne, B.A. "Programmed cell death, apoptosis and killer genes." *Immunol Today*, 1993;14(12):582-90.

Shen, J., et al. "Electroacupuncture for control of myeloablative chemotherapy-induced emesis: A randomized controlled trial." *JAMA*, 2000;284(21):2755-61.

Stamey, J.A., et al. "The prostate-specific antigen era in the United States is over for prostate cancer: what happened in the last 20 years?" *J Urol*, 2004;172(4 Pt 1):1297-301.

United States Department of Health and Human Services. *Benign Prostatic Hyperplasia: Diagnosis and Treatment*. Rockville, MD: United States Department of Health and Human Services, February 1994. AHCPR Publication No. 94-0582.

CHAPTER 6

Adhami, V.M., et al. "Molecular targets for green tea in prostate cancer prevention." *J Nutr*, 2003;133(7 Suppl):2417S-24S.

Bemis, D.L, et al. "Zyflamend®, a unique herbal preparation with nonselective COX inhibitory activity, induces apoptosis of prostate cancer cells that lack COX-2 expression." *Nutr Cancer*, 2005;52(2):202-12.

Biri, H., et al. "Activities of DNA turnover and free radical metabolizing enzymes in cancerous human prostate tissue." *Cancer Invest*, 1999;17(5):314-9.

Chun, K.S., et al. "Curcumin inhibits phorbol ester-induced expression of cyclooxygenase-2 in mouse skin through suppression of extracellular signal-regulated kinase activity and NF-kappaB activation." *Carcinogenesis*, 2003;24(9):1515-24.

Darshan, S. & Doreswamy, R. "Patented antiinflammatory plant drug development from traditional medicine." *Phytother Res*, 2004;18(5):343-57.

Dorai, T., et al. "Therapeutic potential of curcumin in human prostate cancer. I. Curcumin induces apoptosis in both androgen-dependent and androgen-independent prostate cancer cells." *Prostate Cancer Prostatic Dis*, 2000;3(2):84-93.

Dorai, T., et al. "Therapeutic potential of curcumin in human prostate cancer. III. Curcumin inhibits proliferation, induces apoptosis, and inhibits angiogenesis of LNCaP prostate cancer cells *in vivo*." *Prostate*, 2001;47(4):293-303.

Eisenberg, D.M., et al. "Unconventional medicine in the United States. Prevalence, costs, and patterns of use." *N Engl J Med*, 1993;328(4)246-52.

Fremont, L. "Biological effects of resveratrol." *Life Sci*, 2000;66(8):663-73.

Ghafar, M.A. "Regression of prostate cancer following administration of Genistein Combined Polysaccharide (GCP), a nutritional supplement: a case report." *J Altern Complement Med*, 2002;8(4):493-7.

Ghosh, J. & Myers, C.E. "Arachidonic acid stimulates prostate cancer cell growth: critical role of 5-lipoxygenase." *Biochem Biophys Res Commun*, 1997;235(2):418-23.

Ghosh, J. & Myers, C.E. "Inhibition of arachidonate 5-lipoxygenase triggers massive apoptosis in human prostate cancer cells." *Proc Natl Acad Sci*, 1998;95(22):13182-7.

Goel, A., et al. "Specific inhibition of cyclooxygenase-2 (COX-2) expression by dietary curcumin in HT-29 human colon cancer cells." *Cancer Lett*, 2001;172(2):111-8.

Gupta, S., et al. "Lipoxygenase-5 is overexpressed in prostate adenocarcinoma." *Cancer*, 2001;91(4):737-43.

Hussain, T., et al. "Green tea constituent epigallocatechin-3-gallate selectively inhibits COX-2 without affecting COX-1 expression in human prostate carcinoma cells." *Int J Cancer*, 2005;113(4):660-9.

Kinghorn, A.D., et al. "Natural inhibitors of carcinogenesis." *Planta Med*, 2004;70(8):691-705.

Kuo, C.L., et al. "The anti-inflammatory potential of berberine *in vitro* and *in vivo*." *Cancer Lett*, 2004;203(2):127-37.

Lai, P.K. & Roy, J. "Antimicrobial and chemopreventive properties of herbs and spices." *Curr Med Chem*, 2004;11(11):1451-60.

Liu, B.Q., et al. "The flavonoid baicalin exhibits anti-inflammatory activity by binding to chemokines." *Immunopharmacology*, 2000;49(3):295-306.

Matsui, Y., et al. "Improved prognosis of postoperative hepatocellular carcinoma patients when treated with functional foods: a prospective cohort study." *J Hepatol*, 2002;37(1):78-86.

Matsushita, K., et al. "Combination therapy of active hexose correlated compound plus UFT significantly reduces the metastasis of rat mammary adenocarcinoma." *Anticancer Drugs*, 1998;9(4):343-50.

Matsuyama, M., et al. "Expression of lipoxygenase in human prostate cancer and growth reduction by its inhibitors." *Int J Oncol*, 2004;24(4):821-7.

McNeal, J.E. & Bostwick, D.G. "Intraductal dysplasia: a premalignant lesion of the prostate." *Hum Pathol*, 1986;17(1):64-71.

Mioro, T. "Isoflavone aglycone produced by cultured soybean extracts with basidiomycetes and its anti-angiogenic activity." *Bioscience, Biotechnology and Biochemistry*, 2002;66(12):2626-31.

Myers, C.E. & Ghosh, J. "Lipxoygenase inhibition in prostate cancer." *Eur Urol*, 1999;35(5-6):395-8.

Nelson, W.G., et al. "Preneoplastic prostate lesions: an opportunity for prostate cancer prevention." *Ann NY Acad Sci*, 2001;952:135-44.

Nelson, W.G., et al. "The role of inflammation in the pathogenesis of prostate cancer." *J Urol*, 2004;172(5 Pt 2):S6-11; discussion S11-2.

Newmark, Tom. E-mail communications, November 27 and 28, 2004.

Nie, D., et al. "Role of eicosanoids in prostate cancer progression." *Cancer Metastasis Rev*, 2001;20(3-4):195-206.

Obertreis, B., et al. "[Anti-inflammatory effect of *Urtica dioica folia* extract in comparison to caffeic malic acid]." *Arzneimittelforschung*, 1996;46(1):52-6.

Pezzato, E., et al. "Prostate carcinoma and green tea. PSA-triggered basement membrane degradation and MMP-2 activation are inhibited by (-)epigallocatechin-3-gallate." *Int J Cancer,* 2004;112(5):787-92.

Redman, C., et al. "Inhibitory effect of selenomethionine on the growth of three selected human tumor cell lines." *Cancer Lett*, 1998;125(1-2):103-10.

Richwine, L. "Arthritis drug recall sparks criticism of FDA." Reuters, Monday October 4, 2004.

Schroeder, C.P., et al. "Eicosanoid metabolism in squamous cell carcinoma cell lines derived from primary and metastatic head and neck cancer and its modulation by celecoxib." *Cancer Biology & Therapy*, 2004;3(9):847-52.

Singh, S. "Mechanism of action of anti-inflammatory effect of fixed oil of *Ocimum basilicum Linn*." *Indian J Exp Biol*, 1999;37(3):248-52.

Vahlensieck, W., Jr. "[Drug therapy of benign prostatic hyperplasia]." *Fortschr Med*, 1996;114(31):407-11.

Venkateswaran, V., et al. "Synergistic effect of vitamin E and selenium in human prostate cancer cell lines." *Prostate Cancer Prostatic Dis*, 2004;7(1):54-6.

Wang, W., et al. "Chronic inflammation in benign prostatic hyperplasia is associated with focal upregulation of cyclooxygenase-2, Bcl-2, and cell proliferation in the glandular epithelium." *Prostate*, 2004;61(1):60-72.

Williams, C.S., et al. "Host cyclooxygenase-2 modulates carcinoma growth." *J Clin Invest*, 2000;105(11):1589-94.

Yuan, L., et al. "Inhibition of human breast cancer growth by genistein combined polysaccharide (GCP) in xenogenic athymic mice: involvement of genistein bio-transformation by B-glucoronidase from tumor tissues." *Mutat Res*, 2003;523-524:55-62.

CHAPTER 7

Augusston, K., et al. "A prospective study of intake of fish and marine fatty acids and prostate cancer." *Cancer Epidemiol Biomarkers Prev*, 2003;12(1):64-7.

Cohen, J.H., et al. "Fruit and vegetable intakes and prostate cancer risk." *J Natl Canc Inst*, 2000;92(1):61-8.

Davis, J.N., et al. "Genistein-induced upregulation of p21WAF1, downregulation of cyclin B, and induction of apoptosis in prostate cancer cells." *Nutr Cancer*, 1998;32(3):123-31.

DiLuzio, N.R. "Immunopharmacology of glucan: a broad spectrum enhancer of host defense mechanisms." *Trends in Pharmacol Sci*, 1983;4:344-7.

Giovannucci, E. "Nutrition, insulin, insulin-like growth factors, and cancer." *Horm Metab Res*, 2003;35(11-12):694-704.

Giovannucci, E., et al. "Body mass index and risk of prostate cancer in U.S. health professionals." *J Natl Canc Inst*, 2003;95(16):1240-4.

Giovannucci, E., et al. "A prospective study of cruciferous vegetables and prostate cancer." *Cancer Epidemiol Biomarkers Prev*, 2003;12(12):1403-9.

Golden, R.J., et al. "Environmental endocrine modulators and human health: an assessment of the biological evidence." *Crit Rev Toxicol*, 1998;28(2):109-227.

Kampa, R., et al. "Antiproliferative and anti-apoptotic effects of selective phenolic acids on T47D human breast cancer cells: potential mechanisms of action." *Breast Cancer Res*, 2004;6(2):R63-74.

Lee, M.M., et al. "Case-control study of diet and prostate cancer in China." *Cancer Causes Control*, 1998;9(6):545-52.

Miller, S.J. "Cellular and physiological effects of short-chain fatty acids." *Mini Rev Med Chem*, 2004;4(8):839-45.

Ramos, J.G., et al. "Prenatal exposure to low doses of bisphenol A alters the periductal stroma and glandular cell function in the rat ventral prostate." *Biol Reprod*, 2001;65(4):1271-7.

Santibanez, J.F., et al. "Genistein inhibits proliferation and *in vitro* invasive potential of human prostatic cancer cell lines." *Anticancer Res*, 1997;17(2A):1199-204.

Sarkhar, F.H. & Li, Y. "Indole-3-carbinol and prostate cancer." *J Nutr*, 2004;134(12):3493S-8S.

Tymchuk, C.N., et al. "Effects of diet and exercise on insulin, sex hormone-binding globulin, and prostate-specific antigen." *Nutr Cancer*, 1998;31(2):127-31.

West, D.W., et al. "Adult dietary intake and prostate cancer risk in Utah: a case-control study with special emphasis on aggressive tumors." *Cancer Causes Control*, 1991;2(2):85-94.

CHAPTER 8

Black, P.H. & Garbutt, L.D. "Stress, inflammation, and cardiovascular disease." *J Psychosom Res*, 2002;52(1):1-23.

Blake-Mortimer, J., et al. "Evidence for free radical-mediated reduction of lymphocytic 5'ectonucleotidase during stress." *Int J Stress Manage*, 1998;5(1):57-75.

Carey, J., et al. "Beware 'sick-building' syndrome." *Newsweek*, January 7, 1985:58.

Carlson, L.E., et al. "Mindfulness-based stress reduction in relation to quality of life, mood, and symptoms of stress and levels of cortisol, dehyrdoepiandrosterone sulfate (DHEA), and melatonin in breast and prostate cancer patients." *Psychoneuroendocrinology*, 2004;29(4):448-74.

Coker, K.H. "Meditation and prostate cancer: integrating a mind/body intervention with traditional therapies." *Semin Urol Oncol*, 1999;17(2):111-8.

Gale, K. "Stress may promote aging of cells." Reuters, November 29, 2004.

Irie, M., et al. "Psychological mediation of a type of oxidative DNA damage, 8-hydroxydeoxyguanosine, in peripheral blood leukocytes of non-smoking and non-drinking workers." *Psychother Psychosom*, 2002;71(2):90-6.

Lemonick, M.D. "The ravages of stress." *Time*, December 13, 2004:45.

Miller, G.E., et al. "Chronic psychological stress and the regulation of pro-inflammatory cytokines: a glucocorticoid-resistance model." *Health Psychology*, 2002;21(6):531-41.

Tanner, L. "Can laughter relieve pain and help us heal?" Associated Press, Sep. 4, 2001.

Index

3,3"-diindolylmethane
(DIM), 180
5 alpha-reductase
inhibitors, 21-24,
27, 40, 47
Avodart
(dutasteride), 21
Proscar (finasteride),
21-24, 41, 92
5-HETE, 137,
141-142, 151
5-lipoxygenase (5-LO), 140-144,
146, 151

Active Hexose Correlated Compound
(AHCC), 151-152, 227
acupuncture, 63, 76-77, 119-120, 150,
213, 221
adrenal glands, 7, 122
African Americans, 8, 17, 82, 84,
93-94, 106, 154, 170
Agent Orange, 86-87
Alkylglycerols, 120
allopathic medicine, 4-5, 9, 21-37
allopurinol, 64-65
alpha-blockers, 21, 24, 25-26, 41, 57, 63
Cardura (doxazosin), 24

Flomax (tamsulosin), 22, 24, 26,
41, 57
Hytrin (terazosin), 22, 24, 57
Uroxatral (alfuzosin), 24, 25-26, 41
alprostadil, 112, 113
American Cancer Society, 8, 17, 38,
92, 94
American Urological Association
(AUA), 94
Symptom Score, 25
amino acids, 49, 53, 188, 190
antiandrogen therapy, 122, 124
antibiotics, 8, 21, 33, 56, 57, 58, 59,
62, 63, 68, 70, 71-72, 78, 93, 97,
133, 194, 195, 196
antioxidants, 51, 72, 79, 84, 131, 135,
145, 146, 147, 149, 150, 152, 156,
158, 163, 179, 180, 181, 188, 191,
194, 195, 213
apoptosis, 89-90, 144, 146, 148, 151,
152, 159, 162, 180, 206
arachidonic acid, 135, 136, 137,
138-139, 141, 170
aromatase, 46, 47, 161
Atkins Center, 4, 40
autoimmunity, 50, 59, 60, 133, 138, 195
Awad, Atif, Ph.D., 160

bacteriocins, 195
baicalin, 155
baldness, 26
barberry, 83-84, 155
Ben-Eliyahu, Shamgar, Ph.D., 208
benign prostatic hypertrophy (BPH),
    7, 11ff., 39ff., 78, 85, 130, 135,
    144, 161, 226
    diagnosis, 16-20, 94, 95
    medications for, 21-26
    natural remedies, 142, 160, 184, 39ff.
    prevalence, 7, 13
    surgery for, 28-38, 100
    symptoms, 13, 14-16, 91-92,
    134, 141
    therapy, 26-28
benign tumors, 101
Benson, Mitchell C., M.D., 4, 164
Berberine, 83, 155
beta-carotene, 84, 196
beta-glucans, 195
beta-sitosterol, 62, 67, 166
biofeedback, 36, 74, 124, 212
biofilms, 81-82
bioflavonoid, 84, 192
biopsy, 33, 103, 105, 106-109, 112,
    115, 141, 164, 170
bladder, 6, 7, 12, 13, 14, 15, 18, 19-20,
    22, 24, 28, 29-30, 33-34, 35, 36,
    37, 45-46, 66, 74, 78, 91, 134
    cancer, 16, 18-19, 96, 140, 153, 218
    diverticula, 20
    infection, 6, 74
    stones, 6, 15
blood in urine, 91, 95, 96, 108
brachytherapy (internal radiation
    therapy), 107, 115
buchu, 74, 76
butyrate, 191

calendula, 117
Cancer Information Service, 125, 226
Capodice, Jillian, L.Ac., 76, 119
Casodex (bicalutamide), 122
catheterization, 28, 12, 30, 32, 33,
    34, 106
CaverMap, 108
cavernosography, 112

cavernosometry, 112
Center for Holistic Urology, xvii, xviii,
    xx, 4, 5, 21, 44, 51, 63, 119,
    149, 223
Cernilton, 47-48, 52, 78-79, 225
chemoprevention, vi, 104, 129ff., 226
chemotherapy, 60, 90, 118-119,
    180, 152
    side effects, 90, 117, 118,
    119-120, 152
Chen, Richard, M.D., L.Ac., 63
chi (qi), 77, 212, 219
chi kung, 200, 212-213, 214, 228
Chinese goldthread, 74, 148
Cialis, 110, 113
clinical trials, 4, 40, 43, 102, 125-126,
    143, 145, 222
color Doppler imaging with
    microbubble contrast, 95, 98
comfrey, 74
complementary medicine, xvii, 8, 130
conformal/proton beam therapy, 115-116
copper, 49, 53
couch grass, 72, 74
Cousins, Norman, 211
cramp bark, 74
cranberry, 71, 74
cruciferous indoles, 14
crucifers, 14, 181-182
cryosurgical
    ablation/cryotherapy/cryoablation,
    9, 105-107
CT scan, 100, 106, 116
cyclooxygenase (COX), 134, 135, 138,
    139, 140, 170, 172
    1 (COX-1), 138, 139, 143
    2 (COX-2), 136-137, 138-139, 140,
    141, 143, 144, 145, 146, 147
cystitis, 78
cystoscopy, 18-19, 66, 95-96

daidzein, 153, 185
da Vinci Surgical System, 103, 105
deep breathing, 208, 209, 210
Delisea pulchra, 70
Detrol LA, 33
diet, 84, 131, 133, 134, 135, 137,
    152, 165ff.

and prostatitis, 57, 67, 72
and prostate cancer
chemoprevention, 129
dietary fat, 169-173
diethylstilbestrol (DES), 123
dihydrotestosterone (DHT), 14, 21,
42-43, 46, 49, 159-160, 162
digital rectal exam (DRE), 8, 16, 95,
107, 124
Ditropan, 33
diuretic, 45, 46, 64, 72, 74, 75
dong quai, 74, 75
dry orgasm, 110
dysplasia, 132

echinacea, 75, 76
edamame, 185
eicosanoid, 133-134, 138, 139, 144, 170
electroacupuncture, 63, 120
endorectal coil MRI, 100
endorphins (endogenous opiates), 213
enlarged prostate, *see* benign prostatic
hypertrophy (BPH)
enterodiol, 161, 163
enterolactone, 161, 162, 163
Enzymatic Therapy, 51, 159, 192, 225,
226, 227
Epel, Elissa S., M.D., 205-206
epidermal growth factor (EGF),
159-160
erectile dysfunction (ED), 6, 77, 107,
111-114
essential fatty acids (EFA), 50, 53, 190
estramustine phosphate (EmCyt), 118
estrogen therapy, 122, 123
Eulexin (flutamide), 122
Exceptional Cancer Patients (ECaP),
211-212
exercise, *see* physical activity/inactivity

feng shui, 218-219
fermentation, 157, 184, 189-191
fiber, 49, 50, 160-161, 169, 171,
178-179, 185
fish oil, 50, 53, 193-194, 227
flax oil, 163-164, 171, 227
flaxseeds, 50, 161, 162-164, 171, 178,
Foley catheter, 33

food allergies, 67
Food and Drug Administration (FDA),
21, 24-25, 27, 28, 31, 32, 37,
43, 105
frankincense (*Boswellia serrata*), 142,
150-151
free radicals, 130-131, 179, 204
furanones, 70-71

garlic, 75, 173, 182, 183, 186, 188, 226
genistein, 152-153, 161, 184-185, 187
Genistein Combined Polysaccharide
(CGP), 151, 152-154, 227
genitoanal syndromes, 55
ginger, 51, 137, 142, 143, 146, 180,
182, 186, 192
Gleason grading/score, 94, 100-101,
105, 106-107
goldenseal, 71, 72, 75
green tea, 51, 137, 142, 146-147
GreenLight PVP, *see* photoselective
vaporization of the prostate
guided imagery, 127, 207
gum disease (gingivitis), 70, 71

headache in the pelvis, 73
Health Professionals Follow-Up Study,
174, 176
herbal medicine, 15-17, 25, 87, 155
holy basil (*Ocimum sanctum*), 145,
152-153
hormone-refractory prostate cancer,
128, 155, 160-161, 165
hot flashes, 129, 132-133
humor, 214-215
Hu zhang (*Polygonum cuspidatum*), 155
hydrotherapy, 84
hyperinsulinemia, 174

impotence, 23, 28, 102, 103, 108,
110-111, 116, 117, 123
incontinence, 15, 28, 29, 30, 35, 74,
75, 102, 103, 104, 107, 111, 114
indole-3-carbinol (I-3-C), 180, 181
inflammation, 6, 7, 16, 45, 46, 50, 56,
57, 59, 60, 61, 66, 73, 74, 90, 131-136,
138-139, 141, 142, 143-144, 148, 149,
150, 151, 170, 172, 181, 203, 204

insulin-like growth factor 1 (IGF-1), 154, 170
integrative medicine, 21, 88, 222
Intensity Modulated Radiation Therapy (IMRT), 116
International Prostate Symptom Score (IPSS), 25
intracavernosal injection test, 112
intravenous pyelogram, 95
IP$_6$ with inositol, 158, 159, 226

juniper, 75

Kaplan, Steven, M.D., 61
ketoconazole, 25, 124
kidney infection (pyelonephritis), 75, 78
kidney stones, 65-66
Knowles, David R., M.D., 158
kombu (laminaria), 187-188

Lactobacillus acidophilus, 190, 196
Lactobacillus bifidus, 190
Lactobacillus rhamnosus, 190, 196
laser surgery (for BPH), 46-48
leukotriene, 133-134, 138, 141
leukotriene B4, 151
Levitra, 36, 110, 113
lignans, 160-162, 163-164, 178
lipoxygenase (LO), 52, 133-134,135, 138-139, 140-142, 143, 144
lithotripsy, 65-66
Long, John P., M.D., 107
Lupron (leuprolide acetate), 123
leutinizing hormone (LH), 121
leutinizing hormone releasing hormone (LHRH), 122, 123, 124
analogue therapy, 123
lycopene, 72, 84, 150, 155, 158

MD Anderson Cancer Center, 139
Medical Therapy of Prostatic Symptoms (MTOPS) Trial, 24
Medicare, 28, 105
medicinal mushrooms, 150, 151, 191, 226
meditation, 127, 200-201, 207, 208-209, 210, 211, 213
metastasis, 146, 205
microflora, see probiotics

micturition reflex, 18
minimally invasive therapy, 26-28, 105
miso, 172, 182, 184, 185, 187, 190, 194
monounsaturated fat, 172
multivitamin/mineral, 192
myofascial release, 62-63

Naparstek, Belleruth, 127
National Cancer Institute (NCI), 38, 86, 94, 125, 126, 225, 226
National Center for Complementary and Alternative Medicine (NCCAM), xix
National Institutes of Health (NIH), 43, 63, 140, 148
natural killer (NK) cell, 152, 159, 205
nerve-sparing, 100, 107, 109-110
nettle root, 46-47, 52
New Chapter, 51, 142, 149, 190, 192, 226, 227
Nickel, Curtis, M.D., 59, 63
Nilandron (nilutamide), 122
nocturia, 25
nocturnal penile tumescence and rigidity (NPTR) test, 112
nonsteroidal anti-inflammatory drugs (NSAIDs), 137-138, 139, 140
nori, 187

obesity, 85, 135, 167, 169
obstructive symptoms (of BPH), 22
olive oil, 142, 170, 172-173, 182
omega-3 fatty acids, 50, 53, 137, 141, 170-171, 193, 194
omega-6 fatty acids, 135, 137, 141, 166, 170-171, 176, 193, 194
open simple prostatectomy, 27, 30-31
orchiectomy, 121-122, 123
oregano, 137, 147
Oregon grape, 71, 72
organochlorines, 170
oxidation, 130-131, 135, 156, 166, 184, 204

painful ejaculation, 91
Pao pereira, 164
patch graft urethroplasty, 67
pelvic muscle training (PMT), 114

penile arteriography, 112
penile implant, 109, 110, 114
penile ultrasound, 112
Petrylak, Daniel, M.D., 118
pesticides, 86, 166, 173-174,
    215-216, 218
phenolic acids, 191
photoselective vaporization of the
    prostate (GreenLight PVP), 32
physical activity/inactivity, 32, 39, 48,
    50-51, 73, 85-86, 127, 169,
    200-202, 212, 213-214, 222
phytates, 184
phytoestrogens, 161, 183, 184
PhytoPharmica, 19, 226
pipsissewa, 72, 75
priapism, 114
probiotics (microflora), 67, 149, 189,
    190, 191, 194-197, 227
progressive relaxation, 207
Prostabel, 169-170, 226
prostaglandins, 59, 142, 144, 147
Prostate 5LX, 66, 150, 194, 226
prostate cancer, 83ff.
    chemoprevention, 129ff., 226
    diagnostic tests, 95-99
    risk factors, 82-87, 135
    symptoms, 91-92
    treatments (allopathic), 101ff.
Prostate Specific Antigen (PSA), 8, 17,
    23, 65, 67, 81, 83, 84, 91, 92-94,
    95, 96, 99, 100, 106, 107, 119,
    124, 126, 132, 145, 153, 155, 158,
    164, 169, 225
    PSA density, 17
    percent free PSA, 17
    PSA velocity, 17, 158
prostatic antibacterial factor, 69
prostatic intraepithelial neoplasia
    (PIN), 52, 131-132, 134, 135, 144,
    145, 146, 149, 158
prostatic stents (Urolume
    Endoprosthesis), 37
prostatic stones, 65-66
prostatitis, 55ff., 7-8, 16, 45, 47, 52
    abacterial, 62-63, 64
    acute, 55-56, 57, 72
    bacterial, 56, 58, 59, 65, 68

chronic prostatitis/chronic pelvic
    pain/prostatodynia, 56, 57, 60,
    61-62, 63, 65, 66, 67, 68, 69, 72,
    75, 76-77, 78-79
    medications for, 68
    symptoms, 55-57, 61
Prostatitis Foundation, 64, 225
prostatodynia, 57, 62, 79
protease inhibitors, 25, 184
Provail, 163, 227
Provenge, 119
psychoneuroendocrinology, 207
psychoneuroimmunology, 207
pumpkin seeds, 49-50, 53, 142, 171
Pygeum africanum, 43, 44-47, 51, 52,
    73, 160, 225

qi, *see* chi
queen of the meadow, 75
quercetin, 72, 180, 188

radiation, 9, 105, 106, 114-118, 120,
    121, 125, 130, 152, 154, 184, 187
radiation dermatitis, 117
Rauwolfia vomitoria, 164
relaxation techniques, 61, 63, 68
remission, 127-128, 130
resveratrol, 147, 191
retrograde ejaculation, 26, 30, 36
rosemary, 51, 53, 137, 142, 147
Ryan, Regina Sara, 201, 228

Saccharomyces cerevisiae, 157, 190
Samadi, David, M.D., 105
saponins, 184
saturated fat, 170, 172, 193
Sawczuk, Ihor S., M.D., 158
saw palmetto, 41-44, 46, 51, 52, 73,
    75-76, 142, 159-160, 192
scutellaria, 148
seaweed, 187-188, 189, 226
second opinions, 31, 38, 124-125
selenium, 51, 72, 84, 156-157, 158,
    178, 188, 226
Selenium and Vitamin E
    Chemoprevention Trial (SELECT), 157
sex hormone-binding globulin (SHBG),
    169

Shabsigh, Ridwan, M.D., 111-112, 114, 225
shiitake mushrooms, 151, 188
short-chain fatty acids, 191
Shoskes, Daniel, M.D., 60
Siberian ginseng, 76, 192
Siegel, Bernie, M.D., 211, 228
soft tissue mobilization, 62
soy, 48, 150, 152-153, 158, 161, 166, 172, 175, 182, 183-187, 188, 189, 190
staging, 99
Stoll, Andrew, M.D., 193
stress, 199ff.
  and health, 203-206
  management, 207ff.
support groups, 126, 150
sympathomimetic, 15

tai chi, 200, 212-213, 214, 228
Taxol (paclitaxel), 118
Taxotere (docetaxel), 118
telomere, 206
tempeh, 172, 179, 184, 185-186, 194
testosterone, 7, 13, 14, 21, 42-43, 46, 47, 48, 87, 113, 120, 121, 122, 123, 124, 159-160, 161-162, 167, 169, 178
tofu, 176, 179, 182, 183, 184, 185, 186-187
total androgen blockade (TAB)/maximal androgen blockade (MAB), 122
Traditional Chinese Medicine (TCM), 73, 76-77
transrectal ultrasonography/ultrasound, 95
transurethral incision of the prostate (TUIP), 30, 37
transurethral microwave thermotherapy (TUMT), 27
transurethral needle ablation (TUNA), 27, 28
transurethral resection of the prostate (TURP), 27, 28, 29-30, 31-32
Travis, John W., M.D., 201, 228
trigger points, 62
trolamine, 117
tumor flare, 123
turmeric, 137, 146, 149, 180, 227

unsaturated fat, 170
urethral stricture, 18, 66, 79
urethritis, 78
urethrotomy, 67
uric acid, 64
urinalysis, 16, 95
urinary obstruction, 37
urinary retention, 12, 15, 26
urinary tract infection (UTI), 15, 21, 66, 70, 78, 93, 95
urine flow study (uroflow), 17-18
urodynamic testing, 19-20
  cysmetrogram (CMG), 19-20
  fluoroscopy, 20
  electromyograph (EMG), 20
Us TOO, 222, 226

vaccine therapy, 119
vacuum constriction device (VCD), 113
valerian, 76
venereal disease, 85, 135
Viagra (sildenafil), 36, 109, 110, 111, 113
visualization, 208, 211
vitamin A, 85, 226
vitamin B_6, 48, 53
vitamin C, 72, 124, 157, 211, 226
vitamin D, 154-155
vitamin E, 34, 40, 50, 53, 72, 84, 97, 155-156, 157, 158, 194, 226
vitamin K, 181, 195

watchful waiting, 16, 21, 38, 104, 107, 124, 132, 154, 222
watermelon seed, 72
Weiss, Jay, Ph.D., 205
Wise, David, Ph.D., 61

xenoestrogens, 170, 177

yeast infection, 67
yoga, 127, 200, 207, 210-211, 214

zinc, 48-49, 53, 59, 72, 79
Zoladex (goserelin acetate), 123
Zometa (zoledronic acid), 123
Zyflamend, 143-144, 145, 148, 149, 164, 190, 226

About the Author

AARON E. KATZ, M.D., is director of the Center for Holistic Urology at Columbia University Medical Center, and an associate professor of clinical urology at Columbia University College of Physicians and Surgeons.

His pioneering work in advancing the technology of cryosurgery to treat prostate cancer helped Medicare approve this therapy for treating radiation-recurrent tumors. Dr. Katz has trained nearly 100 urologists in the United States and Europe to perform cryosurgery in their hospitals.

During a fellowship at the New York Academy of Medicine, Dr. Katz developed a novel test that could detect small numbers of prostate cancer cells in the blood. Known as RT-PCR (Reverse Transcriptase Polymerase Chain Reaction), it was the first to stage urologic cancers using a molecular assay. He has received several awards and grants to further his research.

Dr. Katz has published over 50 scientific articles in peer-reviewed journals and has written for urologic textbooks. In addition, he has lectured throughout the United States, Europe and Japan.